NETWORKS, EXCHANGE
AND COERCION

NETWORKS, EXCHANGE AND COERCION

The Elementary Theory and Its Applications

Edited by

David Willer
University of Kansas
Lawrence, Kansas

Bo Anderson
Michigan State University
East Lansing, Michigan

ELSEVIER
New York • Oxford

Exclusive Distribution
throughout the World by
Greenwood Press, Westport, Ct.
U.S.A.

Elsevier North Holland, Inc.
52 Vanderbilt Avenue, New York, New York 10017

Sole distributors outside the USA and Canada:

Elsevier Science Publishers B.V.
P.O. Box 211, 1000 AE Amsterdam, The Netherlands

© 1981 by Elsevier North Holland, Inc.

Library of Congress Cataloging in Publication Data

Main entry under title:

Networks, exchange and coercion: the elementary theory and its applications.

    Bibliography: p.
    Includes index.
    1. Exchange theory (Sociology) I. Willer, David.
    II. Anderson, Bo.
HM24.N375   303.3'3   80-21586
ISBN 0-444-99078-X

Desk Editor   Louise Calabro Schreiber
Design   Edmée Froment
Design Editor   Glen Burris
Mechanicals/Opening pages   Virginia Kudlak
Art rendered by   Crestwood Press
Production Manager   Joanne Jay
Compositor   Crestwood Press
Printer   Haddon Craftsmen

Manufactured in the United States of America

To
Fritz Heider, Torgny Segerstedt and Joseph Berger

Friends, mentors and masters
of the sociological imagination

CONTENTS

II MACROSYSTEMS

PREFACE

Can the structure of social relationships determine the course and outcome of human interactions? Is it true, as some have claimed, that coercive relationships are infrequently found and thus theoretically insignificant? Can social exchange be understood in isolation from relationships of other types? Is there unequal exchange and, if so, how is it related to exploitation? Do normative systems work exclusively through internalized values or are norms enforced through a structure of power?

The investigation of these and related issues such as the structural basis of domination is the focus of this volume. To further understanding and encourage new ideas we introduce a new theory for social structure and interaction, the elementary theory.

This is not a book of readings but is instead an integrated set of studies guided by a common theory. The perspective here is strongly antireductionist. When a behavior occurs, when an order is given—or obeyed, when a structure is reproduced, we look first for theoretically significant properties of the social structure.

The elementary theory has a modeling procedure based on network theory. The modeling procedure, with the other parts of the theory, is used to analyze the social relationships of exchange, conflict and coercion and to represent a variety of structural arrangements of these and other relationships. The theory has procedures for relating variations in structure to variations in power, domination, exploitation, normative control and other properties of interactions in the theoretically formulated structure. The research contained in this volume investigates the relations between structure and consequent interactions as guided by the formulations of the theory.

Though more formal than other broad scope theories, the elementary theory is mathematically simple. It can be simple because of the ways that networks are used. The beginning point of the theory is a few simple ideas which are then combined in various ways to generate the more complex ideas of social relationship, interaction and structure.

Investigations found in this volume include ethnographic research, the analysis of ethnographic and primary and secondary historical sources, as well as institutional and experimental research. The elementary theory provides integration for these diverse investigations in spite of differing research methods, widely differing structures and the number of scholars engaged in the research.

The work presented in this volume has been generously supported by a variety of institutions. We would like to thank the National Science Foundation for fellowship and grant support to Willer, and the college fellow program in the College of Social Science, Michigan State University, for support to Anderson. A conference on social networks and exchange at which this volume was planned was held at Michigan State University in the Spring of 1977. We want to thank Dr. Gwen Andrew, dean of the College of Social Science, for making funds available for this conference and for travel, making possible subsequent work sessions with individual contributors. A second conference included further work on the volume and was held at the University of Kansas in 1978, supported by the College of Liberal Arts and Sciences, Robert Cobb, Dean. Professors Jay W. Artis and Scott McNall, chairmen of the sociology departments at MSU and KU, respectively, gave helpful support when the conferences were being organized. Dr. Robert Glenn, Provost, Northern Michigan University and the Institute of Cultural, Environmental and Heritage Studies at that University provided necessary support, as did the Swedish Social Science Research Council. Marilyn Lovall and her secretarial staff in the MSU sociology department efficiently and patiently typed various portions of the manuscript as they evolved. We thank all these institutions and persons for their help and support.

The editors and contributors of this volume owe much to a wide circle of kind and helpful scholars, only three of whom are mentioned on the dedication page. We would like to single out for special mention Professor Douglas Heckathorn, whose early work on the development of the theory was invaluable.

The theory presented and applied in this volume is a working theory. Yet work with the theory has only begun. Being flexible, its domain and scope of application could be considerably extended. This extension implies extensive theoretic and empirical work. It demands the intellectual labor of many more minds than now involved. Both substantive and critical contributions from our readers will be welcomed.

David Willer

Bo Anderson

CONTRIBUTORS

Anderson, Bo
Department of Sociology, Michigan State University, East Lansing, Michigan

Brennan, John S.
University of Kansas, Lawrence, Kansas

Carlos, Manuel L.
Department of Anthropology, University of California at Santa Barbara, Santa Barbara, California

Davis, Nanette J.
Department of Sociology, Portland State University, Portland, Oregon

Gilham, Steven A.
University of Missouri, Kansas City, Missouri

Hansen, Knud L.
Wayne State University, Detroit, Michigan

Hurst, Richard
The Social Science Research Bureau, Michigan State University, East Lansing, Michigan

Loukinen, Michael
Northern Michigan University, Marquette, Michigan

Morris, Ann
University of Kansas, Lawrence, Kansas

Southard, Frank
Department of Sociology, State University College at Buffalo, Buffalo, New York

Willer, David
Department of Sociology, University of Kansas, Lawrence, Kansas

NETWORKS, EXCHANGE
AND COERCION

Bo Anderson

David Willer

INTRODUCTION

A. What Is the Elementary Theory?

This book is about a scientific theory of social relations and social structures, and about the applications of this theory to a number of different empirical cases and theoretic issues. The issues addressed in this book have all been longstanding concerns of social theory and research.

The cases to which the theory is applied include a variety of different community systems, legal systems, a political network, certain "strong structures," and selected experimental cases. Included among the theoretic issues considered here are the relations between exchange and coercion, the differentiation of social and economic exchange, the nature of property in differing social settings, the role of structure in the determination of social interaction, and the relationship between micro- and macrosystems. These cases and issues are addressed by a number of different people working with a common theory. Since it is informed by a common theory, *their work forms an integrated whole*.

The theory of this book is called *the elementary theory of social interaction*. The basic concepts and procedures of the elementary theory are presented in the two chapters that introduce the two major sections of this book. The first section concentrates on microsystems, the second on macrosystems. The relations between micro- and macrosystems are dealt with at a number of points in each section.

To use the theory it will be helpful first to understand its domain of application. What elements of human behavior is this theory intended to comprehend? What elements have been excluded and why? It will also be helpful to know which theoretic traditions and issues are germane to this theory—and the theories to which it stands opposed. Finally, it will be *essential* to understand the conception of scientific theory upon which the theory is based.

B. Social Phenomena and the Elementary Theory

Human events contain in varying degrees elements of at least three separate phenomena: biophysical, social and cognitive. Biophysical phenomena include the physical and biological conditions of the human environment, as well as the biological and physical characteristics of humans themselves. Also included are the tools, techniques and procedures by means of which people relate to that environment. In Marx's theory these phenomena come under the terms "nature" and "the forces of production." Often, they are called "material conditions" or the "material substratum."

Social phenomena include social relationships as they occur among human beings, and the processes of interaction which those relationships imply. Also included are the structural arrangements of these social relationships as well as the boundaries (permeable or not) that divide "clusters" of relationships into diverse groups, associations, organizations and other identifiable social units. Weber's theory of "social action" is perhaps the most general set of formulations for social relationships and social interaction to date. Marx's concepts for relations of production are a somewhat more limited formulation.

Cognitive phenomena include humans' patterns of thought, their values and beliefs, and the systems of knowledge in which they are organized. Considered in its broadest sense, the study of the cognitive would necessarily include the study of human language, of the social construction of reality, and of information theory in its diverse applications. The sharing of cognitions among humans has been studied from as diverse viewpoints as Durkheim's formulations for the *conscience collective* and Heider's balance theory. Marx's concern with ideology and Weber's with "world images" fall into this domain.

A *fully general* theory of human behavior would contain fully adequate theoretic formulations whose domain of application included all three phenomena. A fully general theory would also relate the biophysical, social and cognitive parts into an integrated whole. Furthermore, the theory would be historically and cross-culturally grounded so that its formulations could be brought to bear upon *any* historical or contemporary sociocultural case—not "just" western society of the 20th century—and could be brought to bear upon any case with equal effectiveness. The formulation of a fully general theory of human behavior is a formidable task.

Why is the formulation of a fully general theory at issue? The formulation of such a theory is difficult in the extreme, but the *reason why* such a theory is needed can be easily seen. As social scientists, we are necessarily concerned with why any particular human behavior occurs. In answering that "why" we are led to consider biophysical, social and cognitive conditions. To deal systematically with these conditions we need a theory general to these phenomena. To deal with these conditions, as they have occurred at different times and places, we need a fully general theory.

The task of developing a fully general theory was too formidable for Marx and Weber. It will also be so for us. Since the task as a whole is too difficult, what is the best place to begin? What domain of phenomena should be considered first? Let us consider the works of Marx and Weber as a guide for the selection.

Marx selected social and biophysical phenomena (and the relations between them) as the focus of his concern. What is a "mode of production"? A mode of production consists of the *social* relations of production, the (biophysical) forces of production (technology and its relation to nature), and the relations between the social relationships and forces of production. [See Marx (1964:94ff; 1969:503).] How then did Marx deal with the cognitive? Here a vitally important simplifying assumption was used—the assumption that human cognitions could be treated as if they were *reflections* of the social and biophysical. [See Marx and Engels (1947:14ff).]

What is the reflective assumption? Take the case of a capitalist in a capitalist system. If the capitalist's enterprise is to be reproduced, then the capitalist must buy labor as cheaply as possible. Any reflective capitalist would necessarily recognize and act on this interest. Refeflective capitalists would *necessarily* recognize and act on that interest because their beliefs and values are a consequence of the structure of capitalism and position of capitalists in the structure.

That the use of simplifying assumptions (such as Marx's reflective assumption) is legitimate in science can be seen by example. In his study of dynamics, Galileo treated all falling bodies as accelerating at the same rate (Galileo, 1954:161ff). This treatment simplifies the problem because it means that the air resistance of falling bodies is ignored. Since it simplifies the problem of falling bodies, it simplifies the theory of falling bodies.

What is lost when simplifying assumptions are used? Clearly, Galileo's formulations would be of no use in explaining or predicting the fall of feathers and leaves in air. They are of use, however, in explaining the fall of rocks and cannon balls. Simplifying assumptions limit the scope of cases to which the theory can be applied.

Since simplifying assumptions limit the scope of application of a theory, they must be selected very carefully. It is possible to imagine a simplifying assumption that so limited the scope of a theory that its application could only be to trivial cases—or even to cases that never existed. For example, have there ever been perfect markets? If not, much of microeconomic theory has no application to real world cases, either contemporary or historical. The fact that Galileo's (and Marx's) theories have been fruitful implies that there are cases that closely approximate the simplifying assumption(s) and that the cases are not trivial.

A simplifying assumption is *not* an assertion about the world. Instead, it simplifies a theoretic problem so that it can be dealt with by means of a simple theory. Galileo knew perfectly well that, in air, feathers did not accelerate at the same rate as cannon balls. [See Galileo (1954:256ff).] Marx knew perfectly well that people's values and beliefs do not necessarily reflect their conditions of existence (Marx and Engels, 1947:72ff). (Why else the concept of "false" consciousness?) Furthermore, simplifying assumptions can be withdrawn as the theory is elaborated such that empirical cases that had been outside the theory's scope can be included. It is because elaborated theories are *much* more complex that the first development of theory needs simplification. Without that simplification the development of any theory would be too difficult.

Marx's reflection assumption is, potentially, as important to the development of the social sciences as Galileo's treatment of falling bodies was to the physical sciences. That assumption will allow us to treat the preferences and the beliefs of social actors *as if* they were a reflection of their social relationships. This treatment greatly simplifies the problem of modeling social actors in social relationships. Again, as in the case of any simplifying assumption, it will be possible to withdraw it (wholly or in part) as that need arises in the application of the theory.

Weber selected social and cognitive phenomena (and the relations between them) as the focus of his concern. Weber's social action theory contained formulations for social relationships of a wide variety of types. Weber's cognitive formulations for Protestant and Confucian ethics, and for legitimacy as it relates to systems of domination, are generally known in the field (1951:226ff; 1978:213ff,952ff). The subtlety of the relations drawn between social and cognitive conditions is particularly well illustrated in Weber's *Religion of China* (1951).

Biophysical conditions were not central to Weber's theoretic formulations and drew only occasional mention in his substantive work. There is, however, a way of dealing with the biophysical in Weber's theory—a procedure that was occasionally used by Weber himself. Social actors can have material interests. In turn, these material interest can be conditioned by biophysical factors. Thus, biophysical factors can be used as *initial conditions* that determine the material interests of actors. [See Weber (1949:165.]

Weber also proposed the imaginary (mental) experiment as a procedure for the meaningful interpretation of social interactions (Weber, 1978:10). However, Weber said very little concerning the methods of mental experimentation. Interestingly, Weber's contemporary, Einstein, was also using mental experimentation (Einstein, 1954:233ff). In its use Einstein stood as part of a long tradition in physical science. [See Galileo (1954:153ff) and Newton (1966:551ff).] In fact, there are important parallels in the use of mental experimentation between sciences.

A mental experiment is a theoretic procedure in which a case is imagined and thought through to its conclusion. To aid mental experimentation a good theory will contain a vivid image of the world. In the exact sciences various interpreted geometries have been used to express that world image (see references to

Galileo, Newton, and Einstein). The elementary theory uses interpreted networks in its mental experiments.

Mental experimentation is the single most important theoretic procedure in science. It is the core procedure in both theory development and theory application. It is in daily use in other sciences. Why has it not been developed and used in the social sciences in spite of suggestive passages in Weber? The answer lies in the structure of theory. To use mental experimentation exactly requires that the theory have a *modeling procedure*—that is, an interpreted geometry that can give a precise abstract image of the world. How is mental experimentation carried out? That question will be addressed later in this chapter. Furthermore, mental experiments with the elementary theory will be found throughout the book.

Only social phenomena were core concerns of Marx and Weber. If we are to follow their lead, social relations and social structures should be the core concern of the elementary theory.

Given that selection, how will the elementary theory differ from these earlier ones? It will be more limited in its domain of concern—not being directly concerned with theoretically explaining either biophysical or cognitive phenomena. The elementary theory will be more systematic in its treatment of social relationships and social structures. To that end, theoretic procedures new to the social sciences, such as mental experiments with geometric models, will be used.

The elementary theory will not ignore biophysical and cognitive phenomena. In any application of the theory, biophysical and/or cognitive factors can be used as *initial conditions* for mental experiments. The structure of the theory is such that as any of these conditions vary, the processes and outcomes of the interactions modeled in the mental experiments can vary. The elementary theory is not a theory of the biophysical or the cognitive, but there are theoretic procedures such that both can condition application of the theory to social phenomena.

Nor will Marx's reflection assumption be ignored. As will be seen, the most simple formulations for any application of the theory are always formulations in which the actors are reflective. Both their values and their beliefs are a consequence of the social structural conditions of the system.

Weber's concepts for social interaction will be reformulated. The ideas for social actor and social action will be central to all theory use.

Marx's view of humans as actively creative will be incorporated. The elementary theory is a scientific theory of human behavior. Unlike microeconomics and game theory, it sees actors not as passive but as sometimes active and sometimes passive, depending on the conditions of the action system.

Social phenomena will be the subject of the formulations of the elementary theory. Its formulations should be as systematic and flexible as possible so that a wide variety of social relationships and social structures can be precisely examined.

C. The Bearing of the Classical Tradition on the Elementary Theory

The theories of Marx and Weber each give a complex image of social history. Yet, these theories both have important applications to the contemporary world. Both theories have their advocates, yet neither theory has displaced the other.

In any science, more powerful theories displace less powerful ones. Why is it that Weber's theory has not displaced Marx's or vice versa? There are at least three reasons. First, as discussed in the last section, the domain of phenomena of the two theories differs. Second, the two theories are not systematic enough to assure unambiguous application—thus it is by no means always clear how well either theory fits the "facts" of its concern. Third, in sociology criteria other than scientific ones are commonly used to evaluate theories. (In that regard sociology and other social "sciences" are not scientific.)

In fact, the theories of sociology fall into two types: broad yet relatively unsystematic ones such as Marx's and Weber's, and ones that are narrow and more systematic. Due to the narrow scope of the latter type, precise applications have been largely limited to experimental research. How can a broad yet systematic theory be developed—one whose scope allows less restricted application? Our strategy in the development of the elementary theory has been to select a part of Marx's and Weber's theories and systematize, for it seems to us that the continued durability of both theories is perhaps the best indication of their ongoing utility.

If, as we believe, the theories of Marx and Weber are still the best broad-gauge social theories, then the elementary theory should be grounded in both. However, there are important differences between these theories. How will it be possible to ground a new theory in both the theories of Marx and Weber and not introduce inconsistencies?

Certainly there are differences in these two theories. Some are only differences of emphasis. Marx emphasized economic phenomena, whereas Weber emphasized the political. The more fundamental difference lies in Marx's connection of the social to the biophysical in contrast to Weber's connection of the social to the cognitive. These differences are immediately evident in any application of either theory.

Consider Marx's treatment of capitalism. At the core of that treatment is the concern for biophysical factors (the forces of production) such as human labor power (human energy) as it is expended through technology on nature. The forces and social relations of production jointly condition one another. Out of these formulations came an understanding of the capitalist *social* relations of production as they occur in the individual factory and in society as a whole. [See Marx (1967a,b:passim).]

At the core of Weber's treatment of capitalism is the concern for cognitive factors such as the development of modern procedures of cost accounting. The introduction of Arabic numerals at an early point in capitalist development allowed the calculations of (and thus the comparison of) rates of production—a calculation and comparison that had been effectively impossible with Roman numerals. These cognitive factors were important conditions for *social* organization of the modern factory and its social relationships with the market. [See Weber (1978:86ff).]

Marx's and Weber's treatments of capitalism are different. However, that difference lies in the different scopes of the theories, not necessarily in different conceptions of social relations and social structure.

What similarities do we find when Marx's partly developed biophysical formulations and Weber's partly developed cognitive formulations are removed? In fact, the purely social conceptions of the two are strikingly similar. Marx's concept of consciousness is very similar to Weber's concept of meaning. Both these conceptions have the same role in their formulation of social relationships. Both theorists saw the relation between exchange and coercion in ongoing systems and recognized that social relationships formed ongoing systems of varying structure. Both saw social structure as a determinant of behavior. It is upon similarities of this order that future work departs.

Both Marx and Weber suggested certain elementary terms out of which a systematic social theory might have been developed. [See Marx and Engels (1947:3–78) and Weber (1978:3–62).]

Neither theorist systematically interrelated and developed these elements. Thus, both theories become increasingly awkward to use as the application in question becomes more complex. Furthermore, there is considerable disagreement concerning the meanings of particular concepts and interpretations.

In fact, scientific theories do begin with certain simple elements that are built up into more complex formulations. Neither Marx nor Weber followed through to develop a systematic scientific theory of social phenomena to be used in their substantive studies. That they did not was due to a crucial missing part in both theories, a *modeling procedure*. In fact, no social theory up until now has developed a modeling procedure. That will be the first task of the elementary theory.

Having developed a modeling procedure, it will be possible to investigate the idea of social *structure* as a determinant of human behavior. In so doing we will follow leads jointly suggested by Marx and Weber. In addition, having a modeling procedure to represent social structure will allow us to discover new structures not suggested or investigated by either theorist.

Two further similarities between the theories of Marx and Weber should be noted—similarities that become particularly evident in historical applications. First, each theory recognizes that the social relationships, and the dynamics that develop out of those relationships, can be fundamentally different in different societies. For example, Marx treated each stage of history as having its own laws (Marx, 1967a:270).

We agree that each stage of history has its own fundamental social relationships and dynamics. The modeling procedure of the elementary theory was especially developed to represent the structures of social relationships and their resulting dynamics. However, the methodological structure of our theory is different from Marx's (and Weber's) theory. Thus, our use of the term "law" is different. The two laws of the elementary theory apply to any model developed from the theory—thus, they are (in principle) transhistorical. Yet, in application, models drawn from the theory will evidence the different structures and dynamics Marx insisted upon in *his* meaning of the term "law."

The second similarity between the theories of Marx and Weber is their use of certain transhistorical and transcultural concepts. Consider the concept of "economic interest." People in the widest possible variety of social conditions can be said to have economic interests. That these interests can stand in the greatest possible contrast to one another does not make the concept "economic interest" any less transhistorical or transcultural. Of course, the economic interest of a Roman patrician was very different from that of a southern planter, although both were slaveholders, just as the economic interest of the planter was different from that of the modern entrepreneur, although both were capitalists. Interests vary as structures vary. The point is that the term "economic interest" can be brought to bear upon a variety of epochs and structures.

However, the emphasis upon diversity can blind us to similarities that can occur regardless of epoch or culture. The footpads of late medieval London coerced their victims, threatening them in order to receive their valuables. So do the muggers of modern cities. Both exchanged the results of their coercion on a market. Muggers and footpads may have used different weapons, but their *social relationships were effectively identical.*

Even social structures at different times and different places exhibit important theoretic similarities. According to Marx, the high rate of "coercive exploitation" of slaves in Jamaica in the 19th century was due to the availability of new slaves to take the place of those worked to death in production (1967a:266ff). Coercive exploitation varied by the size of the "reserve slave army." Precisely the same point was made by Weber in his analysis of the fall of ancient civilization. As Rome's expansion stopped, slaves were not replaced as quickly as they died—there came to be no reserve slave army—thus, the rate of coercive exploitation declined. As the effects of that decline ramified through the system, Rome declined and fell (Weber, 1963:passim). Taken together, the implications of the two treatments of slavery are clear. Slavery may differ from place to place in certain important details, but the fundamental dynamics of slave systems as they are determined by the presence or absence of a reserve slave army are the same regardless of those variations.

As we will model these systems, the *coercive* relations of master to slave should be similar regardless of time and place. On the other hand, *exchange* relations can vary considerably more from case to case.

The elementary theory will begin with certain concepts of elements of social behavior, and, by combining those elements in a number of forms, will build up concepts for social relationships and structures of social relationships. The theory is called *elementary* because it begins with these elements and systematically builds its formulations on them. Our aim is to ground these formulations in the thoughts of Marx and Weber with the ultimate aim of broad historical applications. The applications and derivations of this work, though broad in scope by contemporary standards of sociology, remain narrow when compared to the works of either Marx or Weber. Certainly, much important work remains to be done.

D. What Is Wrong with Operant Exchange Theory?

The elementary theory can be applied to systems of exchange, but is not an operant theory of exchange. In sociology, so called "exchange theory" has been predominantly operant. This brief critical review of operant theory will indicate why the elementary theory does not use operant concepts.

According to operant psychology, reinforcement is of two types: positive reinforcement and negative reinforcement. Positive reinforcement is a means of increasing the organism's frequency of emission of an operant (activity) by making a "rewarding" reinforcement contingent upon the operant. If the organism emits the operant, the organism is reinforced. The fundamental sequence is first the act of the organism (the emission of the operant) and then the reinforcement. The reinforcement is known to be positive by the pattern of operants that results. If the frequency of operants (activities) increases, the reinforcement following each of these emissions is said to be positive.

The paradigm experiment is the lever-pushing pigeon. Place a hungry pigeon in a cage with a lever and feed the pigeon when it pushes the lever. If the frequency of lever pushing increases over time we know that the food was a positive reinforcement for the pigeon.

Schedules of reinforcement can vary such that, for example, food may follow not every lever push but every tenth push. Random numbers can be used to generate intermittent patterns of reinforcemnt. One aim of such schedules is to avoid too rapid satiation of the organism, for, once satiated, food is no longer a reinforcer and activity will decline.

Negative reinforcement involves making the *withdrawal* of an "adversive" reinforcer contingent upon the emission of the operant. For example, the cage could contain an electric grid. Any pigeon not pushing the lever at a given frequency could be subjected to a shock. Analogous to the meaning of positive reinforcement, we know the shock was a negative reinforcer if its withdrawal schedule resulted in increasing frequencies of emission of the operant (i.e., the act). [For an excellent treatment of operant concepts, see Burgess and Bushell (1969:27–48).]

The term punishment has a particular technical meaning within operant psychology. A punishment is an *extinguisher* of behavior. Something is known to be a punishment if the frequency of an organism's behavior is *reduced over time*. Like reinforcements, punishments are contingent on act emissions.

Logically, it follows that punishments, like reinforcements, may be positive or negative. A "positive punishment" schedule would make application of the positive contingent upon the emission of the act by the organism. If the pigeon were not fed if it pushed the lever, and the frequency of lever pushing declined, that schedule would be one of "positive punishment." Negative punishments can be used by making them contingent upon emission of the act—the pigeon would be shocked if the lever were pushed.

The strength of operant psychology lies in the extreme simplicity of its basic concepts and the linkages between them. Its weakness lies in the total absence of any formal procedures by means of which these ideas could be built into a complex whole in any application. Any scientific theory does begin with very simple ideas. But any scientific theory has procedures by means of which it can build up more complex ideas from these simpler ones. Because such procedures are lacking in operant psychology, the operant sociologist is left with only these very simple ideas and the simple linkages among them.

One general consequence of the primitive level of theory development in operant psychology is its inability to deal effectively with complex objects and events. Anderson and Bower explain that Skinner's behaviorism is "just not powerful enough to capture the complexity of human memory or language" (1973:33). This limitation is vitally important insofar as its application to social events is concerned. Let the concept, "operant man" be characterized by all of the behavioral capabilities and all of the *limits* of operant psychology as a theory of human behavior. It immediately follows that operant man cannot speak. Is operant man then capable of social exchange? We shall see at a later point. First some narrower yet critical problems of operant *reductionist* sociology must be considered.

The first problem of operant reductionist sociology is its reduction of social to psychological phenomena. To understand reduction as a problem, it is first necessary to see why social phenomena cannot be reduced.

Consider the case of two persons exchanging. In fact, most exchanges do happen between two people. One type of two-person exchange is a bilateral monopoly in which the two are treated as if they were effectively isolated from any other possible exchange. As an isolated dyad, the two must work out for themselves the rates of exchange to be agreed upon. It may be that individual characteristics of the two who are engaged in the exchange can affect the agreed upon rate of exchange.

But two people exchanging in a market are also *only two people exchanging*. As members of a market the process and outcome of their interaction will be determined by others who are not necessarily present at their interaction. In fact, the others may not be actively exchanging. What will any exchange rate be? That rate will be determined by the structure of the market, not by the individual characteristics of the two. This treatment of the market as the determinant of the rate of exchange is common to neoclassical economics, Marxist economics and the elementary theory—though the treatment of the market structure, in each case, is different.

The structure of a market is not a consequence of the characteristics of the individuals exchanging in the market. Nor is the structure a consequence of the numbers of individuals so engaged. The market structure (and *any* other social structure) is not even the sum of the individual characteristics of the individuals engaged in the relationships.

The idea of structure is as important in sociology as it is in chemistry. Coal and diamonds are composed of carbon atoms. They are distinguished by their chemical structure, not by their physical elements.

However, George Homans, the leading operant-exchange sociologist, has taken the position that, "there are no general sociological propositions . . . and that the only general propositions of sociology are in fact psychological" (1964:817). Take this assertion as a statement, not of provable fact on Homans's part, but of a program for operant exchange theory. The sense of that program is to reduce social phenomena to psychological ones, and in particular to ones that can be covered by operant psychological theory. Call this the *operant reductionist position*.

From the operant reductionist position, human behavior is most fundamentally (in Homans's view, wholly) a consequence of the reinforcement histories of the individuals that make up the system in question. [See Homans (1961:passim).] Since there are no general social "propositions," the network in which relationships occur cannot matter. *Thus, everything that is social can be understood by examining dyads*—that is, by examining two-person groups in isolation from all other relations that can occur or do occur in the system. In fact, the only possible bearing of any other people upon any two-person exchange would be through their historically prior acts as those acts determine the *reinforcement histories* of the two people in the relationship.

The reduction of social phenomena to individual reinforcement histories and to dyads of individuals is fundamentally wrong. Worse, it is fundamentally misleading. Its wrong and misleading character can be seen in the following example.

Consider the capitalist hiring in an overfilled labor market. What wage will he pay? From the operant reductionist point of view, he will pay the wage most rewarding to himself. But the wage settled upon is very low. It must follow that capitalists have reinforcement histories that lead them to find low wages for workers most rewarding. It must also follow that the workers have reinforcement histories that lead them to find low wages most reinforcing.

The idea that workers find low wages most reinforcing is absurd. It is precisely to such absurdities that reductionism necessarily leads. Has the appeal to reinforcement histories explained the case? It has assuredly not explained the rate of exchange. Once the rate of exchange was given, an appeal is made to reinforcement histories as self-evident "explanations" of the exchange rate. But no derivation of the rate from given conditions is offered. Thus, no explanation is offered.

The determination of the reinforcement histories of particular people is crucial to any explanation of human behavior offered from Homans' point of view. To study reinforcement histories, a theory of stimulus discrimination and generalization would have to be developed and used. However, Homans does not develop or use such a theory and does not study any reinforcement histories. [See Homans (1961:53).] Thus, Homans offers no explanations whatsoever.

The reason why the rate of exchange was for a minimal wage was because of the structure of the relationship system. The job market is overfilled. Thus, any attempt by any worker to demand a wage higher than the minimum would be rejected by the capitalist in favor of any lower offer. If other potential workers prefer work at the lower wage to not working, the wage will be bid down successively to the observed minimal wage. Thus, the wage is not a consequence of reinforcement histories, the relationship cannot be seen as dyadic between only the capitalist and one prospective employee, or as a sum of a number of those relationships. Thus, the reductionist position is wrong and fundamentally misleading. Reductionism is the first fundamental fault of Homans's (and others') operant exchange theory.

The second fundamental fault of operant exchange theory is the view that, of all the possible kinds of social relationships, only exchange relationships matter. More specifically, both Homans and Peter Blau have rejected the significance of relationships that contain "negatives." (Both coercive and conflict relationships contain negatives.) For example, Homans has stated that

> The use of punishment is an inefficient means of getting another person to change his behavior: it may work but it seldom works well. . . . Punishment or its threat is still less efficient when it is used not just to stop a person from doing something but to get him to perform a particular action . . . punishment makes rewarding *any* action that allows him to avoid or escape the punishment and not just the one we have in mind. (Homans, 1974:26)

Similarly, Blau stated that

> Punishment is not a very effective method of influencing behavior, as has been increasingly recognized. . . . Later experiments by Skinner and Estes essentially confirmed the conclusion that punishment is a poor reinforcer. (Blau, 1964:224)

The first point of note is that neither Homans nor Blau seems to have a clear grasp of operant theory. Homans stated that punishment does not work well in getting someone to act. That is hardly surprising since punishment, by its operant definition, is a method of extinguishing behavior. Blau states that punishment is a poor reinforcer. But Blau is wrong. Punishment is not a *poor* reinforcer—it is not a reinforcer at all. Punishment reduces the frequency of behavior. Reinforcers increase the frequency of behavior. Therefore, it is *formally* and *theoretically* incorrect to state, as does Blau (and imply as does Homans), that punishment is a poor reinforcer, for punishment is *not a reinforcer* at all but rather an extinguisher of behavior.

The effect of this confusion is to leave the impression that operant *psychologists* consider negative reinforcement to be an ineffective method of reinforcement. *Nothing could be further from the truth.* Some operant psychologists have asserted that punishment is not very good at performing one task: suppressing firmly established patterns of behavior. But negative reinforcement, far from being dismissed as ineffective, has consistently been shown to be a powerful and effective means for establishing and maintaining patterns of behavior (Don Bushell, personal communication).

Homans suggests that negatives do not work very well as means for altering behavior because they chase people away. He stated, for example, that

> either two persons reward one another in more than one way, like each other on more than one count, and increase their interaction, or they will hurt one another in more than one way, dislike one another, and decrease interaction. (Homans, 1967:46)

Thus, if people do not exchange, but attempt to coerce, then their relationship will always be transient. This may be the case where some types of small groups are concerned. For example, a guest who was violent and insulting would probably not be invited back for dinner. Sometimes people are able to escape negative sanctions, and when they can be escaped without undue cost, those negatives will not be very effective.

The implication is that of all possible relationships, sociologists need only study exchange relationships. But the evidence is overwhelmingly against that position. Are we to deny that we know that slave states endured over periods of many centuries, that most people pay their taxes to avoid fine or imprisonment, and that robbery, though not one of the more respectable professions, is nonetheless a means of livelihood for some? Coercion works whether we like it or not, and sometimes it works very well indeed.

However, in modern societies, most social relationships that do occur are exchange relations. Is this prevalence of exchange in modern society because it is (as implied by Homans and Blau) a more effective social relationship than (for example) coercion? Precisely the opposite is the case. Because coercion is so highly effective, systems of coercion have grown very large and highly centralized. These systems are the organizations of modern states. In modern states the power to produce negative sanctions is highly centralized, so much so that fewer and fewer people have the means of negative sanctioning available to them. Thus, the only sanction basis for their relationships is positive sanction and consequently their relationships must necessarily be ones of exchange. Thus, exchange relationships are so all-pervasive because coercion is such a very effective social relationship. Again, we see how reductionist operant exchange theory can be misleading.

However, the problems that result from the rejection of coercive relationships go deeper. Having rejected coercion, exchanges are treated as if they were independent of all other kinds of relationships. This is consistent with the operant reductionist position and is similar to the treatment of exchange in neoclassical economic theory. However, economic theorists increasingly recognize that exchange cannot be treated independently from other kinds of relationship.

Consider only the case of two individuals entering into an exchange in a modern society. That these two people can conceive of the possibility of the act of exchange is first of all dependent upon their joint recognition that both have enforceable property rights. Nor is this recognition a psychological quirk that is limited to two persons. Instead it rests quite solidly upon the enforcing powers of the political state and the property rules that it enforces. Both Marx and Weber recognized these points, which are also discussed in Chapter 8 of this volume.

Systems of exchange vary considerably from one society to another. However, almost all exchanges occur within a larger coercive network. Sometimes that network is the state, and sometimes it is not. But in no case can the larger coercive network be ignored if the exchanges that can occur and do occur are to be understood. Ignoring coercion is the second fundamental fault of operant reductionist exchange theory.

However, the most fundamental fault of operant social exchange theory is that it is operant, and not very sophisticated operant at that. The image of social exchange given by Homans is of two operant men somehow encountering one another in which the act (operant) emitted by the first is a positive reinforcer for the second. The second, then, emits an operant to the first that is a positive reinforcer for the first. This sequence of emissions and reinforcements continues to satiation as affected by certain other conditions. The explanation of the interaction rests upon the reinforcement histories of the two. Since Homans explicitly rejects investigation into reinforcement histories, no explanation of any behavior can be offered.

Is a sequence of reinforcements, as in the case of Skinner and his pigeon (a case explicitly mentioned by Homans) a *social* relationship? Could any social relationship be properly seen as a sequence of reinforcements? Consider the case of a modern economic exchange.

Any modern economic exchange occurs only if there is joint agreement on the rate of exchange—that is, upon the price of the commodity. But no operant exchange includes any verbalizations concerning rules, such as the prices that govern these relationships. An economic exchange may occur only once—it need not be part of any sequence. Thus, economic exchange cannot be treated as if it were simply a sequence of reinforcements.

The plausibility of the operant position in sociology rests upon an *accidental similarity* between a sequence of reinforcements and some (not all) exchange relationships. Some exchanges have sequences but do they necessarily end at satiation? A consumer may buy only some commodities from one store because she knows that the others can be bought more cheaply elsewhere. The sequence of exchange would thus end prior to satiation. (Nor could the conclusion of that exchange be explained by any other conditions offered by Homans.) But operant actors do not use language, cannot read prices, and thus cannot maximize in markets—or elsewhere for that matter.

Accidental similarity as the basis for Homans' operant exchange theory is immediately evident in the case of coercion. Take the case of the mugger and victim. Muggers typically encounter their victims only once. Furthermore, most victims are not mugged regularly by sequences of muggers. The valuables of the victim are extracted by *threat* of negative sanction, not by the transmission of a sequence of negative sanctions. Mugging does not rest upon a past reinforcement history of the victim or upon the use of negative *reinforcements* by the mugger. It is the *rule*, "Your money or your life," and the understanding of the rule by the victim that matters. Perhaps it was wise of Homans and Blau to ignore coercion.

In examining and rejecting operant exchange theory it has been seen that we must be sensitive to the systems in which exchange occurs, and within those systems to the relations between exchange and coercion. However, it has also been seen that human social relationships are rule governed. In some exchange relations these rules are prices, in some offers, and in others orders. Other exchange relations are governed by rules of other kinds. In coercive relations rules in the form of threats occur. One aim of the elementary theory is to account for the *generation of rules* in systems of relationships.

E. The Methodological Foundations of the Elementary Theory

The fundamental reason why we need theory to understand the world was explained to us by Fritz Heider:

> The world undoubtedly has a pattern. But we cannot know that pattern directly for the information which we receive from the world comes to us in little bits (quanta). We must reconstruct the world in our minds and we call that reconstruction theory. I form patterns in my mind. My whole life has been a search for these patterns. When these patterns correspond to information from the world, I write them down as a theory. That is how I understand. (Personal communication)

There are indeed very important limits upon our knowledge of the external world. We can observe objects and we can observe events, *but we cannot observe the connection between objects and events*. This has been known since Hume.

There are two fundamentally different solutions to this problem of knowledge. To the empiricist Hume, the answer lay in observation and habit. If we see one billiard ball roll, contact a second and see the second roll, and if we observe this sequence of events time and time again, then a habit is formed which conjoins the first with the second event in our minds. We express this "constant conjunction" by saying that the first billiard ball *caused* the second to roll—the first event is called the cause, and the second the effect. Modern systematic empiricism was intended to be an extension of Hume's empiricism. But its probably related independent and dependent variables, causal inferences and statistical analyses lack even the "predictive" power of Hume's empirical method.

The second solution to the problem of knowledge is scientific theory in the sense implied by Heider. In scientific theory, as explained by the physicist Heinrich Hertz:

> We form for ourselves images or symbols of external objects: and the form which we give them is such that the necessary consequences of the image in thought are always the images of the necessary consequences in nature of the things pictured. (Hertz, 1956:1)

Taking Heider and Hertz together we find that the core of any scientific theory is *patterned mental images,* and, by extension, the procedures by which they are formed. *When written down,* these patterned mental images are called models. The parts of these models are abstract objects and abstract events. The procedures for forming these models we call a *modeling procedure.* In the elementary theory an interpretation of network geometry will be our modeling procedure—our means for writing down and communicating the theory's mental images.

Now here is the key for understanding why the complicated conceptual apparatus of a scientific theory is developed. The abstract objects and events of the theory can be made similar to observable objects and events. Thus, in thought, they stand for objects and events of the world. *But the abstract objects and events of theory are connected to one another by definitions, principles and laws.* These connections of objects and events of the theory, when interpreted empirically, allow us to understand the patterning of objects and events in the world which could not have been understood empirically because empirical patterns and connections (if any) are fundamentally unknowable. Thus, a model drawn from a theory can be used to understand certain structures and processes of the world.

But a well-formed theory does more than form a single model for the world and interconnect its parts. A theory with a modeling procedure can be used to form a wide variety of models whose objects and events, structures, processes and outcomes vary considerably from one to another. This kind of theory can be used for understanding cases of widely differing observable qualities. Thus, it is said that this type of theory has wide scope of application.

What will the models of the elementary theory look like? How will they be interpreted? The networks shown in Figure I are examples of how some parts of an elementary theoretic model will appear. The points a and b will be interpreted as social actors, the arcs between them will be interpreted as social acts. In Figure I two types of social acts are represented, one having a positive and one a negative sign. These will be called (respectively) positive and negative sanctions.

Models are not simply maps. A map is drawn to represent an object that exists or an event that has occurred. A model is drawn for theoretic purposes. One theoretic purpose may be mapping—that is, to represent what has occurred in a

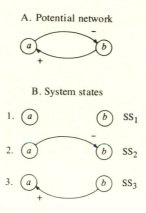

A. Potential network

B. System states

FIGURE I. A coercive social relationship.

social relationship. Another theoretic purpose can be to represent what *could* occur in a social relationship.

Let A of Figure I represent all of the social acts that *could* occur between a and b. The actor a could transmit a negative sanction to b. The actor b could transmit a positive sanction to a. Alternatively, neither act could occur.

Seeing networks as models of possible occurrences, not simply as maps of actual occurrences, leads to certain distinctions. For example, Figure IA is a *potential* network if it represents all of the acts possible for the two actors. This network represents a coercive relationship. For example, a could be a mugger and b the potential victim. If Figure IA is the potential network of a coercive relationship, then a may or may not "transmit" the negative sanction to b, and b may or may not transmit the positive sanction to a.

Assume for this relationship that either a sanctions b, b sanctions a, or neither acts. This "assumption" is an *initial condition*. Under this initial condition there are three possible *events* for the relationship. These events are represented as B1, B2 and B3 of Figure I. We will call each of these possible events a *system state*. Any system state is always a subset of a potential network. Conversely, the union of an exhaustive set of system states is the potential network.

System states (abbreviated as SS_n) can have a number of purposes. If exclusive and exhaustive as in this example, one of the system states will be the outcome of the modeled relationship—the *actual* network. Assume that B3 is the actual network. Why then did the actor b transmit the positive sanction to a? In answering that question two further uses for system states will be seen.

It may be helpful to know what the actor b values, and how those valuations are ordered in a preference system. How can we construct a preference system for b? One way is to order the system states. Since this is a theoretic exercise we can order the system states as we choose. Let that order be $SS_1 > SS_3 > SS_2$. Since these system states are exhaustive under our initial condition, the representation of b's preference system is exhaustive for this relationship.

Now we must ask, since the actor b prefers SS_1, why is the outcome of the relationship SS_3? In answering that question a second use for system states will be seen.

Let a communicate b the following rule, $SS_3 \lor SS_2$. The rule means either b transmits the positive sanction or a will transmit the negative sanction. (In ordinary language this might mean, "Your money or your life.") The expression "$SS_3 \lor SS_2$" is called a *contingency rule*. Thus, a second use for system states is to express contingency rules.

Contingency rules include prices, offers, orders and threats. The contingency $SS_3 \lor SS_2$ is a threat. First notice that the threat, if it is true, *has cut down the number of alternatives possible for the relationship from three to two*. Now SS_1 is not possible, for if b does not act, a will. If b does not transmit the positive sanction to a (SS_3) then a will transmit the negative sanction to b (SS_2).

Let us take the threat as true and believed by b. Now we can infer why SS_3 is the actual network—that is, we can infer why b chose to transmit the positive sanction to a. The threat is believed by b, and b prefers SS_3 to SS_2. Thus b selects SS_3 (the best of the two possibilities) and transmits the positive sanction to a.

In the example we have shown how the system states are drawn out of a potential network and have shown two uses for system states, first to represent a system of preferences for an actor and second to represent a contingency rule communicated by one actor to another.

A third use of system states was implicit in this example. Remember that it was assumed that b *believed* the rule communicated by a. The *content* of that belief was the rule, $SS_3 \lor SS_2$. Thus, system states can be also used to represent the beliefs of actors.

This example demonstrates how to begin the modeling of a dyadic coercive relationship with the elementary theory. This demonstration was a mental experiment. Beginning with some very simple ideas such as positive and negative sanctions, potential network and system states of that network, it demonstrates how theoretically precise meanings can be assigned to ideas such as preference systems, contingency rules and beliefs. Since system states were a referent of preferences, contingency rules and beliefs, the meaning of each in relation to the other was immediately clear and unambiguous. By extension it will be possible to develop a precise theoretical vocabulary of terms that are interrelated by their content and by the procedures of the theory.

However, this was *not* a complete demonstration of how a social relationship is treated as a system of interaction. What is the origin of a's contingency rule? Why did b believe it? Why didn't b develop a contingency rule and communicate that rule to a?

These questions refer to further theoretic *procedures* that need to be introduced. The introduction of those *procedures* is the aim of the next chapter. That chapter will begin by introducing the sanction concepts and will build up concepts for social actor, social act and social relationship. Further *procedures* will extend these to formulations for social interaction. Procedures for the

analysis of structures are introduced in later chapters. Clearly, theoretic procedures are the core of this theory.

With these procedures you, the reader, will be able not merely to follow the
analyses offered in this volume, but, by extension, will be able to bring this
theory to bear upon cases not yet considered. In sociology, theories are typically
presented as the end product of research. Such theories have no procedures.
Thus, they have no utility for future research. Because it is a theory for use, the
core of the elementary theory is its procedures.

Though the foregoing example was incomplete it can be used to illustrate an
essential difference between physical and social theory. The objects of application of physical theory are not social activities, but objects and events that are
external to people as conscious actors. Correspondingly, when a physical system
is modeled it is viewed from the *outside* by the theorist. The theorist may begin
the construction of a social model from that same outside viewpoint. However,
the analysis of social interaction immediately requires that the theorist take the
viewpoint of the actor(s) involved in the relationship. That is, the theorist takes a
viewpoint from *inside* the actor. In fact the theorist will typically take the
viewpoint inside one and then inside another actor working out the interaction by
sequentially thinking it through from the point of view of each (type of) actor.

The theoretic procedure of thinking through the interactions from the points of
view of the actors—of being able to do so with precision—is the first aim of the
theory. If the basic concepts are precise then that procedure will be so precise that
two or more theorists will think any fully conditioned interaction through
identically. That is, they will *see* it in exactly the same way and will be able to
exactly communicate that viewpoint to each other.

It is possible to think through interactions from the point of view of the actors
precisely, because the actors are not concrete individuals but theoretic constructions. Because they are constructions of the theorist, the theorist specifies the
actors' preferences and beliefs—which is to say their *meanings*. Because they are
constructions, theoretic actors are *transparent*. People's meanings cannot be
directly observed. Thus they are subjective meanings. However, social actors, as
theoretic constructions, have *objective meanings*.

The objective meaning of abstract social actors is but an instance in the
elementary theory of the more general condition of all scientific theory—that all
parts of any theory are known and are interconnected. As pointed out at the
beginning of this section, the relations of the observable world cannot be known
by observation. The purpose of any theory, physical or social, is to produce
models whose parts are theoretically connected.

Causes cannot be observed. Since they cannot, the empirical use of cause has
been dispensed with in the physical sciences. [See Toulmin (1953:119).]
Similarly, meanings cannot be observed. Thus the *empirical* use of meanings has
been dispensed with in the elementary theory.

Since the elementary theory has a modeling procedure, a wide variety of types
of models can be developed. From these possible models one or more can be
selected to compare to an empirical case of interest. The case and the model may
correspond. If they correspond, the relations among the parts of that model will

help us understand (and explain) the connections (if any) among the parts of the empirical case—connections that cannot be apprehended by observation.

F. Summary and Final Comments

Following Hume, the objects and events of the phenomenal world are not connected by relations that are themselves observable. This point has important implications that are recognized by all sociologists. In observing people, the individual not trained in social science may see no more than individual activities. The sociologist will infer from those acts the presence of social relationships. The first priority of any social theory should be to present constructs for those inferred relationships, their structure and the connections among their parts. Up till now no social theory has addressed this first problem in a general way.

The elementary theory addresses that problem by developing a modeling procedure which is an interpretation of network theory. Interpreted networks represent the (inferred) social relationships of the empirical world. The "space" in which they are drawn is quite literally (abstract) *social space*. To that space belong the abstract concepts of social acts, relationships, meanings, structures and so forth.

However, it is also possible to project nonsocial but socially related phenomena onto that space. At a point late in the next chapter procedures for representing biophysical and cognitive conditions for action systems will be introduced.

The elementary theory does not use ideas drawn from operant psychology for a complex of reasons. It does not use game theory for somewhat different reasons that can now be briefly noted. The theory is intended to interpret individual acts as they occur in structured relationships. The calculus of game theory is probabilistic and thus cannot be used to interpret individual acts but, in effect, only the average of a number of acts. Thus, game theory will not be used.

The actors of the elementary theory are abstract constructs. That they are constructs and not people must be continually emphasized. This continual emphasis can be made by gender reference. As theoretic constructs social actors have no sex. Thus they cannot be he or she. They are abstract objects and as such each actor is an *it*. By referring to any actor as an "it" a continual reminder will be given that these are constructs, not people—though these constructs may be useful for the interpretation of the acts of people.

What direction of development should the elementary theory take? The broad-gauge theories of Marx and Weber are the most useful ones yet offered. Whether we are or are not successful in reflecting their insights in our work must be left to the judgment of the reader. In any case, we will offer a flexible modeling procedure for representation of social relationships to a field as yet devoid of such procedures.

References

Anderson, J. R., and G. H. Bower
  1973 *Human Associative Memory*. New York: Halstead Press.

Blau, Peter
  1964 *Exchange and Power in Social Life*. New York: John Wiley and Sons.

Burgess, Robert L., and Don Bushell, Jr.
  1969 *Behavioral Sociology*. New York: Columbia University Press.

Einstein, Albert
  1954 *Ideas and Opinions*. New York: Crown Publishers.

Galilei, Galileo
  1954 *Dialogues Concerning Two New Sciences* (tr. Henry Crew and Alfonso deSalvio). New York: Dover.

Hertz, Heinrich
  1956 *The Principles of Mechanics*. New York: Dover.

Homans, George C.
  1961 *Social Behavior: Its Elementary Forms*. New York: Harcourt, Brace and World.
  1964 Bringing the men back in, *American Sociological Review,* 29(5):809–818.
  1967 Fundamental social processes, in Neil Smelser (ed.), *Sociology: An Introduction*. New York: John Wiley and Sons.
  1974 *Social Behavior: Its Elementary Forms*. New York: John Wiley and Sons.

Marx, Karl
  1964 *Pre-Capitalist Economic Formations* (tr. Jack Cohen, ed. E. J. Hobsbawm). New York: International Publishers.
  1967a *Capital* (Vol. 1) (ed. Frederick Engels). New York: International Publishers.
  1967b *Capital* (Vol. 3) (ed. Frederick Engels). New York: International Publishers.
  1969 Preface to a contribution to the critique of political economy, in *Karl Marx and Frederick Engels: Selected Works* (Vol. 1). Moscow: Progress Publishers.

Marx, Karl and Frederick Engels
  1947 *The German Ideology* (ed. R. Pascal). New York: International Publishers.

Newton, Isaac
  1966 *Principia* (Vol. 2). Berkeley: University of California Press.

Toulmin, Stephen
  1953 *The Philosophy of Science*. New York: Harper.

Weber, Max
  1949 *The Methodology of the Social Sciences* (tr. and ed. Edward Shils and Henry Finch). Glencoe, IL: Free Press.
  1951 *The Religion of China* (tr. and ed. Hans Gerth). Glencoe, IL: Free Press.
  1963 The social causes of decay of ancient civilization, in Russel Kahl (ed.) *Studies in Explanation*. Englewood Cliffs, NJ: Prentice-Hall.
  1978 *Economy and Society* (ed. Guenther Roth and Claus Wittich). Berkeley: University of California Press.

I

The focus of this section is on relatively small systems and their processes of social interaction. The first concern of the section is certain theoretically pure dyadic relationships considered in isolation. The concern then shifts to small "communitarian" systems. Do undifferentiated communities have social structures? The answer given in this section is yes. However, the structure is by no means fixed but varies by the conditions of the system.

In Chapter 2 the basic concepts and procedures of the elementary theory are put forward. For simplicity of presentation the methods of modeling and of mental experimentation are limited to two-person groups. In most empirical cases, the interactions between two people cannot be treated as if they were isolated from all other interactions. Thus most (but not all) of the cases considered are empirically unrealistic. However, the procedures presented for the treatment of two person groups can be immediately extended to larger and more complex structures. Thus the utility of the ideas of Chapter 2 is not limited by the examples worked out there.

MICROSYSTEMS

Using the basic concepts and procedures of the elementary theory, Chapter 3 deals with the problem of structure in undifferentiated groups. In that chapter an answer is given to the question, "How do undifferentiated communities maintain order?" Also addressed is the question, "How are the systems of social exchange controlled in the absence of a state?" That is the Hobbesian problem. Models built up within the elementary theory give a new answer to the Hobbesian problem of order.

Is there evidence supportive of the model developed in Chapter 3? This question is addressed in Chapters 4 and 5. In Chapter 4 a small system of social exchange among artisans is discussed. This system is formally illegal — thus the term, "black" exchange. This investigation finds evidence for a system of controlled exchange that corresponds well to that expected in light of the model.

Chapter 5 extends this analysis to a small community as seen over time. There is evidence that, at one time, social exchange was a very important element of this community and further evidence that the basis for that exchange first changed and then declined as the larger economic system penetrated further and further into the community.

What are the relations between communities and the larger systems in which they can be embedded? That question is the concern of Chapter 6, the concluding chapter of this section. By considering again the model for order and exchange in smaller systems, a new understanding is gained concerning the weakening of the power of the local community to reproduce itself as an effective social structure.

2

David Willer

The development of the theoretic formulations of this chapter was supported in part by Grant Number SOC 76-02753 from the National Science Foundation, Faculty Fellowship in Science, and by grants from the General Research Fund of Kansas University. The author would like to thank Professor Douglas Heckathorn for contributions to the development of formulations included in this chapter. Contributions have also been made by Professors Bo Anderson, John S. Brennan, Steven Gilham and Frank Southard. The author would also like to thank Professor Robert Antonio for his occasionally brilliant comments on the manuscript. Needless to say the author takes full responsibility for the faults of formulation and presentation.

THE BASIC CONCEPTS
OF THE ELEMENTARY THEORY

A. Introduction

As the basic concepts of the elementary theory are introduced in this chapter, an abstract image of a social world will develop. When that image is sufficiently developed, the system of concepts can be applied to observable phenomena.

The theory contains two kinds of concepts: fundamental and derived. Fundamental concepts, such as sanction, actor and potential network, are defined by properties attributed to networks. Derived concepts, such as exchange, coercion, interest and system state, are defined by the fundamental concepts. The relations among the concepts are given by their definitions, the procedures of modeling, and the two principles and two laws of the theory.

Many concepts of this theory, such as interest, exchange and agreement, have meanings that are very similar to their meanings in ordinary sociological discourse. (Others such as system state and potential network are new.) Making conceptual meanings similar to those of ordinary discourse has the following advantage. If a theory is to be effectively used, it must be intuitively grasped as a whole. Intuitive understandings are strongly related to familiarity. Keeping theoretic meanings of concepts as close as possible to those of ordinary discourse aids intuitive understanding.

Often the fundamental concepts of the theory, for example "potential network" and "positive sanction," will not be familiar. In contrast, derived concepts, even when built up out of unfamiliar fundamental ones, may be familiar. "Exchange" is a derived concept whose meaning corresponds closely to its meaning in ordinary discourse. However, exchange is defined as a network in which only positive sanctions are potential. In the elementary theory the concept of interest is derived from the preferences of an actor. Both actor and preferences are fundamental concepts. Yet anyone familiar with Marx's theory would use interest in a manner similar to its use in the elementary theory.

In fact most of the concepts of ordinary sociological discourse are complex ideas. Thus, they cannot be fundamental, but instead must be derived concepts in any systematic theory. Having formed them as derived concepts offers this advantage—that the relations among them are made explicit through their derivation from more simple, fundamental ideas. The meaning of the more complex ideas can be made more precise.

Any systematic theory must begin with fundamental and move to derived concepts. However, that means that the elementary theory will begin with less and move to more familiar ideas. That order is unavoidable given the nature of systematic theory and the kinds of concepts of ordinary discourse.

The following is a presentation not only of concepts but of *procedures* of concept formation and concept use. In later chapters further procedures will be introduced so that complex structures can be built up out of the simple structures introduced here.

B. Some Objects and Events of the Elementary Theory

The abstract objects and events of the elementary theory are built up by attributing properties to network geometric figures. The purpose of this construction is to generate social actors, social relationships and structures of relationship in a Marxian–Weberian mode.[1] The result of this construction is a set of mental images which can be used for the understanding of n-person groups. For purposes of illustration, at this point group size will be limited to two.

In A of Figure I a network of two points connected by one arc is represented. Both the arc and the points are abstract objects of the theory. The points a and b are called actors — the arc is an act by a oriented to b. The act is a "transmission" by a and a "reception" by b. Let the property of a positive sign be added to the arc and placed at the reception end. This arc is now called a *positive sanction*. (See Figure IB.)

The sign is a property of the arc. It is, however, also interpreted as a property of the actor b in the following sense. If b could choose to receive or not to receive the act, if the act is a positive sanction b would choose to receive it. The sign of any arc will be treated as a joint act and actor property. If a negative sign is

---

[1] The aim here is not to claim a legitimation but to acknowledge a debt. The elementary theory begins from the same kind of theoretic and historic concerns as Marx's and Weber's. Its value concerns, muted as they are in this volume, are much closer to the former than the latter. One purpose of the elementary theory is to provide the theorist with a system of somewhat greater precision and flexibility than is found in the classical tradition. The reader, however, should take these thoughts for what they are worth given the evident misuse of the work of both theorists in both theory and practice. Knowledgeable scholars will recognize the influence of each at subsequent points of this and later chapters. That that debt is hereby recognized in no way implies that the author disclaims responsibility for evident faults and errors.

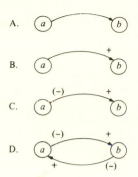

FIGURE I. Some objects and properties of the elementary theory.

placed at the reception end of the arc a negative sanction is represented. Here the interpretation is similar to above with the proviso that if *b* could choose between no reception and the reception of the negative sanction, the former would be selected.

A sign can also be placed at the transmission end of the arc, and to distinguish it clearly from the first sign it is enclosed in brackets as in C of Figure I. The sign is again a property of the act and, in this instance, of the actor *a*. We now have a "bisigned" arc which can be called a *negative–positive* sanction. Since these signs are properties of the arcs and the actors, it is proper to say that they are properties of the network. Other types of acts will be introduced later by attributing other properties to network geometric representations.

In the elementary theory sets of abstract objects can be put together to represent more complex objects as in Figure ID. That representation is a simple model for a dyadic economic exchange relationship. An economic exchange system is defined as one in which all sanctions are negative– positive sanctions. It stands for empirical cases in which the giving up of money or a commodity is a "loss" (the negative sign at the transmission end of the arc) and the reception of same is a "gain" (the positive sign at the reception end of the arc). Let this representation be treated as exhaustive of all the (types of) acts possible for *a* and *b*. This representation is then called a *potential network*.

Beyond signs, the property of quantity can be attributed to any arc (and thus to the actors of the network). Let the *a–b* sanction arc vary in descrete units of one from zero to 40 and the *b–a* arc vary discretely from zero to one. Now the *object*, the economic relationship, contains 82 possible *events*.

Figure II contains representations for three of the 82 possible events. These events are called *system states* and are numbered in an arbitrary order. System states then are events which are possible, and if our list is exhaustive, will contain the event(s) which "actually" occur(s) in the relationship. Any representation of an actual event is called an *actual network* and will take a form identical to system states.

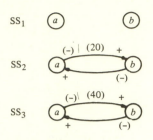

FIGURE II. System states as abstract events.

For present purposes let us arbitrarily limit the system states possible for the exchange to the three of Figure II. Thus either no exchange will occur or an exchange will occur at the rate of 20 or 40 to one. These networks can now be used to attribute a further property, *preference system,* to actors a and b.

Let any preference system be an ordering of system states. Let the preference system of a be $SS_2 > SS_1 > SS_3$ and the preference system of b be $SS_3 > SS_2 > SS_1$. (As we shall see, these actor properties are by no means independent of properties of larger network systems in which they occur.) Further properties, such as *beliefs,* can be attributed to the actors a and b. One element of the beliefs of b could be an accurate (or inaccurate) knowledge of a's preference system.

A wide variety of types and structures of relationship can be generated either by constructing further n-actor systems with presently defined properties or by the introduction of further properties. Proceeding in this way has at least two clear advantages. An internally consistent and unambiguous technical vocabulary for describing abstract objects and events is generated, and the *structure* of any system of action can be given a clear representation which is consistent with actor-related terms such as preferences and beliefs.

But what will actors a and b do? Which of the "possible worlds" will be selected in their interaction? To move to questions of interaction requires that we know the principles (and laws) upon which any actor will act.

C. Why Scientific Principles and Laws Are Not Generalizations

The first principle of the elementary theory is

> P_1 ALL SOCIAL ACTORS ACT TO MAXIMIZE THEIR
> EXPECTED PREFERENCE STATE ALTERATION.

Let the three ordered system states for a and b be their possible preference states; let the actors' beliefs be complete and accurate; and let the interaction begin at SS_1. By examination of the preferences and application of the first principle, we can infer that the only system state (other than SS_1) that is possible is SS_2 [for a prefers SS_1 (no exchange) to SS_3, the 40-to-one exchange rate]. SS_2 will be the actual network of the specified interaction. This event follows from the application of the first principle to the formulations.

System state two also exhausts the interaction process for this particular system. This follows as a consequence of the comprehensive beliefs attributed to each of the actors. Since each actor has full information concerning the preferences and beliefs of the other, no communications are needed by either in their decisions to act. More realistic interaction process models will be possible, but this model needs no apology. Any theory should be capable of producing realistic models, but it should also be capable of producing unrealistic ones, particularly when they are theoretically simple.

The first principle is not a utility maximization principle in the normally accepted sense of that term. As a theoretic exercise, the 82 system states possible for the economic exchange system could be given any order for either actor. Only a small subset of these would result in anything like "utility" maximization of the possible action outcomes. Given the appropriate conditioning even the most idiosyncratic actors can be modeled.

[*General note*: The reader may have noticed that, if we allow every possible ordering of system states (as just suggested) a possible inconsistency has been introduced between the idea of sanction as a property of an actor and preference system as a property of an actor. For example, one possible preference system for the actor *a* would rank the system state of no exchange higher than a system state in which *a* received the positive from *b* and did not transmit any sanction to *b*. The problem is this—must we allow this theoretic inconsistency in order to allow the theoretic possibility of actors with "irrational" preference systems? This problem is resolved later in the chapter by the introduction of the idea of reflexives. With the introduction of reflexives, any of the orderings discussed above and immediately below can be introduced without generating inconsistencies between the ideas of sanctions and orderings within the preference system.]

Why is the first principle not a generalization? Is it not a falsification of the principle if my Uncle Mike likes to make himself miserable? On the contrary. Here we only need to use the principle to construct a preference system appropriate to the actor "Uncle Mike." That actor's first-ranked world is the one of greatest misery, the second world is the one of next greatest misery and so forth. Now by application of the principle to this actor in a given relationship, along with other elements of the theory yet to be introduced, we can determine the type of action selected.

The first principle of the elementary theory is a theoretic tool and, like the principles "all bodies accelerate at the same rate" and "all light travels in straight lines," cannot be falsified, for its referent is not any empirical event but the abstract objects and events of the theory. Similar statements could be made concerning the second principle and the two laws of the theory to be introduced in Chapter 7.

D. "Objective Meaning" and Initial Conditions

In constructing a model for any interaction system the conditions that are specified for actors include preferences and beliefs. These conditions have as their referent what Marx called consciousness and Weber called "subjective meaning." It is true, for any *empirical* interaction, that *people's* meanings, their preferences and beliefs, are in certain regards subjective. But this is not the case at the theoretic level. All *theoretic actors* have known meanings — or, stated differently, explicit conditions for actors' meanings are introduced as initial conditions of any model. Thus, theoretically, actors' meanings are always known, and in that sense, not subjective but "objective."

At the theoretic level it could be said that our actors are transparent — we can look inside the actor and know *its* preferences and beliefs. (Remember, actors are abstract objects, not people, thus they have no gender and are not he or she but *it*.) Thus we will not say that an actor's preferences are *likely to be* this or that, or what the actor's beliefs *probably are*. In fact probability has no place in the theory. Thus models for particular cases, not just statistical averages of a number of instances, will be constructed. When interpreted we may find that a model constructed for a given case is not sound; that is, we have made an error in one or more of the specified conditions. But we want to know when a mistake has been made, so that the appropriate model can be constructed. No theory is proof against error, but as we shall see the application of the elementary theory contains self-correcting mechanisms.

In the constructing of any model certain conditions must be specified at the outset. These are called *initial conditions*. In any dynamic application, inferring or calculating with the theory then leads to *final* condition(s) or outcomes. Often certain processes or *intermediate* conditions are implied.

Initial conditions are not independent variables and final conditions are not dependent variables. We are not doing empiricism here.

E. First- and Second-Order Models

Theories are always simpler than the empirical world to which they are applied. But this fact is often misunderstood for it is thought to mean that theories are simply idealizations whose fit to the world is, at best, only approximate. On the contrary, any theory with a modeling procedure can be used to construct models that are as similar as desired to the objects and events within its scope of application.

Consider the following. If we were interested in doing an experiment on falling bodies, our model for the system would require the determination of certain initial conditions such as g, the gravitational constant, air resistance of the body, and so forth. (These determinations are empirical questions in which we are guided by the theory.) But the color of shirt worn by the experimenter, his/her intentions, the time of day, the phase of the moon, the price of gasoline—none of these possible observations have anything whatsoever to do with the application of the theory to the falling body problem. Better results would not be gained by somehow adding these further facts to the analysis. Empiricists have no theories; thus there are no formal limits to observation. But in the application of any scientific theory we are always guided toward the facts needed and away from the facts that are irrelevant. This is the *first* sense in which any theory is simpler than the empirical world to which it is applied.[2]

There is a second sense in which a *model* drawn from a theory may have further simplifications beyond those considered above. Consider the following example. A football bounding down a rough hillside is a falling body. Physical theory could be used to generate a model, albeit a very complex one, that would be isomorphic to this instance. But models of this complexity, though valid scientific concerns, generally fall outside the work of science. Typically, there must be a technical reason for a construction of particularly high complexity that is particular to one empirical case.

The simplest model that captures the scientifically interesting characteristics of a phenomenon will be called a first-order model. (What counts as first order is a consequence of the way a theory is formulated and can vary from one theory to another. Most discussions in this chapter will be limited to models that are first order from the point of view of the elementary theory.) First-order models are very general in the sense that they are approximately accurate in their fit to a broad scope of empirical cases. Seen from the theory's point of view, in light of the approximate fit, the *cases* are said to be "dirty." On the other hand, the first-order model may *exactly* fit some empirical case that would never exist if we did not construct it experimentally—thus the need for experimental work with the elementary theory *and* the reason why these experiments use simple first-order models.

Second-order models are constructed by elaboration of first-order models. Thus they are always more complex. But the need to model more exactly certain "nonexperimental" cases will lead us, at times, to carry forward these elaborations. Again, as in the case of the football and the hillside, second-order models are more exact for some applications (or limited set of applications) but may be more limited in their approximate fit to a broad scope of empirical cases.

In science empirical generalizations are not used. There is no interest in enumeration of the common qualities of cases. Instead science gains its "generality" through the use of *abstract* theories of broad scope. In the use of scientific theory, its procedures for modeling will allow a nonlimited set of models to be drawn. These models will vary considerably in their abstract objects and events. Some of these are first-order models which we use to gain a general understanding of a broad range of empirical cases. Some models are second-

[2] For explication of these points the reader should see such standard sources as Butterfield (1957), Einstein and Infeld (1938), and Galileo (1954). These same sources are relevant to the variety of methodological points made above. Also, see Willer and Willer (1973). For the importance of modeling procedures and the difficulty even brilliant scientists have in recognizing that importance, see Watson (1968).

order elaborations which are used to gain a precise understanding of a narrower range of empirical cases. It is by these means that science can be said to produce general knowledge.

The use of abstract theory requires mental habits that are different from those typical of much mainstream sociology, political science and anthropology. To those accustomed only to generalization and other empiricist modes of thought, mastering the theory will require a radical shift of perspective. (Two other groups, however, may be immediately comfortable with the elementary theory: classical theorists, particuarly those concerned with Marx or Weber, and formalists.) This chapter is addressed as broadly as possible. Thus procedures of theory use are emphasized again and again. To that end only simple and, for the most part, first-order models are used, leaving more complex derivations to later chapters as they are needed for explanation and interpretation. The models of this chapter are so simple that little can be said concerning structure. Dyadic systems are treated in unrealistic isolation. If the end point of the elementary theory were the end of this chapter, then we would be subject to many of the criticisms that we have leveled at other "theories" of exchange. But, as will be seen, the introduction of the basic concepts and procedures of the theory is only a beginning.

F. A Typology of Social Acts

A sanction is a social action transmitted by one actor and received by another, which alters the preference state of the actor *receiving* the sanction. Positive sanctions are differentiated from negative sanctions by the direction of the preference state alteration of the receiving actor. Note that an act is a sanction if and only if it affects the preference state of the receiving actor. A sanction may or may not affect the preference state of the transmitting actor. A positive sanction that does not affect the preference state of the transmitting actor is called a zero–positive sanction. A negative sanction that does not affect the preference state of the transmitting actor is called a zero–negative sanction. A sanction that lowers the preference state of the transmitting actor and increases the preference state of the receiving actor is called a negative–positive sanction, and similarly for the remaining types.

Certain conventions are followed when sanctions are named and represented which will now be made explicit. When only one sign is mentioned in the naming of a sanction (positive sanction or negative sanction) then that sign *always* refers to the valuation of reception. When two "signs" are mentioned in the naming of a sanction (negative–positive sanction or zero–negative sanction) the first "sign" *always* refers to the valuation of transmission and the second sign *always* refers to the valuation of reception. The conventions for representing sanctions in networks were introduced in Figure I. Remember, for any bisigned arc, the sign for the valuation of transmission is always enclosed in brackets.

It needs to be added that there can be acts which affect the preference state of the transmitter only. These negative–zero and positive–zero acts are not sanctions given the definition of that term.

Why has the term sanction been limited in its meaning only to those acts that affect the preference state of the receiving actor? The reader will recognize that that limitation does introduce a kind of "asymmetry" such that a zero–positive act is a sanction while a positive–zero act is not a sanction. Why the asymmetry? Consider the following points. When sanction was first mentioned it was pointed out that if *b* (the receiving actor) could choose to receive or not receive the act, if the act is a positive sanction, *b* would choose to receive it. Similarly if *b* could choose to receive or not receive another act, if the act is a negative sanction, *b* would choose not to receive it.

But consider again the phrase, "choose to receive or not receive a sanction." Actors choose or choose not to *transmit* acts. A transmitted act need not be received. For example, actor *a* intends to transmit a negative sanction to *b* (a blow with a mace), but the act is avoided by *b* (the mace strikes a shield) —*a* shouts an insult, but it is not heard by *b*. By plan or happenstance a transmitted act may not be received, but immediate choice of action lies not with the receiver but with the transmitter.

Thus for any sanction the preference state of the receiver is always affected (by definition) *but* immediate choice of action or nonaction is always the choice of the transmitter of the act. Thus there is an apparent dilemma in the separation of *choice* and *necessary preference effect* of any sanctioning act.

Meaningful social interaction is the solution to that apparent dilemma. Why does actor *a* make attributions of meaning (of preference and belief) to actor *b*? Because *b* can choose to transmit or not transmit a negative or positive sanction to *a*. Why does *b* make attributions of meaning to *a*? Because *a* can choose to transmit or not transmit a negative or positive sanction to *b*. Why do actors develop rules relating their acts to those of other actors and transmit those rules to those other actors? Because other actors and only other actors can select the sanctions to be transmitted to them.

Thus if *b* believes that *a* has an interest in transmitting to it a negative sanction, if *b* cannot avoid the act by escape or other means, then *b* has an interest in transmitting a threat to *a*, which is a *rule* contingently relating *a*'s action selection to *b*'s. Again, *b* cannot make the choice of action for *a*, but by transmitting the rule, *b* can affect *a*'s choice conditions. Similarly, I cannot *make* another exchange with me. But I can make a rule which is an offer to the other contingently relating our activities such that the other can have an interest in exchange and will choose exchange at the offered rate.

Stated conversely, sanctioning acts are the foundation upon which meaningful social interaction develops, for the *interest* in meaning attribution by any actor rests on the separation of action choice and necessary effect of any sanctioning act. When social theorists ignore these points, social activity is reduced to the meaningless semirandom acts of positive and negative reinforcements—that is, social activity is reduced to operant exchange theory.

Now material and symbolic sanctions will be differentiated. Any material sanction affects the preference state of the receiver through the changes in the actor's physical system or resources. Thus what counts as a material sanction is at least partly a biophysical question which will not be discussed here. But what counts as a resource which has been received as a material sanction or could be transmitted as a material sanction is a social question which is tied to ideas of property (see Chapter 8). Consider the following case. My friend and I have jointly bought a lawnmower. The lawnmower is in my garage and my friend asks to use it. I pass it to him. Should this act be modeled as a material sanction flow? No, for the object in question was a joint resource. Take another case. A hunting community uses nets which are a community resource. One member of the community asks another for the use of a net. The net is passed over to the first. Though this interaction is a social activity, it cannot be an exchange, for all actors of the system shared the resource in question. These issues are dealt with further in later chapters. At this point it is sufficient to note that at least some of what has been called primitive exchange cannot be viewed as such in light of the foregoing distinctions.

Any symbolic sanction affects the preference state of the receiving actor through the actor's beliefs. That effect may or may not be accompanied by a change in the beliefs. For example, an insult is a negative symbolic sanction in that it affects the actor's preference state but it may not change any element of the actor's beliefs. It should go without saying that what counts as a positive symbolic sanction in one relationship or in one society may be a negative symbolic sanction in another relationship or society. Sanctions are not defined by their content, but by their modeled effects. The determination of typical contents of, for example, insults and compliments, is (largely) an empirical question.

It is now possible to complete the typology of social actions by the introduction of the concepts of information and communication. The content of any information flow can be any (believed or disbelieved) condition of the system and any derivation from the conditions. Often a model for a system will only include its sanction flows. However, any model can be elaborated to include information flows, each of which is drawn as an arc with an adjacent "I."

A *communication* is an information flow that affects the beliefs of the actor receiving the flow. The effect can be of two types. If the communication is *believed* when received, then the content of the communication is added to the beliefs of the receiving actor. (Under that condition it can be said that the receiving actor attributes veracity to the transmitter of the communication.) This type of communication can be modeled by an arc with an I^+ "sign" adjacent to the receiving actor. (Note: for this presentation of the elementary theory, actors' beliefs are treated *as if* they were simply *lists of information*. Though this is the simplest possible formulation and is adequate for many uses, power and scope could be gained for the theory by the incorporation of the idea of *structured belief systems*. When that idea is included, then I^+ communications can, beyond being added to beliefs, have further ramifying effects within the belief system of an actor.) A communication with an I^- "sign" adjacent to the receiving actor is disbelieved by the receiver and, although it is not incorporated into the beliefs, can have specified effects upon the elements of the beliefs. (Since beliefs are not treated here as structured, the particular effects of an I⁻ communication would have to be specified as a particular condition for a given model.) Finally, a sign for the transmission of information can be included for any model, such that an I⁺ adjacent to the transmitting actor would indicate an information flow consistent with the transmitting actor's beliefs, preferences and resources (i.e., a truthful statement) and an I⁻ sign would indicate an information flow inconsistent with the above (i.e., a lie, false communication and so forth). Needless to say, the I "signs" of any arc can, as in the case of the sanction signs, vary independently from one another—thus we can model believed lies and disbelieved truthful communications and so forth.

The ideas of sanction and communication should be reviewed in light of the concept of social actor. Social actors have preference systems. When a social act that affects the actor's preference system is received by the actor, that act is called a sanction. Social actors also have beliefs. When a social act is received which affects only the actor's beliefs, that act is called a communication. For the transmitter of both types of acts there can be a preference state alteration which can be indicated graphically and included in the theoretic description of the act. A single social action can have dual effects upon the receiver of the act—both the belief and preference system could be altered. Such an act can be called a sanction–information flow and is dealt with accordingly.

G. The Three Ideal Types of Social Relationship, Some Types of Networks and a Mental Experiment

In this section only the reception sign of sanctions will be considered. Given that limitation for dyadic relationships in which only two sanctions are potential, an exhaustive list of types can be given as in Figure III. There are three (ideal) types: the first system is exchange in which both sanctions are positive; the second is conflict in which both sanctions are negative; and the third and fourth system (which together represent the third ideal type) are coercion, in which one sanction is positive and the other negative. The three ideal types will now be used to illustrate some types of networks that will be consistently used in the analyses of these and other systems.

A *potential network* is a system that contains all of the social acts that are theoretically considered for a given instance. All, some or none of the acts included in the potential network may occur in the relationship. Each of the three ideal types modeled in Figure III will be treated as potential networks. If, for example, a dyadic exchange *could* occur, then its potential network is that given in the figure. To model the occurrence or lack of occurrence of the relationship, a different type of network would be used. Similarly, a conflict relationship, if it is potential, would be modeled as in Figure III. In coercive relationships it is normal that only one of the two potential sanctions flow. Nevertheless, its potential network includes all of the sanctions which could flow regardless of

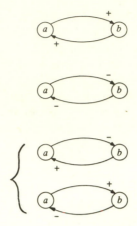

A. Exchange

B. Conflict

C. Coercion

FIGURE III. The three ideal types of social relationships.

whether or not they flow. Since potential networks are exhaustive of all social acts that are theoretically relevant, all other types of networks are subsets of the potential network.

Possible network is a general term for any subset of the potential network. For example, for the exchange relationship of the figure, one possible network is identical to the potential network, another is a network that contains no sanctions—other possible networks contain one positive sanction each, one from *a* to *b* or one from *b* to *a*. There are a number of types of possible networks that are useful in the analysis of relationships and systems of relationship. At this point only system state and actual network will be introduced.

A *system state* (SS_n) is a conditioned possible network. System states can be drawn in light of any theoretically significant conditions. For example, consider all of the system states of the coercive relationship drawn for the conditions (1) that any sanction flow rate is either zero or one and (2) that no more than one sanction can flow for any given time period. Under those conditions there are only the three system states illustrated in Figure IV.

An *actual network* is any system state (or set of system states) which occurs in the relationship. Let the system states of Figure IV be exhaustive and exclusive. It follows then that one and only one of the three system states would be the actual network, which in turn is the outcome of the process of interaction. The aim of the elementary theory is to determine, in light of the conditions initial to this or any other relationship, both the process of the interaction and the system states that will be actualized.

A coercive relationship could represent a mugger (the *a* point) and a victim (the *b* point) or could represent a master (the *a* point) and a slave (the *b* point). The instance of the mugger–victim relationship will be followed through in the mental experiment.

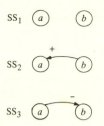

FIGURE IV. Coercive system states.

To model the coercive relationship we need to generate the preference system for each actor. What is the best of all possible worlds for the mugger, the second best and so forth? What is the best of all possible worlds for the victim, the second best and so forth? Let these "worlds" be the system states of the relationship. All that is needed then to generate the preference system for the actors is to order the system states of each of the actors from most to least preferred "world." For this example, let b, the victim, be given the preference system $SS_1 > SS_2 > SS_3$, and a, the mugger, be given the preference system $SS_2 > SS_1 > SS_3$. These preferences are given graphically in Figure V.

Now that we know the preferences of the actors we can consider their interests in the system. *Interest* is a *comparative* term which has as its referent the preference system of the actor. For any system an actor has an interest in attaining its first-ranked system state as compared to any other system state, an interest in attaining its second-ranked system state as compared to any system state ranked lower and so forth.

FIGURE V. Preference systems in coercion as ordered system states.

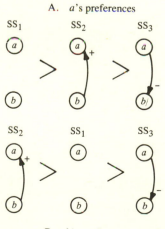

A.   *a*'s preferences

B.   *b*'s preferences

For the coercive relationship b has an interest in attaining SS_1 as compared to any other system state, whereas a has an interest in attaining SS_2 as compared to any other system state. Since b either transmits the positive sanction to a or b does not transmit the sanction, these two system states cannot occur simultaneously. Thus this is a system in which there is an *opposition of interest*.

In a social relationship there is an opposition of interest to the extent that there is not a correspondence in the ordering of preference of the actors. If there is a correspondence in the ordering of the preferences of the actors, then there is a *complement of interest*. For some relationships, particularly economic exchange, these terms are not exclusive in the following sense. A buyer wishes to pay the lowest price possible while a seller wishes to receive the most money possible. To that extent there is an opposition of interest in economic exchange relationships. However, if *both* actors prefer the occurrence of the exchange (over a range of prices) to no exchange, then there is a complement of interest in economic exchange. Thus economic exchanges are, as Weber pointed out, relations of "opposed but complementary interests" (Weber, 1947: 156). (At times opposed interest has been rendered as "conflict of interest." However, in the elementary theory, the term conflict has been preempted by the social relationship of opposed negative sanctions—thus *conflict of interest* will not be used here.)

Returning to the coercive relationship, the initial conditions thus far set forward are as follows. We know (1) the potential network and (2) the system states for the relationship. By ordering those system states we know (3) the preference orders of the actors, and know (by definition and inspection) that there is an opposition of interest in the system.

Now let the initial conditions for the beliefs of the actors be specified. Let it be specified that a (the coercer) has correctly attributed b's preference order and has also attributed to b a lack of information concerning a's preference system. To the actor b let us attribute no beliefs concerning a's preference system, and that information received by b from a is believed. Thus a has full information and believes correctly that b does not. Finally, let it be specified that b cannot escape from the domain of a's coercion, and both actors "know" that it cannot.

Now that the initial conditions for the system have been specified, consider the relationship from the point of view of a. The actor a knows that if it does nothing b will choose its best of all possible worlds, SS_1, and, as a consequence, a will not receive the positive sanction that a has an interest in receiving. How can a act so that b will transmit the positive sanction? As a social actor, a knows (as we do) that the first principle is operative—that is, that all social actors act to maximize their expected preference state alteration. If a hopes to receive b's positive sanction than a must block b's preferred system state (SS_1), leaving b with only the choice of SS_2 and SS_3. Since a believes that SS_2 is preferred to SS_3 by b, a infers (in light of the initial conditions) that b will choose SS_2 if SS_1 is blocked.

How then can a make SS_1 impossible for b? By adopting the rule, "if b were to choose SS_1, a would transmit the negative sanction to b." This rule transforms

SS_1 into SS_3. If a adopted that rule then it would not be possible for b to choose SS_1—that is, SS_1 would be blocked by a's rule and its act upon that rule.

But it is not sufficient that a simply adopt that rule, for a knows (as we do) that b does not have sufficient information to infer that a will adopt that rule; b cannot infer a's rule. If a did not tranmit the rule to b, b would do nothing, thereby selecting SS_1. But if b selected SS_1, a would transmit the negative, transforming SS_1 into SS_3 and SS_3 is a's worst world. Thus a has an interest in transmitting its rule to b. The transmission of the rule is a *threat*.[3]

The reception of the rule, together with b's belief of it, results in its incorporation into b's beliefs. Thus b believes that its alternatives have been narrowed to SS_2 and SS_3 and, preferring the former, transmits the positive sanction to a. As a consequence a attains its best of all possible system states, SS_2, which is the (theoretically) predicted actual network.

The central ideas of *this* mental experiment are the central ideas for the analysis of social action as it occurs in social relationships, whether they be coercive, exchange, conflict or a variety of other types. *The core idea is that the theorist must think through the relationship, not as an outsider, not from the point of view of one actor, but from the point of view of all of the (types of) actors engaged in the system.* By exactly specifying the conditions for the relationship, particularly the preferences, beliefs and potential sanctions of the actors, a consistent set of inferences concerning the course and outcome of the interaction can be made. Essential for that consistency is the exact specification of conditions, which has been made possible by the properties attributed to network representations and by the procedures for working with those networks which have been introduced prior to and within this example. Let us return to the example beginning with a full statement of its initial conditions and again follow through the processes of inference that lead to the conclusion that SS_2 would be chosen by b.

The following is an exhaustive list of the initial conditions for the process and outcome of the coercive relationship modeled above:

1. The system states of Figure IV as an exhaustive list of the outcomes possible for the relationship.
2. The preference systems of Figure V as an exhaustive statement of the preferences of the actors in the relationship.
3. The actor b's inability to escape *(circumscription)*, and correct information of this condition in a's and b's beliefs.
4. The full knowledge of the system by the actor a (i.e., its correct attribution of b's preferences and correct attribution of b's lack of information).
5. The incomplete knowledge of the system by b (especially its lack of information of the order of a's second and third world), and b's belief of the information received from a.

---

[3] It should be noted that a threat is an information flow and may be a communication as are offers and orders. See the Glossary.

In light of these initial conditions, certain elements of the theory are brought to bear. As in all analyses we begin with the first principal, which, stated in terms of interest, is that all actors have an interest in gaining the highest-ranked (and avoiding the lowest-ranked) system state which is believed possible. In light of these ideas the next step is to infer the processes of choice of contingency rule for one of the actors, in this case the actor a. [Note: were we to begin with b the system would remain static at SS_1 (the vacuous system state) until we had moved to the processes of calculation of a. Thus the process and outcome are not affected in this system by which actor is modeled first.] The processes are as follows:

1. *(For a)* The actor a (1) attributes correctly b's preferences, (2) infers that no sanction will be transmitted by b in the absence of initiation of the relationship, (3) decides upon the rule "SS_2 ∨ SS_3" to block b's most preferred world, and (4) decides to communicate the rule. [In light of our knowledge of a's preferences we know (as does a) that this information

2. *(For the system)* The actor a transmits SS_2 ∨ SS_3 to b.

3. *(For b)* The actor b, having received (and believed) the information and not knowing a's preferences, chooses SS_2 because it is preferred to SS_3 and because SS_1 is (believed) blocked.

4. *(For the system)* The actor b realizes SS_2 by transmitting the positive to a. The modeled interaction ends.

The procedure for modeling the processes and outcomes of a social interaction begins with the complete statement of the initial conditions. The initial conditions can be constructed (as in this instance) for theoretic purposes alone, or can be drawn in varying detail for a known social relationship. The process is then modeled by following the processes of choice of one actor, what that actor does vis-à-vis the other(s) and, in turn, the processes of choice of the other actor(s) and their resultant acts. The coercive dyad as modeled here was a very simple system and thus the process of interaction was simple and short. For more complex structures and more complex actors, the processes of interaction can be longer than the simple, four-step process modeled above.

The instance modeled resulted in the transmission of the positive sanction. This mental experiment was conditioned by the lack of information of b and b's belief of a's transmitted rule. However, a was not telling the truth to b when the contingency was transmitted! The fact that the information was false can be easily seen by reference to a's preferences, and the following extension of the mental experiment. Let it be assumed that the initial conditions were altered such that b would not accede to a's threat. What then would a do? If b did not transmit the positive sanction to a, then a could only choose between SS_1 and SS_3 and, since the former was preferred, a would not choose to transmit the negative sanction to b! In other words, a was bluffing.

H. Confrontation and Agreement

In a system of social relationships an *agreement* occurs if two or more socially related actors adopt common and consistent rules.[4] In a system of social relationships a *confrontation* occurs if two or more socially related actors adopt distinct and inconsistent rules. The concepts of agreement and confrontation have important implications for the analysis of systems of interaction. Some of these implications will be drawn out in this section in light of a second model for the dyadic coercive relationship.

The activity of a mugger, shooting and killing the victim and lifting the valuables from the lifeless body, can be interpreted as a biophysical event not a social action. (The event is not social action if it depends only upon the intention of the mugger, not upon the mugger's attributed meanings concerning the victim. See Section L below.) This event will be called "physical coercion." The occurrence of events of this type will be called physical states (PS).

The prospect of physical coercion can condition the outcome of the social relationship. Consider the expanded preference systems given in Figure VI. To the system states considered in the foregoing mental experiment has been added the physical state (PS) of physical coercion which has been ordered and included in the preferences of the actors a and b. In order to indicate that a and b are not acting socially in PS, the "points" representing the actors are "square points." [Note: for the physical state the arcs are not sanctions, but instead indications of the effects of the physical acts.]

For the mental experiment only two initial conditions will be added to the preference systems of Figure VI. First it is specified that b cannot escape. Second

FIGURE VI. Expanded preference systems in coercion as ordered system states (SS_n) and physical states (PS_n).

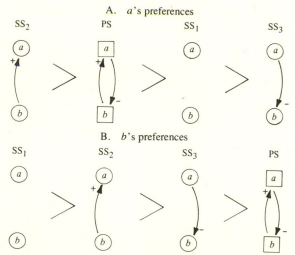

A. a's preferences

B. b's preferences

[4] The term "rule" is introduced below in Sections K and L and in the Glossary.

it is specified that the interaction is a full information system. That is, both a and b have correctly attributed the preference systems of the other and know that b is circumscribed.

First consider the rule that a would adopt in this system. The actor a knows that b is circumscribed and knows that SS_1 will be made impossible if a *alone* chooses to physically coerce b. Thus a can offer b the alternatives of SS_2 and PS. The threat (in ordinary language, "Your money or your life") is "SS_2 v PS." **Because a prefers both of these alternative to any other alternative, a has an unambiguous interest in adopting that rule, and transmitting it to b.**

Now turn to b who has received the rule from a. Since this is a full information system, b knows that a has an unambiguous interest in adopting the rule. In other words, b can map the rule back onto its (correctly) attributed preference system for a and evaluate its implications. One consequence of that evaluation is that b can infer that the communication is true—that is, that a has adopted the rule and will act upon it.

The actor b now has two alternatives. First, it could adopt a's rule, map the rule on to its own preference system, make its decision and act. Let us follow through this alternative first. The rule adopted by a has blocked SS_1 and SS_3. The actor b knows that were it to attempt to select SS_1 it would be transformed into PS by a's physical coercion. Since b prefers SS_2 to PS, b would transmit the positive sanction to a ending the relationship.

However, a second alternative line of action is possible for b—b can also generate a rule that can block a's preferred world. For example, b can adopt the rule, "never transmit the positive sanction to a." This rule makes SS_2, a's preferred system state, impossible. [That rule would have been a viable course of action in the example discussed in the last section. In that example, a's threat was false and, as a consequence, if b had adopted the rule never to transmit the positive sanction, SS_1 (its best of all possible system states) would have resulted. But b did not then have the information needed to formulate that rule!] For this system, b could form that rule but its adoption would result in PS which is *the intersection of a's and b's rules. The consequence of adopting a's rule, SS_2, is preferred by b to PS, the consequence of adopting its own rule.* Thus b accedes to a's rule (the threat) and *agreement* occurs with the transmission of the positive sanction.

If b had not agreed to a's rule, then the system would have been in *confrontation*. Let us now consider the distribution of the *costs of confrontation* and compare them to the distribution of the *costs of agreement* for the two actors. For a real system corresponding to the one modeled here (assuming that a mugger such as a did not believe that he would be caught, prosecuted and imprisoned), the cost of confrontation for the mugger is the cost of a bullet, which must be balanced against the expected "benefits" of the valuables. However, for a victim such as b the costs of confrontation are loss of life and valuables, whereas the cost of agreement is only the loss of the valuables. Therefore this coercive relationship is characterized by highly *differential costs of confrontation*.

Social actors are linked by their interdependent *activities,* which are independently evaluated for each actor in light of their preferences and beliefs. At no point in these or any other analyses with the elementary theory is it necessary for the theorist to compare preferences of actors directly, a comparison that, in any case, is normally disallowed by economists and other social scientists. Nevertheless, for a given system when agreement and confrontation result in distinct system states, the consequences of each can be evaluated for each of the actors as a basis for inferring the process and outcome of the interaction. For the example of coercion, the states of both agreement and confrontation were preferred to any other alternatives by a — an indication of the low cost of confrontation to that actor. For b, the system state resulting from agreement, SS_2, was preferred to PS, b's worst of all possible worlds, thereby indicating that the costs of confrontation for b were high. Since the costs of confrontation were low for a within its preference system and high for b within its preference system, it is possible to characterize the relationship as one of *differential costs of confrontation.*

The analysis of the costs of confrontation and their distribution in social relationships is of the greatest possible importance in the understanding of the course and outcome of interactions. Power, as that term is normally used in sociology, is importantly conditioned by the distribution of the costs of confrontation in relationships. For example, if we were to say that the mugger exerted power over the victim, then it could be added that power was exerted because of the differential costs of confrontation in the relationship.

I. Four Types of Conflict Systems and a Simple Mental Experiment

If both transmission and reception signs of sanctions are considered, an expansion of the three ideal types of social relationship is possible. In Figure VII that expansion is shown for the conflict relationship. These four potential networks will be used as a point of departure for a simple mental experiment.

In Figure VIII initial conditions for a conflict relationship are given. (In drawing the system states for the preferences of a and b, only the actors' own transmission values are included for reasons that will become evident as the mental experiment unfolds.) First consider only the preferences of a and b. Standing outside the system, we know that all valuations arc negative, and thus a and b are "peace lovers" (i.e., actors who would prefer the vacuous system to any system in which sanctions were to flow). However, were sanctions to flow, each would prefer to transmit a negative sanction, then conflict, and then to receive the negative of the other without the transmission of a negative in return. Had this been a full information system, no conflict would occur.

However, now consider a's belief concerning b's preferences. In fact a has attributed an incorrect preference system to b. In light of that error, what will a do? Clearly a's threat to transmit a negative to b would not be believed effective

44

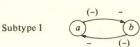

Subtype I

Subtype II

Subtype III

Subtype IV

FIGURE VII. Potential networks for four conflict subtypes.

FIGURE VIII. Conflict system states ordered as preferences.

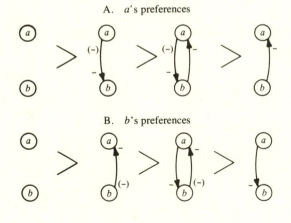

A. *a*'s preferences

B. *b*'s preferences

C. *a*'s belief concerning *b*'s preferences

by a because a believes that the threat *will not block* a world preferred by b to any world in which b transmits a negative sanction. Given a's belief, a can only choose between its third- and fourth-ranked worlds; a selects the third and transmits the negative sanction to b.

This act of "aggression" by a may well be a rude shock to b. The act may lead to a change in the beliefs of b about a. But, regardless of b's beliefs (which have not been specified), b's course of action will be determined by its preferences and a's act. Now b has only the choice of its third- and fourth-ranked worlds, and selects the third, transmitting its sanction to a.

This interaction exhibits some interesting characteristics. Initially neither actor wanted conflict to develop. However, given a's belief concerning b, conflict was inevitable. This belief could, using Merton's terms, be called a self-fulfilling prophecy and is an instance of the "Thomas theorem" (i.e., that which is believed to be true *is* true in social interactions). The Thomas theorem does not apply to all interactions, but its scope is broad. That b subsequently did transmit the negative to a could easily be believed by a as "proof" that its original belief was correct, while b could believe that a was an aggressive actor. Seeing the system as a whole we know that a preferred no conflict and acted "only in self-defense."

J. Social Actors and Reflexives

The actors that have been modeled up till now were social actors in the sense that they engaged in social relationships. However, the modeled actors have been (implicitly) constrained by the following conditions. The components of the actors' preference systems were drawn only from the actors' potential network. All elements of actors' beliefs were also beliefs about the system of action. Preferences and beliefs did vary between actors. However, the variations of their preferences were simply functions of their positions and the ordering of system states relevant to those positions, while variations of beliefs were functions of position, completeness and/or accuracy. To conceptualize humans as social actors in the sense given above concentrates our attention upon the social elements of their preferences and beliefs. Nevertheless, humans are not just social, but also are biophysical entities. Furthermore, human behavior can be cognitively conditioned. The purpose of this section is to introduce briefly some of the procedures for extension of the elementary theory to biophysical and cognitive conditions. Consider A of Figure IX. The actor a is represented as having a social relationship with b. The "dashed point" c and the dashed arcs connecting c to a represent a cognitive relationship. (For modeling cognitive relationships, each of these arcs can be given two or fewer signs as the need occurs in the modeling of the system.) The point c represents a belief of the actor a which is relevant to its social action. Let c be an ethical system such that were a to transmit a type of social act to b, a transmission to and/or reception from c

would be believed to occur by a. The point c is, in fact, an element of the actor a which has been *drawn out* of the a point so that processes "internal" to a which could not be represented with the network for social action can be represented.

The point d is a "square point" which together with its arcs can be used to represent an element of the actor's relationship to natural events. The point d may be the actor considered as a biophysical entity. For example, a hungry actor could be represented by a square point with an arc to the actor point wherein the reception value of that arc is negative. On the other hand, the square point could represent elements of the biophysical world. A working actor who disliked work could be represented by an arc from the actor to a square point with a negative sign of transmission.

The most central elements of Marxian theory are concerned with social and biophysical relations. The power of its analyses comes from the subtlety of

FIGURE IX. Models for biophysical and cognitive elements.

A.

A. The point a is a social, biophysical and cognitive actor;

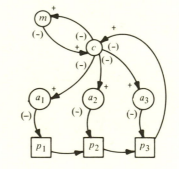

B.

B. a model for an assembly line;

C.

C. a value-rational actor (a) socially related to the actor b.

relations drawn between social relationships and the relations of social actors to their biophysical environment. A model for a simple capitalist productive enterprise is given in Figure IXB. The c point is the capitalist who pays the a worker points. The a points "work" on a set of p linked processes. The result of the processes is owned by the capitalist—thus the vector to the capitalist who exchanges the results in a market (the m point) for money. Here it can be seen that the relationship between capitalist and worker is not, strictly speaking, an exchange, for it is mediated through the square points. However, were we to simplify the model by elimination of square points (collapsing them into the a points) the result would be an economic exchange system between workers and capitalist.

Needless to say, there are a great number of models which could be drawn using square points. In a previous section, square points were used to represent the physical state (PS) of physical coercion. Though space will not allow further discussion, you, the theorist will be able to generate a set of uses for this procedure in light of the issues discussed here and elsewhere in this volume.

Now consider the use of dashed points. Figure IXC is a model for interpretation of a Weberian value-rational actor. This actor is modeled to represent an ascetic Protestant whose actions are conditioned by belief in God (the g point). The social actor a is engaged in an exchange relationship with the social actor b. However, a's actions will be affected by its belief in the g point and its "sanctions." [See Weber (1947:154).] Let it be taken as an initial condition that the believed flows are far more important to a than any social sanction. For this instance let it be a condition of the interaction that a believes that there is a "fair price" for the exchange and that if it exchanges at the fair price it will be in God's grace (and thus receive the positive flow from the g point) and if it agrees to any other price it will not be in God's grace (and thus will receive the negative flow from the g point). Let it also be a condition of the system of exchange that a's believed condition of grace be contingent upon the truthfulness of a's communications to b (and to any other actors). The resultant actions of the a point will be quite unlike those of any actor modeled up till now, but will instead resemble the type of actions expected for Weber's value-rational actor. The a actor will offer and will accept only the rate of exchange corresponding to the fair price. Yet this actor is no less rational than any other previously modeled actor—it can calculate alternatives and can act to maximize its (expected) preference state. However, its preference state in this and other relationships is not a consequence of its potential social network but is, instead, importantly conditioned by its belief in God and the contingencies between its and God's actions. The g point is an element of the a point which has been drawn out for purposes of representation. Thus the a actor has an *inner* orientation [See Weber (1956: Kapitel I).] and its behavior is (in all cases) conditioned by that orientation. Finally, the belief system of the a actor is "overly full" when compared to other types of points in the system that do not have a g point in their belief systems.

In contrast to the *a* point, actors that have been discussed in previous sections were characterized by what Weber called an *ausser* orientation [See Weber (1956: Kapitel I).] in that their preferences and beliefs were strongly conditioned by their conditions of existence—that is, by their potential networks. Thus these earlier actors were, in Weber's terms, instrumentally rational. Looking back to A of Figure IX, it is evident that the strength of Weber's sociology is his combination of social and cognitive elements.

In the modeling of complex systems of social interaction, there will be a large set of points representing social actors and a large set of arcs representing their actions. Such a model can be very complex, yet there may be a need to include cognitive and/or biophysical elements for at least some of the actors. For example, in modeling a worker who can be fired, it may be necessary to model the event that if fired it will become hungry.

So that these factors can be included with a minimal increase in the complexity of the model, the idea of *reflexive* will be introduced. A "reflexive arc" is any arc that originates and terminates at a given point. A "reflexive arc" in the elementary theory is constructed by collapsing a dashed or square point and associated arcs into a social actor point such that the arcs to and from either of the former become the reflexive arcs for the social action point. For example, in

FIGURE X. Reflexives.

Unpacked and packed reflexives.

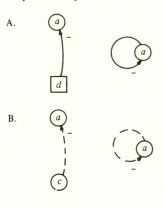

Contingent reflexives.

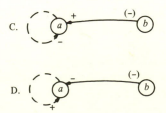

Figure XA, a social actor point is connected to d, a square point, by an arc from d to a. (This could represent the experience of hunger for the actor.) The same relationship can be represented by the reflexive arc of the a point in the right-hand column. In B of Figure X an actor a is related to a cognitive point by a negative arc from c to a. That same relationship can also be represented as in the right-hand column by the negative reflexive arc of the a point.

In the elementary theory, any biophysical or cognitive element that is included in a model is called a reflexive, regardless of the mode of representation used. If the reflexive is represented by a reflexive arc as in the right-hand column of A and B of Figure X, then it can be called a *packed reflexive*. If the reflexive is represented by a square or dashed point and associated arcs, as in the left-hand column, it is an *unpacked reflexive*.

The flow of reflexives can be contingent upon a sanction flow. That contingency can be indicated either by system states or by the context for the potential network. Consider C and D of Figure X. C is a system state representing guilt. The actor a is receiving a positive sanction wherein that flow is associated with the flow of the negative reflexive (the guilt feeling). D could be described as a system state in which a is receiving the negative sanction and feeling virtuous—the feeling of virtue being represented by the contingent flow of the positive reflexive. When properly interpreted, C and D are consistent with Nietzsche's discussion of "transvaluation."

K. Social Rules

The first step in the modeling of any system is the construction of the potential network for the system. For most (though not all) systems this network may include only sanction flows and, for those flows, both signs should be included. The theorist must then specify or derive the system states for the interaction and order them for each actor. That ordering should be consistent with valuational signs of the potential network and the beliefs to be attributed to the actor. Then initial conditions for the beliefs of the actors and for belief change by communication (as needed) are specified.

Given these initial conditions the mental experiment for the interaction process can begin. As that mental experiment unfolds, a variety of communications of the actors can be generated, including, as in the foregoing examples, the rules of the actors.

Space restrictions of this work have not allowed the presentation of formal procedures for rule selection for "qualitative" systems. Nevertheless, the basic ideas of the decision procedure can be described less formally. Each actor has a set of potential rules that could be adopted. The range of potential rules is strongly conditioned by the sanctioning resources of the actors and by their preference systems. The adoption of any rule by an actor can limit the system states possible for both that actor and for the other. *The decision to adopt or not adopt a rule can only be made by an actor by (1) mapping that rule onto the believed preferences (and for some cases, beliefs) of the other to determine the expected outcome of the rule and then (2) mapping that outcome back onto the actor's own preference system.* For example, prior to adopting the threat, the mugger first inferred its expected result by mapping the threat onto preferences that were attributed to the victim, and, having inferred the expected act of the victim, mapped that act back onto its own preference system to determine whether that threat would have a result that was in its interest. Since the mugger inferred that the victim would accede to the threat and would transmit the positive sanction to the mugger, and since that would result in the best of all possible system states for the mugger, the threat was adopted and communicated to the victim.

Nevertheless, for any interaction, not one but a number of rules are normally potential. The number and type that are potential are determined by conditions such as preferences of the actors (blocking!), the resources of the actors, the numbers and arrangement of actors in the system and the information available to each. *In systems of social relationship, actors initially make decisions, not about action* (for in social relationships no one actor can uniquely determine the consequences of an action), *but first about rules.* Only after at least one actor has selected a rule for its behavior can decisions directly concerning action be made by any actor.

Before proceeding to the remaining sections of this exposition, it is strongly advised that you construct and model a number of simple systems. The elementary theory is a theory for use. Since it is, its procedures are at least as important as the terms that it introduces. By use of the concepts and procedures that have been introduced, a remarkably varied number of systems can be modeled and their processes of interaction inferred. Essential to knowing the theory is the ability to use it.

L. The Concepts of Actor, Action and Social Relationship

The models of this chapter have been drawn in "social space." Upon that space are found social actors and their social acts, the most important of which are sanctions and communications. Not belonging to that space are biophysical and cognitive reflexives, which, nevertheless, can be mapped onto it by various procedures. Taken together, sanction flows, communications and reflexives are the most important events in social interactions—as those interactions are seen from the point of view of the elementary theory.

The technical language and procedures of the elementary theory thus far introduced allow us to define certain terms (already used) whose properties have not yet been specified.

The concept *social actor* has two properties, a meaning system and resources.

The concept *meaning* has three properties: preference system, beliefs and decision procedures.

The first property of meaning is a *preference system,* a weak ordering of system states believed by the actor to be potential to a given action system (potential network).

The second property of meaning is *beliefs* which are statements of information that are relevant to the given action system. Note: full and accurate beliefs of an actor are the action system as specified and constructed by the theorist. It includes all other actors' preferences and beliefs and the structure of the system. Because it is a ''reflection'' of the system of action, these beliefs form a system which is a consequence of the theoretic properties of the action system as specified. A fully inaccurate set of beliefs may be specified simply as a list of information ''attributed'' to the actor. (At this point in the development of the theory no procedures for the ''internal organization'' of beliefs as systems of beliefs has been introduced. But partially accurate beliefs may be at least partially structured by their relations to the action system.)

In any empirical application the beliefs of the actor that need to be modeled are only those which can affect the actor's behavior for the system in question. The actor's beliefs may contain elements not considered as part of the modeled action system, but those elements must be connected to at least some action system element to condition the actor's behavior. For example, a model for the beliefs of a ''Sunday Christian,'' professing the Nicene Creed but acting in an exchange only from ''material motives,'' would not contain elements of religious beliefs—for no element of religious belief is connected to any element of the exchange system.

The third property of actor's meaning is *decision procedures.* All actors' decision procedures are the first principle as used above, and the second principle and laws one and two to be introduced in Chapter 7. That all actors use the same decision procedures is not a generalization about the way all people think nor is it an important scope limit for the application of the theory. Remember, the conditions for decisions—preferences, beliefs concerning other actors (and even nonactors) and the structure of action—can each vary. The result of the variation of those conditions is the generation of a wide variety of widely differing kinds of decisions and thus of interaction processes.

Now consider the second actor property, resources. Resources are also treated as initial conditions in any model. The mode of treatment was given in Section J of this chapter and will be treated further in later chapters, particularly Chapter 8.

The introduction of social actor and meaning allow the following specifications:

Social action is an action conditioned by an actor's preferences and by its beliefs concerning at least one element of at least one other actor's meaning system. All sanction flows and communications are modeled as social actions. (Note that the following are not social actions: two cyclists colliding by accident; a mugger shooting a victim and taking the victim's valuables.)

Social relationship is two or more social actors acting socially toward one another. Included in this category are economic exchange, social exchange, social coercion, social conflict and other types.

Contingency rule is a statement that can conditionally relate the actions of two or more social actors.

Rule is a possible contingency rule. In interaction process models, rules occur as information flows between actors. Offers, orders and threats are rules.

System rule is a contingency rule that actually governs the action of at least one actor in the system.

Fully general system rule is a contingency rule that governs the action of all actors in the system.

[*Note:* "Govern" has a particular meaning here. If the content of a law is known, a "law abiding" actor's acts would be so governed. The acts of a "criminal" recognizing the law and attempting to avoid the consequences of its violation are also "governed" by the system rule. Thus even fully general system rules do not determine, instead they govern, behavior.]

The system rules for a given social relationship or system of social relationships give a *fundamental theoretic description* for the system. *This theoretic description is similar to the kind of theoretic description that is given to physical systems when the scientific laws for the system are stated.* In that regard, the system rules for a given social system of relationships are similar to scientific laws found in the physical sciences. On the other hand, an important difference exists. For any given physical theory the laws of the theory are fixed. But for social theory, the system rules are variable by system conditions. These ideas can be compared to Marx's idea that each stage of history has its own laws.

System rules can vary a great deal by system conditions. But that does not mean that a social theory cannot have wide scope. What it does mean is that any one model drawn from a theory will have scope limits—hardly a new idea to the sciences. The problem of generality then lies not in the formulation of any one model but in the variety of models which can be generated.

M. Final Comments

This ends the introduction of the basic concepts and procedures of the elementary theory. In the remaining chapters of this section these ideas will be extended for conceptualization of normatively controlled social exchange systems.

The second section of this volume is concerned with larger structures. To deal with *n*-person structures Chapter 7 will include a quantitative interpretation of the elementary theory. That interpretation will present the two laws of the theory and its second principle.

As an aid to the reader, a glossary of terms is included at the end of the volume. The glossary includes all of the fundamental and most of the derived terms of the theory as they were introduced in this chapter, in Chapter 7 and in the remaining chapters of the volume.

References

Butterfield, Herbert
  1957   *The Origins of Modern Science*. New York: Free Press.

Einstein, Albert, and Leopold Infeld
  1938   *The Evolution of Physics*. New York: Simon and Schuster.

Galilei, Galileo
  1954   *Dialogues Concerning Two New Sciences*. New York: Dover Publications.

Marx, Karl
  1967   *Capital* (Vol. 1). New York: International Publishers

Nietzsche, Friedrich
  1966   *Basic Writings of Nietzsche* (tr. and ed. Walter Kaufmann). New York: Modern Library.

Watson, James D.
  1968   *The Double Helix*. New York: New American Library.

Weber, Max
  1947   *The Theory of Social and Economic Organization* (tr. A.M. Henderson and Talcott Parsons). Glencoe, IL: The Free Press.
  1956   *Wirtschaft und Gesellschaft* (ed. Johannes Winckelmann). Tubingen: J.C.B. Mohr.

Willer, David, and Judith Willer
  1973   *Systematic Empiricism: Critique of a Pseudoscience*. Englewood Cliffs, NJ: Prentice-Hall.

3

Frank Southard

This paper utilizes and modifies certain aspects of the model of social exchange in Chapter 3 in Frank A. Southard, "A Study of Structural Determinants of Population Change" (Doctoral Dissertation, University of Kansas, 1978). I am indebted to Ann Morris and especially to David Willer for their suggestions and comments in the preparation of this chapter.

NORMATIVELY CONTROLLED SOCIAL EXCHANGE SYSTEMS

A. Introduction

This chapter will offer models for some systems of social exchange. The analysis will concentrate on normative control and social exchange in primitive societies. These systems have the advantage of being theoretically cleaner than systems of social exchange that occur in more complex and contemporary societies.

Social exchange systems have been described in various ways.[1] Although variations may be observed among these systems, two features are especially salient. First, they are characterized by the presence of a strong and effective normative system that is coercive insofar as each member is concerned. The effect of this normative system is most clearly seen in those relatively rare cases (in primitive societies) when an individual violates an important norm and steps are taken to enforce that norm. Secondly, social exchange systems are characterized by one-way flows of goods, services, or assistance among members that may frequently shift. These flows may or may not be accompanied by positive and symbolic forms of interaction. In everyday terms, these are systems of sharing. Giving and receiving are social acts and, as social acts, are subject to normative control. Let us begin by examining types of control in a normative system.

B. System of Social Control and Norm Enforcement

Although primitive societies lack codified laws, formal courts and police, norms are nevertheless present and enforced. Since these societies are not hierarchial,

---

[1] For one of the more systematic and insightful attempts to treat social exchange systems recently, see Sahlins (1965). What we call social exchange is treated by Sahlins as generalized reciprocity.

centralized systems, the important condition exists where members have more or less equal ability to both violate the norms and to respond to the norm violations of others.

Models of three different forms of social control are represented in Figure I. Each system is characterized by a distinct means of norm enforcement. Each system is treated as having four actors, *a, b, c,* and *d.* There are two alternative

FIGURE I. Systems of social control.

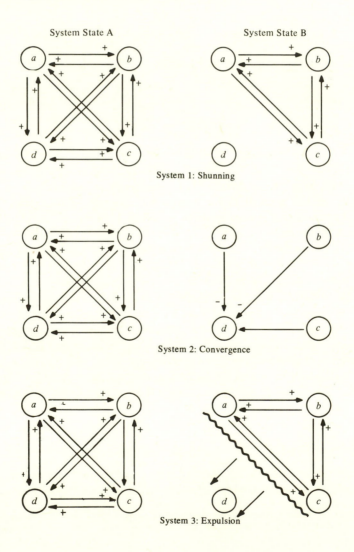

System State A   System State B

System 1: Shunning

System 2: Convergence

System 3: Expulsion

forms of interaction possible for these members. These alternative networks of interaction may thus be said to represent system states A and B for each system of norm enforcement. System state A in each case involves the sharing of goods and services among members (i.e., the flow of positive sanctions). System state B in each case represents the response of $n-1$ actors to nonconformity by actor d. Nonconformity is defined as the commission of act s, from the set s, which other members have an interest in prohibiting.

Each of the systems of social control utilizes a different means of norm enforcement and they are therefore named on this basis.[2] Each system will be interpreted and then compared to an empirical example to demonstrate its usefulness for understanding relevant events and processes.

1. System 1: Shunning

Actor d has committed act s. Actors a, b and c may continue among themselves to transmit and receive positives. Actor d has not disrupted this network between a, b and c but it is shunned by them as a consequence of its act. No other action is taken against d.[3]

The exercise of this form of social control can be seen clearly in the Ontong Java community described by Hogbin. A group of the men had gone fishing and had returned home with their catch.

> . . . at the next house another man, Ohuki, was distributing the fish that had been caught by the men of his expedition. Each of the fishermen received his share and went off home with it. A share was also sent to all but one of the members of the fishing group who had not been able for one reason or another to go out in the canoe. The one exception was Peoa, and he was ignored. . . . He had stayed at home three times in succession without the slightest excuse beyond that he was tired. Ohuki knew the reason for his tiredness; he was much too fond of dancing on the beach at night and as a result he was not fit for work in the daytime (Hogbin, 1961:125).

Peoa had failed to meet his obligation of helping others in the fishing expedition. His violation of this norm was enforced by shunning. He did not receive a portion of the catch from Ohuki who was distributor of the fish that day and he was ignored by others who also did not share with him.

There seems to be little doubt that shunning in itself can be an effective system of control for some groups. It has even been raised to the level of explicit policy on occasion, with the Amish serving as a well-known example. Shunning or *Meidung,* as the process is called, is very much a part of their religious practice (Hostetler, 1970:28, 57–58).

---

[2] Although the three following systems are treated as analytically distinct, the boundary or difference between shunning and expulsion may be a matter of degree. When expulsion involves an actual forcing of the actor out of the system (the case treated here), the difference is clear.

[3] This form of social control was pointed out to me by Ann Morris through personal communication.

2. System 2: Negative convergence

A norm has been violated by actor d by commission of an act, s. In response, actors a, b and c transmit negative sanctions, symbolic or material, to d. Thus, actor d is at the point of convergence for these negatives. Symbolic negatives may be accusations, insults or threats, and material negatives are the use of physical force in some manner.[4]

This formulation may be compared with a particularly vivid and relevant empirical case, the "crime of Cephu," as described by Colin Turnbull (Turnbull, 1962:94–108).

Cephu was an older male member of a Mbuti Pygmy band who violated one of his band's important norms: the placement of hunting nets. The Mbuti Pygmies are a forest people whose hunting relies primarily upon the use of nets to trap game. The nets are owned by each hunter and his family. The nets are placed consecutively, end to end, to form a semicircle. Some members of the band, usually women and children, act as drivers to rout the animals and send them fleeing in the direction of the nets.

On this particular occasion, Cephu had been unsuccessful in the previous casts of the nets. On the last cast of the day, Cephu left the main body of hunters and placed his net in front of the others and out of their sight. The first of the fleeing game was caught and killed by Cephu but he was seen as he rolled up his net.

As members arrived back at the camp, the news of Cephu's whereabouts and activities during the last hunt spread. Within a short time, members of the band began to stridently and publicly berate Cephu. His past errors were recalled and enumerated in speeches, fists were shaken in the air, and insults were shouted at him. That evening Cephu was absent from the usual socializing that went on around the camp fires.

Clearly, elements of Cephu's case are isomorphic with the model. In placing his net in front of the nets of others, Cephu had violated the norm which held that members should place their nets end to end in a semicircle. As word of Cephu's behavior spread among members, opinion quickly turned against him. Cephu became the object of negative convergence, receiving a variety of negative symbolic sanctions.

3. System 3: Expulsion

In this system, violation of a norm by actor d leads to the expulsion of d from the network by the other actors. As a form of control or norm enforcement, it is a

---

[4] Analytically, two stages thus exist for the process of negative convergence: one stage involving symbolic negatives and the second utilizing material negatives. Furthermore, it appears that the mere hinting of possible convergence is sufficient in many systems to stop an actor from further commission of deviant acts. The model here treats the simplest case but it could be readily elaborated to take hinting into account.

more drastic response as it usually entails physical as well as social expulsion from the group.

There is a description of a Cheyenne Indian named Pawnee in Hoebel (1976) that can be interpreted as a form of expulsion. As a young man Pawnee had lived in Oklahoma where he had acquired a reputation as a "no-good." He was disrespectful, he stole meat from people's racks, and he took their horses without permission. Finally, after he had taken two ponies, Pawnee was apprehended by the warriors of the Bowstring band.

> "You have stolen those horses," they cried as they pulled me from my horse. "Now we have trailed you down." They threw me on the ground and beat me until I could not stand; they broke up my weapons and ruined my saddle; they cut my blankets, moccasins, and kit to shreds. When they had finished they took all my food and went off with the horses, leaving me alone on the prairie . . . too weak to move (Hoebel, 1976:146–147).

In the period before the warriors took action against him, Pawnee had violated many norms. Finally, he was humiliated and expelled from his group.

4. Stages in the social control process

As the example of Pawnee illustrates, expulsion was preceded by negative convergence. In fact, expulsion as a form of norm enforcement cannot stand alone since negative convergence acts as a backup should the deviant resist the attempt at expulsion.

C. Interests and Social Control

As we have seen, the normative system can be a very strong and coercive element in a social network. It certainly would appear to be an effective force for maintaining sharing (one-way flows of positives) in social exchange systems. But, what exactly is a norm and how does one form or emerge? What conditions affect norm violations? Let us consider the problems in terms of the interests of actors in an "ideal type" system.

Consider a full information network comprised of n actors where n is greater than three. Let all actors have identical positions in the network and therefore identical interests. A number of activities are of concern to the actors. For any of these activities each actor has two important interests: (a) an interest in its own behavior, and (b) an interest in the behavior of the other $n-1$ actors. These two interests may or may not be distinct or different. In part, this depends upon the nature of the activities, the structure of the network, and the relationship of the network to the environment. Take the case of individuals hunting game. Each hunter has an interest in his success and no reason *not* to wish success for the other hunters. On the other hand, as in the case of thievery, the two interests are quite distinct. The thief has an interest in stealing and also an interest in prohibiting the theft of his property. When the actor in a system has one set of interests in its own behavior and a different or opposed set of interests in the behavior of others, a condition exists that may be defined as a *bifurcation of interest*.

A bifurcation of interest can emerge from or develop around two different types of activities. In the first type, the actor has an interest in committing the act and an interest in prohibiting others from also committing the act. The previous example of thievery is one such case. It is out of these acts and interests that *proscriptive* norms emerge. In the case of social exchange networks, stinginess or hoarding is proscribed.

Around the second type of acts and interests, *prescriptive* norms develop. Here, the actor has an interest in not carrying out a particular act and an interest in seeing that others do carry out the act. Thus, after the acquisition of game, the hunter may not want to share his kill but he has interest in having others share their kills.

Consider now the meaning of bifurcation of interest for our ideal type system. In respect to sharing, let each actor in the system have an interest in not sharing with others and an interest in having others share with it. It is impossible for all actors to act simultaneously upon the second interest and realize the first. Let it be given that actor d has refused to share with a, b and c. Actor d has acted upon its first interest. But this is contrary to the second interest of a, b and c who wish d to share with them. As a consequence of d's action, there is an opposition of interest in the system. How can this opposition of interest be resolved? In the manner suggested above, it can be resolved through some form of norm enforcement.

D. Social Control and Social Exchange Systems

What is the simplest theoretic description of a system in which all actors share with one another? Consider a system of positive–positive sanctions. When al' sanctions are positive–positive, all actors have an interest in receiving sanctions from all others. Furthermore, all actors have an interest in transmitting sanctions to all others. Thus in an exchange system in which there were only positive–positive sanctions, all actors would share their positive sanctioning resources with one another.

Define an actor's "social need" as a condition in which the reception of a particular sanction flow would be positively valued. Clearly, in any real system, such needs will vary from time to time and place to place. If an actor were hungry, the reception of food would be a sanction with a positive value of reception. An actor has a task to complete and needs help. If help were then received, the help would be a sanction with a positive value of reception. In general, as any actor develops a social need that actor can receive a positive sanction flow from another actor.

Over any given time period actors differentially develop certain social needs. Need development is related to both fundamental biological needs as they are related to the group's technology and cognitive factors. Need development is also related to the abilities of actors to individually satisfy their needs. Thus the very young and the very old as well as the infirm have a number of needs that cannot be individually fulfilled and these become social needs.

The development of social needs can be related to periods of work and leisure. For example, in a hunting and gathering society some members may not work on any given day. In the absence of accumulated resources (or if accumulated resources are less valued than ones more recently acquired) those members will have social needs for food.

The development of other needs can be understood similarly. In general, need development can be related to the distribution of skills in the group as well as the occasion of projects requiring the combined work of more than one individual.

Simple social exchange systems have the following system rule: all actors have an interest in acting on the needs of all other actors by transmitting to the others the needed positive sanction. In terms of sanction valuations the system rule is if the value of reception of any known potential sanction flow is positive for one actor, the value of transmission will be positive for the others.

What dynamics would be typical of simple social exchange systems? Such systems would have a great number of sanction flows, wherein these flows were conditioned by the development of social needs over time. Some, but by no means all, of these flows can be reciprocal. Some (the old, the young, the infirm) will have many social needs because of their limited abilities. Such actors will be the point of convergence of a number of long-term, positive–positive sanction flows. Other actors will have few social needs but will produce surplus resources. These actors will be the point of origin of a great many positive–positive sanctions.

In these systems the distribution of durable resources should exhibit interesting characteristics. At one point, a resource will be held by one actor. At a later time the same resource will be held by another. Yet, for the system as specified, no purchase will have occurred. This phenomenon has been commonly observed by ethnographers in a wide range of tribal systems.

There is considerable sharing in social exchange systems, even of resources that are defined as belonging to individuals. There are also resources that are defined as jointly held by some or all members of the group. Although joint resources are shared, their transmission from one to another actor cannot be treated as a sanction flow. This is an issue of property and will be treated further in later chapters of Section I and in Chapter 8.

However, not all social exchange systems are simple. In some the flow of positive–positive sanctions is conditioned by social distance. These complex social exchange systems will be dealt with in subsection F below.

The dynamics of social exchange systems are very different from the economic exchange systems of negative–positive sanctions that are typical of modern societies. They are different precisely because the sanctions are positive–positive. However, it is appropriate to ask upon what basis the positive valuation of transmission is maintained? Why are the modeled actors generous to one another? How is the potential bifurcation of interest resolved? The answer lies in the relation between the normative and exchange systems.

If all actors have an interest in all other actors sharing with them, that interest will be dominant as long as conditions for effective normative control are present—and if certain further conditions yet to be discussed are satisfied. Let us consider the relations between the normative social control system and the maintenance of the positive valuation of sanction transmission.

Actor *a* may initially have an interest in being selfish—that is, in keeping resources it does not immediately need for which others have social needs. But all other actors have an interest in *a* being generous. Given information about *a*'s lack of sharing, any or all of the social control methods would be used. However, *a* knows that it could be subject to social control and that the result would be a lowering of its preference state. Assume that that lowering of preference state is greater than any advantage gained in not transmitting the sanction. Thus because social control is potential, *a* has an interest in being generous. Thus the maintenance of the positive valuation of transmission of positive sanctions occurs.

E. Some Conditions for Social Exchange in Simple Systems

Social exchange systems with a norm of generosity are by no means present in all tribal societies. There is undoubtedly a complex of conditions relevant to the presence or absence of this phenomenon. This discussion will only be suggestive and will be limited to three such conditions: scarcity, the concentration of the means of violence and information.

Actors will share to avoid the consequences of social control. But what if sharing were to result in biological deprivation? Consider the following system. An actor has resources that, if transmitted, would result in a material negative reflexive for that actor. (For example, if food were shared, the person would be hungry.) If the resource were not transmitted, social control mechanisms would be applied. (There could also be contingent cognitive reflexives, both positive and negative.) Will the actor share or not? The answer depends upon the relative effect of the negative material reflexive and the social control.

Now imagine this same actor in a system that moves from resource richness to poverty. At first the actor would be generous and later not. Colin Turnbull (1972) has studied the Ik who, having been deprived of their resource base, were starving. They refused to share with one another. The foregoing discussion may be consistent with the society described by Turnbull.

Poverty as a consequence of exploitation in modern societies can affect social exchange systems. As will be seen in Chapter 5, it is possible for people to believe in the rightness of social exchange and yet to have lost the opportunity for sharing.

Some societies exist in a hostile social environment of ongoing conflict with others. Under that condition there can again be a bifurcation of interest but now focused on interests related to conflict with outsiders. Any actor has an interest in all others being fierce toward any outside threat, yet any actor can have an interest in saving its skin. Thus a norm of ferocity can develop. That development can have two consequences. First, it can take precedence over a norm of generosity. Second, it can result in a concentration of the means of violence in the hands of a few.

If the means of violence are concentrated, the system is no longer undifferentiated. Now some can coerce others. More exactly, those who have the means of violence can, as a group, coerce others in the tribe, extracting positive sanctions from them. Further, such a system can exhibit certain instabilities in the form of intratribal conflict, particularly as obligations of kinship interact with the differentiated system. Chagnon (1968) has studied the Yanomamö. Elements of the foregoing discussion may be consistent with his description.

The working of any social exchange system is dependent upon shared information concerning the needs of others. As will be seen in the next chapter, it is common for members of a social exchange system to seek out others in need. On the other hand, information sharing can be a time-consuming process for it is typically connected with complex associational activities. Lack of time for information sharing is one of the central conditions for the breakdown of social exchange systems.

F. Complex Social Exchange Systems

An important property of social exchange networks in primitive societies is the flexibility in the membership and size of these networks. The networks expand and contract with variations in the resources acquired by members and with the movement of individuals and families from one network to another. Social ties even between nonbiological kinsmen are expressed in terms of kinship. In general, the closer the ties (i.e., the smaller the kinship distance between two actors), the greater the obligation to share. Members maintain their ties to others by social exchange and can also create new ties by extending their sharing.

In more ''modern'' systems, social ties and social distance may also be viewed in terms of friendship and a sense of neighborhood or community. Although there are differences between kinship and friendship networks, both manifest flexibility in size. Also common to kinship and friendship networks is the phenomenon of social distance. In a kinship system, actor c is a relative of a if c is a relative of b and b is a relative of a. In a friendship network, c may be a friend of a if c is a friend of b and b is a friend of a. In both cases, the social distance between c and a is greater than that between c and b and b and a. In the brief formulation of kinship that follows, it should become clear that the flexibility of social exchange networks behaves in accordance with the strength of existing social ties and social distance among members.

Kinship systems can be conceptualized "egosymmetrically" as in Figure II so that kinship distance k_d can be calculated from any given actor, a to other actors (bs or cs). The distance from a to these others equals the distance from them to a. Starting from any given actor in a kinship network, kinship ties radiate outward by degrees of kinship distance. For any given a, these degrees of kinship distance may be viewed as forming a series of concentric circles, each larger than the preceding one and each encompassing more distant relatives. The other actors included within a given circle (e.g., b_1 and b_2 or c_1, c_2, c_3 and c_4) stand in a similar relationship to a. A complete representation of an empirical system would typically result in a series of concentric circles as in Figure II. For that figure, k_d is (kinship) social distance. The value of k_d for the $a-b_1$ relationship is 1 and for the $a-c_1$ relationship is 2 and similarly for other $a-b_n$ and $a-c_n$ relationships.

There is another feature inherent in kinship systems that one must consider when looking at the network of obligations and ties for any actor. This feature is the *branching phenomenon*. As one moves outward from a in the network, the number of potential kinsmen increases geometrically with each additional degree of kinship distance. The actual branching kinship tree for a given a will depend upon the kinship classification system in use and the number of living relatives. The tree shown in Figure III represents the minimal possible branching effect.

FIGURE II. Kinship distance k_d in an ego-symmetrical kinship model drawn for actor a.

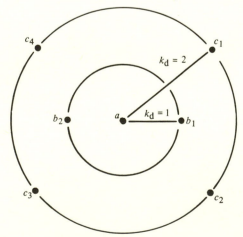

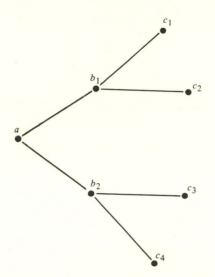

FIGURE III. The branching phenomenon in kinship systems.

Given these features, how do social exchange networks organized along kinship ties function? It is clear that a's obligations are strongest for those relatives closest to it in kinship distance. It is also true, however, that more distant relatives outnumber these closer relatives of a. What is to prevent mutual obligations between them and a from taking precedence over a's mutual obligations with closer relatives?

Assume that a relationship between kinship distance k_d and valuation of symbolic sanction reception v_{r_s} holds because kinship distance is related to strength of ties. What form must this relationship take to prevent a from being swayed by numerous but distant relatives? It is clear that the effect (valuation by a) of symbolics received from relatives must decline at a rate sufficient to offset the branching phenomenon. The relationship between k_d and v_{r_s}, when formulated as an inverse exponential curve, yields a dynamic consistent with our earlier treatment of norm enforcement (see Figure IV). Thus, as kinship distance between actors increases, the valuation of reception of symbolic sanctions decreases exponentially. Conversely, as kinship distance decreases, the valuation of reception of symbolics increases exponentially.

What dynamics are expected of this system? Consider an actor a with only enough resources to share with two other actors. Assume that if a shares with those of least social distance (the bs of Figure III) those of greater social distance (the cs) will negatively converge on a. Also assume that if a shares instead with any two actors of greater social distance (any c of Figure III), those closer (the bs) will negatively converge on a. But a's preference state is lowered more by the convergence of the closer, than by the farther actors—

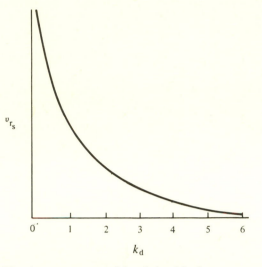

FIGURE IV. The inverse exponential relationship between reception valuation of negative symbolic sanctions v_{r_s} and kinship distance k_d.

even though the latter group is larger. Thus a has an interest in sharing first with those at closer social distance and, only if surplus resources are left, sharing with those farther out in its network.

If over time a does not have enough to share with the cs, they may leave the potential network of a. This brings the potential and actual network sizes into alignment. If resources increase, a can extend its actual (and potential) network. This *alignment of potential and actual network size* is a central feature of social exchange networks. The alignment of potential and actual networks in empirical systems serves to mark their boundaries. Although the world of social relations is seen in terms of kinship or some other form of social distance, boundaries are distinguished by the limits of the actual social exchanges.

G. Embedded Social Exchange Systems

In modern society, social exchange systems are found embedded within the larger social system. Two features of these larger systems that have had important consequences for social exchange systems are the development of the political state and systems of economic exchange.

Kinship has been an important carrier of normative systems that supported and controlled social exchange and, historically, the shrinkage of kinship systems has been associated with the development of certain kinds of political state. Systems of social exchange with a normative system based upon a sense of community (deriving from neighborhood or even ethnicity) have also been weakened in a similar manner. With the development of the political state, the material means of coercion are increasingly monopolized and as a consequence the effectiveness of normative enforcement is weakened for social exchange systems (Weber, 1964: 78). Furthermore, the state through its demands such as taxation and military conscription created external obligations that take precedence over those of the social exchange network.

While there may be arguments over the prerequisites of economic development, there is little doubt that capitalist economic development and the spread of large-scale economic systems have weakened local social exchange systems. As an actor in a local, normatively controlled system becomes involved in a larger economic exchange system, the exchange ratios it finds in the market affect the resources at its disposal for use within the local network. If exchange ratios (i.e., the prices received for products sold and the prices paid for goods or services) become less favorable, more of the actor's resources are "pulled out" of the local network. As a consequence, increases in exploitation dissolve the normatively controlled exchange systems of the dominated. Conversely, increases in exploitation strengthen the normative and social exchange bases of solidarity of the dominant class.

In addition to the unfavorable exchange ratios found by dominated actors in external markets, involvement in external systems has another and possibly more important effect. As actors become involved in these larger systems and demands of the state can be a major stimulus for this involvement, they become very busy. As they devote more time and energy to their activities in these larger systems, they have less time and energy for their local, normatively controlled social exchange systems. The expenditure of time and energy in the local system comes to be judged not only in terms of the local system but in relation to the total demands made upon the individual. In respect to the dominant class, to the extent it is a leisure class the effects are exactly opposite of those noted here for the dominated group.

H. Summary and Further Comments

Social exchange networks are characterized by the one-way flow of goods, services or assistance among members. Both the size of a network and the quantity of flows among members reflects the resources available within the network. For a given actor, when social distance is a factor, the amount that is received on a given occasion will also reflect how close its ties are to the transmitting actor.

The role of the normative system in controlling social exchange through the enforcement of obligations does not imply that (a) obligations are undifferentiated, and (b) all flows of material resources in the system are sanctions and are thus a form of social exchange. In a general sense, resources must be regarded as either a possession of or under the control of an actor in order for the transmission of them by the actor to be regarded as a sanction. This in fact is seen in the bifurcation of interests that is the basis for norms and norm enforcement. But the holding or possessing and the controlling of resources need not be viewed as identical within the system. Thus, social exchange systems show variation according to the way certain resources are regarded.

Variations in norms also occur. Norms may differ in terms of how specific they are about the quantities to be shared and the designation of others to be included in the network. Furthermore, the norms defining an actor's obligations may be conditional: conditioned by factors in addition to the social distance among actors of their previous interaction. Two examples will suffice. A hunter may be expected to share with only the members of the hunting party when the party has three or fewer members and to follow other rules when the party is larger than three (Fried, 1967:65). Obligations may also vary according to the division of labor between sexes so that the resources acquired by women are subject to obligations different from those of resources acquired or controlled by men.

It is ironic that social exchange systems have not received more attention from those sociologists who argue that social order and social control are due primarily to the internalization of norms and moral commitment.[5] On the surface, social exchange systems would appear to be a good case for this attempt to recast the Hobbesian problem of order into a more Pollyannish form. Perhaps it is well that social exchange systems have largely escaped such treatment since the normative-consensus–moral-commitment formula has overtones of the old "cake of custom" view.

Social exchange systems do not fall easily or neatly within the current distinction between social and economic behavior. This view tends to see distinct interests, structures of interaction, and forms of control characterizing each type of behavior. But behavior in social exchange systems is both social and economic. Actors are both instrumentally oriented toward their material self-interests and concerned with their image in the eyes of others. The presence of the first interest does not preclude the presence of the second. There is a system of power in the normative structure that prevents war of all against all but this power resides neither in moral commitment nor in the state, which is lacking in primitive societies. Power is everywhere and elsewhere in the form of potential collective response to norm violation.

---

[5] For the major exponent of this view, see Parsons (1964). The internalization of norms is certainly a factor that may vary among systems. Under the mode of representation employed here, the effect of an internalized norm on the actor would be modeled as a symbolic reflexive. The issue of internalization of norms is complex as it involves among other things the orientation of the actor to the world. Thus, we have not dealt with it here and have not specified it as an initial condition. Social exchange systems may function well without this condition when the other conditions we have specified are present.

References

Chagnon, Napoleon A.
  1968   *Yanomamö: The Fierce People*. New York: Holt, Rinehart and Winston.

Fried, Morton H.
  1967   *The Evolution of Political Society*. New York: Random House.

Hoebel, E. Adamson
  1976   *The Law of Primitive Man*. New York: Atheneum.

Hogbin, H. I.
  1961   *Law and Order in Polynesia: A Study of Primitive Legal Institutions*. Hamden CT: Shoe String Press.

Hostetler, John A.
  1970   *Amish Society*. Baltimore: Johns Hopkins University Press.

Lee, Richard B.
  1969   !Kung Bushman subsistence: An input—output analysis, pp. 47–79 in Andrew P. Vayda (ed.), *Environment and Cultural Behavior*. New York: Natural History Press.

Parsons, Talcott
  1964   *The Social System*. New York: Free Press.

Sahlins, Marshall D.
  1965   On the sociology of primitive exchange, pp. 139–236 in Association for Social Anthropologists (ed.), *The Relevance of Models for Social Anthropology*. New York: Praeger.
  1968   *Tribesmen*. Englewood Cliffs, NJ: Prentice-Hall.

Service, Elman R.
  1971   *Profiles in Ethnology*. New York: Harper and Row.

Southard, Frank A.
  1978   "A Study of Structural Determinants of Population Change." Ph.D. dissertation, Department of Sociology, University of Kansas, Lawrence.

Turnbull, Colin
  1962   *The Forest People*. New York: Simon and Schuster.
  1972   *The Mountain People*. New York: Simon and Schuster.

Weber, Max
  1964   *From Max Weber: Essays in Sociology*. New York: Oxford.

4

Knud L. Hansen

"BLACK" EXCHANGE AND ITS SYSTEM OF SOCIAL CONTROL

A. Introduction

What follows is an account of a normative exchange system that was observed closely during a year's fieldwork in a Scandinavian village. A variety of material and symbolic sanctions are exchanged between persons who are involved in long-term, often multistranded social relationships. Symbolics, in the form of food, drink and sociability accompany the tangible, material transactions. Time spent is not explicitly seen as a cost to participants, as long as the system runs smoothly. Accounts of services (material sanctions) received and rendered are kept and regular visiting and talk assures that all participants are continuously kept informed about any transactions within the group. No service by service reciprocity is expected, on the contrary the members deny vehemently that they have reciprocation in mind when they render a service. That, nevertheless, careful accounts are retained only becomes clear when a member breaks the norms of the system.

Sections B and C of this chapter give a description of the system. Following this, I present a case study of the events that surrounded the violation by one participant of the norms of the system and his eventual exclusion from it.

B. "Black" Service Exchanges

Scandinavia is experiencing rapid social change due to national policies aimed at urbanizing the countryside and centralizing political and economic control. The village represents a microcosm of national policies, resulting in alterations of the traditional social structure.[1] The former consistency and pervasiveness of traditional values and norms have given way to a new social structure providing new choices in many social relationships. This chapter details the functioning of an exchange system that, by its very nature, resists such changes.

Data are drawn from fieldwork done in a village of 525 people, originally craftsmen and laborers working on two very large farms. Although small during most of its history, the village included residents who had a variety of specialized skills required by the two farms and served as a marketplace for surrounding farmers. It had many of the resources of the trade town and an unusually high standard of living, all made possible by a money economy early in its history.

This discussion is limited to the exchanges of either goods or services between individuals who are recognized master or apprentice craftsmen. These exchanges take place "after hours," that is, they are not recorded in daily account books or receipts. They are illegal or, to use the local terminology, *black,* since present laws prohibit a craftsman from plying his trade unless all transactions are recorded in account books open to inspection by the tax authorities. None of the exchanges related here were so recorded. The names of participants are fictional to protect the people who so patiently tolerated my presence and, at times, awkward questions.

There are two kinds of black service exchanges. *First,* there is the *ad hoc form of exchange.* Ad hoc exchanges are between individuals who find themselves in situations conducive to a black exchange, but are not permanent members of a group. Ad hoc exchanges do not entail other obligations such as visitation or gift giving during family events. Ad hoc exchanges, unlike group exchanges, are negotiated and renegotiated at each occurrence even though two individuals may engage in a series of such exchanges.

Subtle approaches and careful probing by a service provider often precede the negotiations for ad hoc exchanges and allow for either individual to back out of a possible exchange before the actual terms of the deal are clearly understood or explicitly discussed. Such care is necessary because some individuals are not interested in illegal exchanges; there are many who fear the zealous pursuit of lawbreakers by tax authorities. Stories abound of months-long investigations of suspects and the persons with whom they have had dealings.

In some situations, the conditions are so clearly defined and limited that the need for negotiations is obviated, and only the obtuse, such as a naive researcher, can fail to see the offer of exchange for what it is: an invitation to deal in an illegal fashion so both may profit. For example, I had work done on a car before I knew the nature of the black exchange. When the mechanic completed his work I was asked if a receipt was needed. It was a small bill, so I said no. I then noticed that the very substantial sales tax was omitted from the

---

[1] For a discussion of the traditional social structure of a Scandinavian village, see Hansen (1976).

bill and I was given a knowing smile with my change.[2] My informant later clarified this exchange and noted that the question regarding a receipt was a test of my willingness to engage in black exchanges, since a receipt was normally given in the transaction. The mechanic implicitly explored the possibility without using the term "black," in a manner that would not have created an embarrassing situation had I refused.

Ad hoc exchanges will undoubtedly represent the most common form of black exchanges in the near future since they are more suitable to a village with a changing social structure. These exchanges are consciously profit motivated and have a beginning and end not intrinsically part of a social exchange network. Who exchanges with whom is a matter of individual needs and the availability of goods and services, and not of a social exchange network with its set of requirements for participation. Thus these exchanges are economic.

The *second* form of black service exchange is *social exchange*. These take place within a select and permanent group of craftsmen. These exchanges are part of a larger set of relationships and obligations that exist among the group members; however, they are primary to the group's existence since violation of exchange norms constitutes sufficient reason to terminate any other social relations.

Black service exchanges performed in the context of the established group do not have the clear beginning and end of ad hoc exchanges; each exchange of an object or service is only a single event in a long chain of interactions made possible by the social organization in a permanent and stable group of persons. Both asking for and providing a service to another is understood to be part of one's obligations as a member, and the result is a continuing cyclical process of paying and incurring debts to fellow members.

Members do not keep written records of the debts and obligations owed. The general consensus, understood although seldom discussed, is that members are obligated to help one another whenever the opportunity arises. One craftsman in the village noted that such exchanges are "just something we do for each other," and another reported that "we help each other, it is expected." When asked if their exchanges constituted a way of paying each other for help received, they were confused over the very language of the question. When the question was clarified they were angered and let me know that such questioning was not acceptable. I was repeatedly told that exchanges in the group's context are "a friend's favor" and nothing more.

The term *friend's favor* is symbolic and in the past represented a gift of assistance from one friend to another without obligations. It is still expected that friends help each other without keeping records of who owes whom. The

---

[2] The savings realized by the provider and customer are potentially great. The customer sees a savings of well over 15% and the provider does not pay an income tax on the purchase that often is in excess of 50% of the income. Such ad hoc exchanges are only possible with labor or objects not recorded in a shop's or store's inventory since auditors can readily discover missing items.

provider of such a gift of assistance responds with "it was so little" when thanked for his services, thereby in effect saying that he does not expect *immediate* reciprocation for a particular gift of help. The established exchange group enters such favors into the *group's* balance of trade. Later, reciprocation is definitely expected. Use of the term *friend's favor* and the expression "it was so little" are statements of the *nature of the exchange* and indicate that the group rules and not the rules for ad hoc exchanges apply. Group members are keenly aware of a balance of trade in spite of the absence of records. The balance is struck by not only helping each other when called upon, but also by *requesting* help whenever possible. In fact, the group expectations are such that *not* asking for help on a regular and frequent basis is considered as serious a violation of the group norm as failure to give help when requested.

Such a tight system is possible because of the cultural homogeneity and resource heterogeneity among group members. Members have a shared social history as craftsmen, evolved over several generations; they know and trust each other.

The method by which a balance of debts and obligations is kept can easily be demonstrated in certain instances. For example, requests for assistance are made only when there is proper knowledge of a similar need by another member. One craftsman, for instance, needed a new expansion tank for his furnace. He did not ask about the new tank until he heard that another member of his group needed a new brick wall for his pig sty. When he had this information, he knew that he had an opportunity for exchange, and broached the issue of the tank. This procedure is a rule for exchanges of major services and expensive objects.

For the innumerable smaller instances of help or exchange of objects there are other means for monitoring persons' needs and the group balance, and members are continually active watching the balance of exchanges. Such monitoring occurs during other social activities. Visits, for example, are used to transmit information about group exchanges. The men discuss their exchanges during the evening and show little tolerance for discussions of other topics. Social activities become incorporated into the exchange system and allow all to remain knowledgeable regarding the activities of group members.

The regular coffee hours of wives of group members serve a similar purpose, since members often instruct their wives to transmit messages regarding the schedule of events for the evening. Wives also sanction potentially deviant members by gossip structured to evaluate and threaten individuals not living up to their responsibilities. One session that was particularly illuminating had the wives discussing and criticizing a craftsman who had allowed his apprentice to charge for minor services. They were incensed by such charges and predicted that his business and friendship with others would surely suffer if he continued this practice since others had freely given him assistance without charge.

Although the wives of members assist with the transmission of information, participants in actual exchanges are men. Women do not participate since they do not have access to the skills and resources necessary for service exchanges, nor have they traditionally been directly involved with such activities. One woman, a skilled beautician, regularly cuts the hair of her husband's exchange partners. Despite the regularity of her services and the recognized skill of her trade, she is not accepted as a contributing member of the group. She is regarded as one of her husband's exchange resources. He, not she, is paid for the service. His partners bring bottles of beer to share with him while she cuts their hair and later prepares coffee and cake for them to enjoy.

C. Rules for Black Group Exchange

The cyclical process of asking and giving represents visible affirmation that all is well within the group and that future exchanges can be expected. As long as the exchange system in the group functions in a cyclical manner all stand to benefit, and it is for this reason that *asking* for assistance is positively valued by the individual asking and that *giving* assistance is positively valued by the giver. Both asking and giving transmits an awareness that one accepts the rules of the system, and giving is equivalent to making a deposit (of services) in a bank where the deposit can be withdrawn when needed. Only positives are exchanged between participants, and the system functions as long as the cyclical pattern continues over time with no disruptions.

There are two rules that apply to this exchange system of positives: (1) as much as possible, group members should strive to keep a *balance* in the long run of services given and received, and (2) members have a *duty* to keep the exchange relationships going over an extended period of time.

Rule 1 is necessary to ensure an equitable distribution of services to all members, and is manifested by the cyclical pattern of exchanges. A cyclical pattern helps to ensure an even flow of exchanges and provides nearly equal access for all members to the benefits of the system. However, such a distribution is difficult to achieve on a groupwide basis and comes about only through careful and complete information transmission about the exchanges in the group. As a result much time is spent discussing the activities of the group and coming to a consensus about the fairness of services given and requests made by individual participants.

Participants view their exchange obligations seriously, and make it a duty to search out partners actively and to ask and give services. There were, for example, several instances where a person would anxiously search the village for a partner because he had heard from others that this partner needed assistance, and he could not rest until he had met his obligations to assist. Telling one that a group member needed assistance was a favorite joke to play on many unsuspecting men right after their return from work in the early evening. It happens that members go to ask for help even when they can do the work themselves.

What we have here is an interactional system in which only positives are exchanged. *Cost analysis by individual members does not occur when the system functions properly because both receiving and giving services are valued positively.* Balance is maintained by the constant flow of information, and a very real sense of duty conditions partners to think of the group and its needs rather than individual profits.

While individual members *do* participate because of the rewards to be gained, they do not sit and calculate the costs and benefits of each individual exchange act. The sense of duty has become enmeshed in a village-centered ideology, and members view their exchange acts as representing all that is good about village life. It is firmly believed that exchanges are *friends' favors* of the traditional kind, and in this belief they find an almost sacred role played out by their activities in the system. Mercenary considerations are not part of their *day-to-day* activities; these motivations are hidden behind the notion that it is rewarding both to give and to receive a service—and it *is* rewarding as long as the cyclical pattern of asking and giving continues.

But, in an exchange system of positive–positive sanctions that is based on a sense of duty and obligation to participate in a cyclical manner, any serious deviation is threatening to the system. A deviant is one who does not reciprocate or ask for assistance when expected. Deviants threaten to alter the exchange system of positive–positive sanctions by forcing members to face the fact that not all of their investments in the group might produce return benefits. And, since the whole system functions because future returns are expected, any deviation breaks the pattern, and these expectations are shattered in a show of resentment and grudge. Every group member is affected and stands to lose.

The danger of deviancy is that the positive value of transmission will become negative and that members will have to divorce themselves from the system rules and act as calculating individuals. Such a confrontation requires a cost–gain calculation based on a long history of investments in the exchange; and in a system where all have given services and where many have services outstanding, there is a great potential for loss. The only alternatives possible are either for the deviant to relent and once again join the cyclical pattern of exchange or to leave, or otherwise the group dissolves. To avoid the latter the conforming members meet, discuss the state of affairs, reaffirm the rightness of their rules, and plot for the righting of the deviant member.

D. A Case of Deviance in the Exchange System

The following account details the sanctions against a deviant member and the turmoil in an exchange group trying to attribute responsibility to regain stability. The case reveals much of the nature of the group and uncovers details of its day-to-day functions. The efforts to reform the deviant failed and he was expelled, but in the process the group became vulnerable to its internal fears and the external pressures of the changing community.

"Mads Pedersen" is an unskilled laborer born and raised in the village. He now works in a mid-sized factory some distance from the village. Since he had never married, he had the time to help "Erling," another group member, on a daily basis. After dinner he would come with a couple of beers to work in his friends' gardens, not requiring any payment other than their friendship.

When Mads's parents sold much of their land and retired, he was left with enough to build a house in the new section of the village. He kept this land for several years while living at home, and did not consider building until he was nearly 30. During his many visits to Erling and "Henrik," another group member, he would talk about his hopes of having a house of his own.

Erling would good naturedly listen to Mads's talk about a house although at first he did not help him realize his hopes. Erling is a skilled craftsman, the product of many generations of craftsmen, and has never left the family home. He is no longer self-employed, and like many others, he could not keep his tiny shop after the war. But despite his new status as an employee, he is still considered a leader in the community. His employer not only gives him great freedom at work but also lets him use the factory's facilities for his own purposes. The use of the factory machines and the freedom to do much work for himself is a key factor to Erling's success at the black exchange. These resources permit the construction of wrought iron lamps and banisters, special tools of hardened steel, and the sharpening of knives, saws, lawn mowers, plows and shovels, all of which he uses as exchange resources.

Great ability as a craftsman, unbounded energy and a seemingly endless number of resources make Erling the natural leader of the group. His energy lets him help others to such an extent that they are continually indebted to him—a fact he enjoys and which gives him feelings of security in the group and the village.

Erling's closest friend is Henrik, who traces his ancestry to a family farm located near the village. Henrik's father and grandfather were regular customers and friends of Erling's father. Henrik became a craftsman when his older brother inherited the family farm, and he was one of the first to build in the new section of the village. Over a two-year period Erling and Henrik exchanged a large number of profitable services. These involved both men at times entering into exchanges with third parties in order to get services for both Erling and Henrik. For instance Henrik entered into exchanges with a third partner to get new ceiling tiles for both his own and Erling's houses.

It was to such an exchange system that Mads gained admittance, and he also received similar benefits in the first year of membership. Mads, Erling and Henrik are the main characters in the following account of the social exchange deviance episode. The other members were present and involved, but played minor parts and at all times deferred to the decisions of Erling.

In 1973 Erling decided to help Mads build a house, since he had willingly given his time for many years, and arranged for the wholesale purchase of the needed bricks and cement. Mads, living with his parents, had saved a large sum of money and with a bank loan had enough to pay for the building material. For the next several months the group built Mads's house. By paying wholesale prices for brick and cement and not paying for labor the house was built for less than 65% of the open market price. While Mads did not command such resources himself, group members could provide needed material through their contacts; and he reciprocated by continuing to help whenever possible, although never able to supply the equivalent services of the other members.

Erling provided both plumbing and heating materials and installed them; Henrik obtained many appliances; and Laurits saw to the windows and woodwork. By accepting these favors Mads joined the group and in so doing became deeply obligated. His once free gifts of help now became incorporated into the group's balance of obligations and payments, and he was now *expected* to offer his help in the gardens and with other odd jobs not requiring actual craft skills.

The invitation to Mads to join the group was an exception and was based on his childhood friendship with Erling and his continual assistance with chores for over 10 years. Membership was not a gift however, and Mads remained on a probationary status, always owing more than he could ever repay with his limited, noncraft skills. Mads's very admittance speaks to the diminishing number of traditional and independent craftsmen in the villages. In earlier years he, as an unskilled laborer, would not have gained entry, but would have remained an outsider limited to negotiating ad hoc exchanges only because of his friendship with Erling.

The group members were the real recipients of benefits from his membership. Because of his lack of skills and the obvious value of their skills, Mads was required to put in much more time than normally expected, and he was also obligated to actively offer his services where he saw a need for them. In a sense Mads became indentured to the group, not free to decide when and where he would give his services, whereas the contributions of the others were essentially completed, bounded by the specific nature of their craft skills. They were now free to concentrate their efforts on more productive endeavors since the house was completed and Mads performed many of the time-consuming chores. He remained obligated as long as he had the house to remind him of their generosity.

Despite the unequal nature of the exchange, Mads was a willing member and did not show any regrets about his position. After all, he did have a home of his own. However, when he met "Gudrun" he had second thoughts and sought a way to limit his time with the group. He did not immediately perceive the danger of this since Gudrun was not a stranger to the group, being related to Erling and his wife, Lis, through her marriage to Lis's brother, now deceased. Gudrun had worked as a secretary to support her three children, and continued her employment throughout her new relationship with Mads.

When Gudrun moved in with Mads they made a verbal agreement to keep their incomes separate. They shared equally in the costs of living, though Mads was still required to pay for all of the expenses directly related to the house. This financial arrangement is important since Gudrun later used it to emphasize the trial nature of their relationship, and Mads knew he had to fulfill her expectations if she were to continue living with him.

There were apparently no changes in Mads's lifestyle during their first three months together. He actively helped the others, assuming little responsibility for Gudrun's children since she continued working and paying for child care. Lis and others in the village were pleased at their success, and made predictions about the actual wedding date. But in the fourth month Mads began to look tired, and his ever-present humor gave way to brooding and silence because of Gudrun's insistence he spend more time at home. While he continued helping the group, his casual visits with beer became less frequent, and Erling and Henrik began teasing him, saying the usual things about a new couple staying awake too late at night. Mads smiled weakly at these jokes but did not really join them in their banter.

During this time Gudrun remained in the background and was not suspected of pressuring Mads to reduce his group activities. Lis and Henrik's wife, Jette, were sympathetic to Mads and spent many hours during the morning coffee discussing Mads's new and strange behavior, wondering how Gudrun could tolerate him. These views and their talks with Gudrun gave Mads the impression that the group still supported the relationship and especially Gudrun, and proved to be problematical for him later when he had to decide between Gudrun and the group.

In the fifth month everyone attended a citizens' council meeting at the school. While the men gathered to discuss their own affairs, Lis and Jette sat and talked with Gudrun, who had been drinking earlier. She daringly said she would never live with men such as Erling and Henrik since they refused to help with the children or other chores at home. Lis came to Erling's defense, saying he had other responsibilities at home, and that it took two people with separate responsibilities to make a home.

This conversation was discussed for some time, and the consensus, unknown to Mads, was that Gudrun was really responsible for his peculiar behavior. By the sixth month Lis and Jette sympathized with Mads and acted friendly and supportive whenever they saw him, and Erling and Henrik stopped their teasing and gave him moral support in an attempt to stabilize the situation. Mads did not know the reason for such support, but accepted it and for a while renewed his efforts to please the group.

Mads assisted with the spring planting, but completely stopped his casual visits with beer since Gudrun was still adamantly pressuring him to assume more responsibilities at home. He was obviously trying to satisfy both Gudrun and the group by limiting his casual visits and concentrating on actual helping activities.

Erling and Henrik, not entirely satisfied, took his continued lack of involvement with the group to be his own decision since they had tried to encourage him to participate fully. They began discussing the situation in earnest and concluded that something had to be done, although they did not yet know how to go about changing Mads's behavior.

In the seventh month Gudrun invited us to an office party and exhibit. Mads was strangely silent during the evening, spending most of his time watching the children while Gudrun asked many questions about American men and my own behavior at home. Kay, my wife, attempted to remain noncommittal, but Gudrun skillfully manipulated the conversation to appear we were in agreement with her. I had the distinct feeling we were invited to help Gudrun prove the rightness of her position to Mads, and she was partially successful because in the weeks that followed Mads failed to appear for several projects to which he had been invited.

One particular incident exemplified the situation confronting the group. Henrik, during this time, required help to install a large CB radio antenna, and pointedly asked Mads to help. Mads apologetically excused himself. In itself that would not arouse Henrik's suspicion, but he was seen caring for the children and tending his own garden while the others were working. At first puzzled by this behavior, Henrik later became very angry.

At this point the mood of the group changed, and Lis began to criticize openly both Gudrun and Mads, calling them unappreciative and lazy. She also repeatedly mentioned that Gudrun had refused produce from their garden because she did not have the time to clean and prepare it. This was reasonable on Gudrun's part since she worked a full week, cared for the three children, and did the cooking and household chores in the evening. Mads's income as an unskilled laborer was not high enough to support them both in a new house, and she had to work to make ends meet. Lis, on the other hand, was accustomed to Erling's relatively high wages and his continuous benefits from the black exchange, and she, as so many others, staunchly believes that the woman's place is in the home. It was therefore incomprehensible to her that Gudrun did not have the time to deal with fresh produce from the garden.

The group, by this time, had gone through the process of determining responsibility for Mads's negligent behavior. When Mads first showed a change of moods and restricted his casual visits with beer, the others knew something was amiss but withheld judgment. It just did not seem possible that Mads would consciously neglect his obligations after all they had done for him. With Gudrun's criticism of Erling and Henrik they immediately attributed responsibility for Mads's behavior to Gudrun and increased their efforts to regain stability. Despite these efforts, Mads continued to further restrict his group activities and this angered them since he was surely capable of resisting her pressure with their help. They proceeded to test his alliance by asking him to help with several projects. He failed, and the group left him alone while Erling and Henrik decided on a future course of action.

Their shunning let Mads know their extreme anger threatened his expulsion from the group, and he tried to make amends by inviting Erling, Lis, Kay and myself to dinner. A dinner offered the ideal situation to casually sit and discuss needed projects and chores, and with Erling present it would be difficult for Gudrun to object. Such parties were frequent among members and Mads chose one as the most secure means of confirming his relationship to the group. Mads had obviously asserted himself and Gudrun, to keep the immediate peace, prepared a splendid dinner.

This was to be Mads's last attempt to remain in the group while also coming to terms with Gudrun, and might have worked had Erling been approachable at this time. Erling, however, was quiet during the party, smiling awkwardly, and spoke only when spoken to—certainly not his usual, boisterous party behavior. After dinner, he retreated to the living room and the television, where he made small talk with Kay and myself. At no time during this dinner did he talk with Gudrun. By 10 p.m. he was ready to leave, a good two hours before he usually left a party; and Mads, despondent by now, gave no objections to the early hour. Mads was left in the position of having only Gudrun for support—a fact upon which she undoubtedly capitalized.

The party failed to reestablish Mads's relationship with Erling because of Erling's stubborn insistance that he be more responsive to the group if he was to enjoy its benefits. Since the decision to exclude Mads had not been formally reached, Erling made it a point to test Mads one more time by asking him to help dig up his lawn the following Saturday. Mads promised to help, and Gudrun said nothing in the presence of the others.

That first Saturday we began working at 8 a.m., each bringing a shovel and wheelbarrow, and Erling and Henrik worked their areas of the lawn at a furious rate, obviously competing with each other. Ulrich and I, not nearly as energetic, worked at a slower rate. At 9:15 a.m. Mads arrived, smiled, and began working on a section left for him. He did not say much, and Erling and Henrik were overly polite, both obviously giving him a last watchful benefit of the doubt.

At 10 a.m. we took a break, and had beer and a few small, open-faced sandwiches in the kitchen where Erling and Henrik enthusiastically discussed plans for future projects. Ulrich went home to feed his animals and I, already tired, silently listened to Mads and Lis talk about the children.

We were back in the yard by 10:30 and the two proceeded at their competitive best while Mads worked slowly, keeping a good three meters behind the rest of us. He became even more quiet and at noon abruptly apologized for having to leave since he had promised Gudrun to care for the children during the afternoon. Erling responded by saying, "We are going to stop soon anyway, see you next Saturday." As Mads left, Erling gave a knowing smile.

Mads was not mentioned again that week, but his area of unshoveled lawn remained as a testimony to his lack of diligence.

The following Saturday we met once again, but Mads was not seen, and Erling finally sent his son to borrow Mads's shovel, which he had sharpened during the week. This was Erling's way of letting Mads know he should come and fulfill his obligations, but the son came back alone and told us that Mads had apologized for not being able to join.

Mads's failure to come produced an immediate reaction in Erling and he began to severly criticize Gudrun for interfering in Mads's life and with the group, and later Mads for letting himself be so dominated. Henrik said little, but acknowledged the correctness of Erling's assessment.

It was significant that Erling ceremoniously suggested they take care of Mads's section of the lawn, and they worked at it smiling and laughing as if to show how little it really was and how easy it would have been for Mads to show his alliance to the group. Between the two of them they finished this area in an hour.

At noon Erling sent his son back with the shovel and wheelbarrow, and instructions to tell Mads that they appreciated his help. He gave a smile to the rest of us as his son left with the insult.

Both Erling and Henrik drank several beers at lunch and began to talk freely, finally mentioning Mads's considerable debts to the group. I was surprised at the number of details remembered, and as they drank and talked a careful accounting took place. It was concluded that Mads had not acted fairly and left the group owing a considerable amount for all of the work they had put into his house.

Erling proceeded to tell how he had made a wrought iron lamp for Mads's house and had charged him a large sum of money. It was the same type of lamp he had made as gifts to the others, and he took special delight in his foresight to charge Mads. On this note Henrik left and Erling continued venting his anger, at one point grabbing a candle holder Gudrun had left to be soldered and said, "Damn if I am going to fix it when they can't even help." Lis said nothing, but later convinced him to fix it and had a neighbor return it.

Mads was only mentioned once more in the next two months; the following Monday, two days after the lawn incident, I made it a point to be at Erling's house as he returned from work. He came home in great humor and about 10 minutes later Henrik came with a couple of beers and the two proceeded to laugh and drink. Lis asked what was so humorous, and Erling, between laughter, said, "You should have seen Mads this morning when we passed him on the way to work." Mads had obtained a ride for the last two years, but this morning he was passed while waiting for the bus. He had apparently known that his failure to come marked the end of this relationship with the group—he was expelled.

Erling and Henrik then drove to the next village for some parts for Henrik's car, and once again they passed Mads, who was walking home from work. This last incident was related in great seriousness a week later by Lis while talking about her fears of not seeing Gudrun's children. Lis had passively accepted

Mads's expulsion, though several times told me of her wish to continue contact because of the children.

In the 12th month Lis's father, who was the children's grandfather, had a birthday. With Erling's consent she invited Mads, Gudrun and the children to a party, hoping to reinitiate contact, however infrequent. Both Gudrun and Mads were uneasy at the party and Mads's behavior was a repeat of Erling's own a few months earlier. It was obvious his future relationship with Erling and Lis would also exclude social visits.

These events occurred in 1975; in 1977 Mads sold his house and land and moved to a village near work. According to Lis, Erling and Mads do not talk to each other at work, nor have Gudrun and the children visited the grandfather since 1976.

Reference

Hansen, Knud
   1976   ''Exchange Networks and Stratification in a Danish Farming Village.''
           Unpublished dissertation, Michigan State University.

5

Michael Loukinen

SOCIAL EXCHANGE NETWORKS

A. Introduction

The focus of this chapter, like the last, is upon social exchange systems. In this report, however, the concern is somewhat broader, for the attempt will be made to briefly draw the outlines of the exchange system, not of a single group but of a community. In the investigation of this community, the contemporary and historical data, which were collected, indicated changes in its social structure over the past 80 years. As will be seen, these changes are consistent with our formulations for normatively controlled social exchange systems.

The fieldsite is Finn River (pseudonym)—a settlement carved in a mixed hardwood forest that covers nine out of every ten acres in a far northwestern county of Michigan's Upper Peninsula. There are 152 households with about 80% standing in scattered clearings and the rest concentrated in a central service area. The service zone is on a 300-yard strip of a two-lane asphalt road lined on both sides with gathering places including a post office, a general store, machine shop, feed mill, building supply warehouse, credit union, two service stations, a community center, skating rink and an elementary school.

Currently there are 420 residents including 162 men, 131 women, and 127 children less than 18 years of age. Slightly more than 85% of the men and 79% of the women had one or more ancestors who were Finnish immigrants, and the remaining families are second- and third-generation Swedish and French-Canadian ethnics. A strong local orientation sets the tone of life in Finn River as 92% of the adults were born within a cluster of backwoods hamlets fitting within a 30-mile radius of the community, with 60.5% of the men and 40% of the women actually being natives.

B. Historical Development of the Exchange System

In the 19th century, Finn River was a French-Canadian settlement of trappers, lumberjacks and subsistence farmers.[1] They migrated westward following the White Pine logging industry at the turn of the century and, as they left, Finnish immigrants moved in. Seventy-one percent of the immigrants came from the company-dominated towns of Michigan's copper country.[2] Most of them settled in Finn River as a way of escaping the violence of the 1913–1914 copper country strike.

Their confrontation with corporate power in conjunction with political developments in Finland divided the immigrant community into two factions: conservative "Church Finns" who opposed the strike and the "Red Finns," a coalition of leftist radicals supporting union activities. This ideological factionalism was carried into the community along with the former miners who began the task of clearing the cutover pine forests.

Distant from the cash economy, most of the Finnish immigrant farmers had meager and relatively equal amounts of capital, skill and household labor. Most were in the same situation, facing a harsh wilderness environment in a severe climate. To maximize what could be extracted from this wilderness environment and to minimize their work and capital investment, they suppressed inter-household competition, avoided confrontations over differences of belief, and cooperated with their neighbors. Visiting among the neighbors became a lubricant for the relations of production.

The early immigrant settlers typically exhausted their cash reserves paying for the downpayment on their land and the few animals and supplies with which to begin subsistence farming. "We were all in the same boat in the early days," is how the surviving oldtimers explain the extensive informal cooperation that developed among the pioneering settlers.

Throughout its history Finn River has had two distinct but related sets of overlapping networks: a network of service exchange and a network of visiting exchange. The dynamics of each and their interrelations will be examined in subsequent sections. Here I will comment upon some of the changes that have occurred in each.

Service exchanges began with neighbors sharing their horses to clear the land of the enormous pine stumps. Distinct neighborhoods, each with its own name, one-room schoolhouse and railroad spur became the site of communal threshing, woodcutting and, in some cases, potato and cabbage harvesting.

The sons and daughters of the immigrants believe that both exchanges of services and visits were more frequent during the period of 1900 to the mid

[1] Sources for these historical comments include both unstructured and systematic interviews with the sons and daughters of the immigrant pioneers as well as official documents—newspaper, church records and county government documents.
[2] Data are based upon a 1978 survey in which the surviving sons and daughters of 100 immigrant families were asked questions about their parents' geographical and occupational route leading to Finn River, their beliefs, and their visiting and labor exchange partners.

1930s. Residents' reports of their immigrant parents' visitors and labor exchange partners indicate that both networks were most intense among neighbors. Within the neighborhood, labor exchanges and some visiting crossed the "Church Finn"–"Red Finn" line, although visiting exchanges were more frequent among those having similar beliefs. Difference of belief did condition visiting when it occurred beyond the neighborhood.

In 1932 a larger school was built in the central village area and the neighborhood schools closed. In 1936 the railroad company pulled up its tracks, and each neighborhood lost its own access point to outside markets. By the end of the Great Depression the second generation farm youth began to migrate to the cities and the era of the self-contained neighborhoods came to a close.

Today, by analysis of survey data, almost half of the visiting exchanges occur among relatives, the remainder being divided about equally among neighbors and friends.[3] Although there is still a relationship between visiting and service exchange today, that relationship does not appear to be as strong as it was in the 1900–1936 period.

Some of the foregoing shifts are simply a consequence of the development of more extensive familial relationships since the immigrants' settlement of the community.[4] The introduction of the automobile and the gradual improvements in the roads made it possible for residents to maintain their increasingly large kin networks.

But the decreasing interaction in service and visiting networks appears to be related to occupational shifts. Virtually all of the immigrants were dairy farmers who worked as lumberjacks in the winter. These relatively complex enterprises provided an important base for the exchange of services. This exchange was, to an extent, based upon some differentiation of skills, but rested more importantly upon the need for cooperative effort in a large number of tasks. Today only about one of six households are actively farming. One-half of the men and one-third of the women work outside the household economy, often in jobs outside the community. This shift has had two consequences. First, the need for cooperative help—the mutual exchange of services—has decreased. Second, particularly for those working outside the community (and for those families in which both husband and wife are employed), time constraints have limited opportunities for both service and visiting exchanges.

There is reason to suppose, however, that these two networks have not shrunk at the same rate but that the service exchange network has shrunk faster. Today almost all residents are involved in visiting networks. About one-third of these visiting networks overlap with networks of service exchange, but in the remaining cases there are few if any services exchanged even among those engaged in intense ongoing visiting networks.

---

[3] Data are based upon a 1974 survey in which 245 second-generation adult residents in 147 of the 152 households reported their visitors names and their relationships to them.

[4] The Finnish immigrant pioneers had an average of 6.5 of their children live to young adulthood and many remain today in or near Finn River.

C. The Service Exchange System

Intense service exchanges can still be found in Finn River. Consider the exchange relationship between two males. Toivo Mäki and Eli Pelkonen are both dairy farmers managing small herds of less than 20 cows. They are old school friends, neighbors, hunting buddies and members of the same parish and farmer's organization. Both sing together in the church choir and participate in the church council. During a typical summer day they work together in the hayfields until noon. Not only do they share expensive haymaking equipment, but they also work together mowing and bailing. If one has a problem, the other will come to his assistance, and both will work together until the job is done. While working together, one will walk over to the well and carry the other a cup of water. They will pause to talk and reminisce about matters totally unrelated to the task at hand. They eat lunch together and converse about topics that range from tasks of mutual concern to politics and the world situation, as they compare and affirm one another's beliefs. After lunch, they enter the fields and resume the complex pattern of material and symbolic transactions. They stop to milk their herds in the evening. After eating supper together, they work in the fields until dark. As the day ends they enjoy a sauna together, then have coffee and pastries at the kitchen table. As Eli says good night, Toivo's wife gives him a tray of baked cinnamon rolls and a few ears of fresh corn she picked from the garden.

The reciprocity conception of social exchange would lead us to believe that in the case just noted the two farmers kept some kind of accounting of the exchanges which occurred, for if they did not, how could they balance the relationship reciprocally? But is this a relationship of balanced reciprocity?

When I asked one of the two farmers mentioned earlier how he "keeps track of the day-to-day give-and-take," he replied,

> Heck! How would I even begin to think about that? We have so-o-o much going on back-and-forth between us, you know . . . [pause] that we just wouldn't want to take the time to sit down and figure it out. I wouldn't know where to begin. We don't worry about who is ahead or getting the short end of the deal. It changes back-and-forth. We just keep helping one another. That's all there is to it.

It is evident that this system is in a condition of information overload, such that an accounting of the particular flows of services is not kept. Thus balanced reciprocity cannot be the rule governing the system. Instead we can infer that the rule is one of "mutual benefit." If, in a system of this type, an actor benefits (in the sense that the actor believes that more has been gained than lost in any relevant time period) and believes that its continued benefit is conditioned by the continued benefit of the other(s), then the actor has an interest in the continuation of the relationship. The information overload consequent upon such ongoing interactions can be supportive of the belief in ongoing benefit and the interests resting on it. Furthermore, as long as any actor believes that benefits have occurred and will occur in such a relationship, that actor has no interest in calculations of exchange rates or in keeping an accounting for that calculation.

On the other hand, as we have seen in the discussion of Mads in the foregoing chapter, as frequency of interaction declines, *if there is an interest in an accounting,* the members of the system are found to have very good memories indeed. In Finn River it is very common to hear residents explain to one another that they have been very busy. Being busy (or at least saying that one is busy) is, of course, a commonly used excuse for not interacting with another whom we want to believe that we value. However, the frequency of this "excuse" in the case of Finn River lends credence to the evidence that service (and visiting) networks are shrinking, a shrinkage which must be excused by each community member.

It is by no means surprising that generosity is a norm typical of the persons of this community. Standing in at least some of the networks of the community is strongly related to adherence to that norm, thus creating an (ideal) interest in helping. Related to this norm is the idea of obligations: both a general obligation to help those in need and a particular obligation to help those who have helped the person in question. Furthermore, members standing closer to one actor can discharge certain obligations to one farther from that actor as evidenced in the following example.

A neighbor boy appeared to be helping an elderly farmer in return for complements, advice across a wide range of subjects, meals and interesting conversation spliced with stories about the old man's youth. I afterwards learned that the boy's father had previously borrowed the old man's hay bailer and in return had sent his son to help with the chores. The boy was a carrier of the pivotal transaction between his father and the neighbor. Seen in the proper perspective the symbolic exchange between the old man and the boy was significant only as a lubricant for the pivotal transaction. Interestingly, the boy saw no relationship between the loan of the hay bailer and his father "suggesting" that he help their old neighbor. He simply knew that his father thought the old-timer needed a hand with the chores. Conversely, when the old farmer loaned the hay bailer he had no intention of receiving this help in return. He simply loaned the machine after he had bailed his own hay because his neighbor needed it and asked to use it. The old man simply took it for granted that neighbors should and would help one another because it is morally correct to do so. However, when the boy came to help him he knew why he had come and was pleased.

That Finn River is not fundamentally a system of balanced reciprocity is even more clearly seen in the less-intense service exchange relations occurring in overlapping networks among those who are not engaged in farming. For any resident the potential service network is conditioned by the task in hand. When a person needs, for example, a plumbing repair, he may construct an imaginary list of persons having that skill and select an actual exchange partner from that list. Priority of position on that list can be given to those in most frequent interaction (and thus to those closer in the resident's network). Here balance has little and perhaps no role. But if the resident must search farther out on his/her network or must cross into another network with the help of a friend or relative, then issues of balance and specific obligation can arise. In general there is evidence that closeness in network and not level of skill is the primary determinant of priority of position when such imaginary lists are constructed.

Distinct religious and secular belief systems support the social exchange system. There are two variants of religious beliefs. A major Evangelical Lutheran tradition defines helping others as the behavior expected of one who, through God's grace, has already been saved. It is believed that one "feels so much joy and love" for others as a consequence of having been saved that one simply wants to help them "out of God's love." A positive valuation of transmission is thus attributed to the act of giving a service.

A minority religious tradition articulated in several variants of the Finnish Apostolic churches presents an image of a God that is an omnipotent accountant observing all the transactions of His flock. At the moment one's life ends a balance sheet is tallied and one is either saved or damned depending upon the outcome on the bottom line. Helping others in this context is seen as a hedge against damnation—a (believed) severe, prolonged negative sanction. It is thus a long-range cost-avoidance strategy, although it is mixed with the positive inner feeling of doing good for others. Both traditions define excessive self-interest and a refusal to help others as sinful behavior, but the minority tradition is much stronger and more explicit on this point.

(The reader should carefully note that the position being taken here is that these beliefs are *supportive* of the system of social exchange. The claim is not being made that such a system could function supported only by such beliefs and in the absence of the system of social control discussed below.)

The secular beliefs supportive of the social exchange system have their origins in a fusion of Finnish immigrant socialism and rural neighborliness. It is believed that it is every person's responsibility to help others for the well-being of the community; and that narrow self-interest is a threat to the common good. It is believed that everyone should help everyone in need and that way all persons benefit.

D. Visiting Networks

Visiting is an activity which can be an end in itself, and, as mentioned above, in many cases in Finn River today there are visiting networks whose members are not engaged to any significant degree in service exchanges. Our focus of interest here, however, will be on the relation between visiting and service exchanges for those cases in which the latter still occur. Space will not be taken to describe the elaborate rituals and etiquette that surround visiting, nor their variations. But this much at least must be said. As will be seen service and visiting exchange systems can be connected. *But that does not mean that a visit can be exchanged for a service.* Instead, visits are valued as ends in themselves. It is believed that people should visit one another because the visit itself is a valued act, and not because it is a means to an end—that end being the opportunity to let another know of one's needs. Thus any request for help must be put as if it were incidental to the visit in spite of the fact that the visit may well have been planned specifically to the end of making the request. (Needless to say those at closer social distance will exercise less concern for the wording and timing of need statements than those at greater social distance.) But need is only one condition determining selection of visiting partners.

Again the initiation of an exchange seems to begin with an imaginary list. Here if no needs condition visiting the order of the list is conditioned by time elapsed since last visit on the one hand and social distance on the other. Thus those last visited and farthest removed from the resident are at the bottom of the list and those socially closest to the resident and for whom the longest time has elapsed are highest on the list. This ordering has important consequences for information sharing. First of all, information concerning the activities of others, *including their service exchanges,* is most fully shared among those socially closest to one another. However, information is spread beyond the limits of smaller groups by the second condition. Thus with the exception of those shunned (see below) almost all members of the community have at least some information concerning the activities of all others. This means of course that were any member to choose to receive help from others and give no help in return to any member of the network, that information would soon spread to other participating members through the visiting exchange system. Finally, given the temporal conditioning of visiting, the relative efficiency of the network as an information pooling device is maximized.

At the other extreme, those having the largest visiting networks are the retired and disabled, neither of whom are significantly engaged in transmitting services to others. These people may be the recipients of services from those whom they visit. Moreover, these people can, given the time available to them, be resources of information exchange.

E. Social Control in the Larger Community Network

Being embedded in a larger state system it is no surprise that social control in Finn River does not include the convergence of material negative sanctions. Negative symbolic convergence can occur particularly in relations of lesser social distance, but the apparent frequency of its occurence is very low, for merely hinting at the possibility of convergence is effective as a social control mechanism. Expulsion from a particular network can and does occur, but, given the state, expulsion from the community is not an option for the community members as a whole.

Insofar as the Finn River community as a whole is concerned, the effective social control mechanism is shunning. For this social exchange system each member has an interest in all other members being generous. Consider the following example in light of that norm. Ahola went off the road while trying to dodge a deer. He knocked down a piece of Lahtinen's fence. Ahola apologized and offered to repair it, but Lahtinen insisted that he pay what the unfortunate motorist (and I) thought to have been an amount exceeding the actual cost of the damage. Most members of the community thereafter shunned Lahtinen. I presented other people in the community with a similar, but hypothetical situation, asking what they would think about the episode and the persons involved. Their responses confirmed the existence of generosity as a system rule and shunning as a social control mechanism.

Nor is shunning an ineffective means of control in a small community such as Finn River. The community has a very small number of stores and few churches. Contact of some kind with others cannot be avoided as in larger communities. Thus Lahtinen and others have found themselves subject to shunning by others in public places, a system condition that approaches negative convergence. Finally, since shunning means the cutting off of a resident from visiting, an activity genuinely enjoyed by practically all in the community, the preference alteration effects of shunning can be quite great.

F. Concluding Remark

The community of Finn River contains normatively controlled social exchange systems that overlap a great deal. In the terms of the next chapter, embedded as they are in larger networks, these are mutual benefit systems. The history of this community seems to demonstrate a continual, ongoing and increasing penetration of larger systems. The need to work outside the community and related changing needs of individuals has reduced the frequency of service exchanges, while the ease of escape and the increasing monopoly of material negatives by the state have weakened but by no means eliminated the effectiveness of normative control. Finn River is still a community today, but there is reason to suppose that it is less so than it once was.

6

Frank Southard

Bo Anderson

David Willer

Nanette J. Davis

John S. Brennan

Steven A. Gilham

Knud L. Hansen

Richard Hurst

Michael Loukinen

Ann Morris

THE THEORY OF
MUTUAL BENEFIT SYSTEMS

A. Introduction

A mutual benefit system is a normatively controlled system of social exchange that is embedded in a larger (exchange and/or coercive) social structure. The theory for normatively controlled social exchange systems was introduced in Chapter 3. The focus of that chapter was upon simple systems such as tribal groupings, which could be treated as being effectively isolated from other structures. Now the focus of concern turns to social exchange systems that are found in larger structures. The aim of this discussion is to account theoretically for the major outlines of the systems reported in the last two chapters.

The main outlines of mutual benefit systems are like those discussed in Chapter 3. Simply put, they work much as a baby-sitting pool. Work time and resources are pooled and joint work is done. In addition the benefits of specialized skills are put at the disposal of the community. When such a system is working all of its members benefit. One important consequence of the system is that its members can, to an extent, reduce their dependence upon larger structures for the goods and services that they need. One consequence of that reduced dependence can be, as in the case of the Danish artisans, an increase in standard of living beyond that otherwise expected of the group in question. In the case of Finn River, the mutual benefit system of this very poor community allowed its members to have a style of life somewhat farther above subsistence than would have been possible in its absence.

Where does this increment in material well-being come from? To an extent its origin can be found simply in the extension of the work day and work week. To an extent its origin can be found in the advantages gained by pooling specialized skills. For example, I know how to repair cars but I don't know how to plaster walls. Of course I could teach myself to plaster but my work rate would be quite low. Far more efficient would be a pooling of skill such that I fix my friend's car and my friend plasters my living room.

But there is a third source of the increment of material well-being which has its origin in the rates of exchange *within,* as compared to rates of exchange *outside,* the mutual benefit system. Consider for example a mutual benefit system in which equity rules were interpreted as the exchange of equal labor time. Such a system, by definition, has no exploitation. Consider that system embedded in a larger exploitative system, in which each member's rate of exchange was unfavorable. It follows that material advantages are to be gained from exchanges within as contrasted to exchanges outside the group.

This advantage is conditioned by technological factors. Mutual benefit groups in modern societies can have tools and simple machinery at their disposal. They do not have at their disposal the complex and often automated machinery of modern factory systems. As a consequence such a group can maintain and repair one anothers' houses, appliances and cars, but cannot hope to make any of these commodities or the parts needed to maintain and repair them [though repair parts can often be obtained at relatively favorable exchange rates (i.e., wholesale) through group members]. In a society of complex technology such as the United States, low technology lifestyles are not a choice option for most members. Coal furnaces are easy to maintain and coal is cheap. But coal is not available on local markets. Public transportation systems have been dissolved by large capitalist interests. [See Snell (1976:passim).] As a consequence of a large number of these facts, simple subsistence is a complex ongoing enterprise. In this context mutual benefit systems can (often) be seen as necessary support systems that minimize the costs of living in structures that limit consumer choices.

In light of the foregoing comments then let us turn to the social dynamics of mutual benefit systems, reviewing their systems of exchange and social control in light of their place in larger structures.

B. The System of Positive–Positive Sanctions

Systems of social exchange in general and of mutual benefit in particular are systems of positive–positive sanctions; that is, the transmitter has a (conditioned) interest in the transmission of sanctions whether the sanction be a friend's favor, a gift, help rendered to a relative or whatever. To understand the dynamics of these systems means first that we understand when a sanction is potential and second the conditions under which its transmission valuation becomes positive. Following Southard's discussion of Chapter 3 the following general conditions can be put forward. First, in a mutual benefit system a sanction such as a service must be potential—the actor in question must be capable of the act. This condition typically becomes indexed in the beliefs of the system's actors. Thus if *a* needs help plumbing its house, *b* who has no plumbing skills will not be asked for the friend's favor. Second, the transmission valuation will be positive if and only if the actor's own (minimal) needs are satisfied first. Thus if a friend is ill, he/she will not have an obligation to do the friend's favor. (Needless to say this is a minimal condition which can and typically is transcended in powerful systems.) And the needs of those closer to the actor have precedence over those at greater social distance. Thus a would like to help c but "cannot" because b who is closer to a needs and is getting help.

Beyond the foregoing conditions we must remember that these systems work as they do (in part) because of the ongoing information overload. As long as the frequency of interactions is high enough no one will be able to keep exact count of the flows, and under that condition no one will have an interest in keeping an accounting. It is only when interaction declines that accountings come to the surface.

Since mutual benefit systems are embedded in larger structures, interaction within the system is limited by demands of the larger structure. Thus activities satisfying its own needs and those of its family (i.e., those closest in the network) may very nearly fill the time available to an actor. Moreover, the time spent in the mutual benefit system is not determined simply by work time but, as we have seen, also includes the time spent in visiting and other work at the symbolic level. That this "work" is typically enjoyed is itself no assurance that anyone will have time to do it *and* make contributions to the service network. In the case of Finn River, the helping network seems to have shrunk faster than the visiting network—the shrinkage of both being conditioned by the demands of the larger system. The Danish artisan system was very small. But even given its very small size we have reason to ask if it could have existed if the *friend's favor* had been taxed at the same rates as other services in the larger system.

More generally we can infer that frequency of interaction is less in modern systems of social exchange as compared to those of tribal systems. Furthermore, there are some typical variations in modern societies among status groups. On the whole "working classes," particularly those in smaller communities such as Finn River, have been able to maintain mutual benefit systems. In contrast, "middle-class" families seem more and more to exist in isolation. Why are these contrasts found? First of all, working classes typically have a variety of manual skills that provide the basis for (the potential network for) the system. The greater the skill level and the greater its diversity, the greater the potential mutual benefits. On the other hand, the demands of hierarchical strong structures on "middles" (see Chapter 9) typically mean that the work day extends well beyond its eight-hour limits. Finally, to the extent that middles have more disposable income, choices outside mutual benefit systems are wider.

To say that systems of social exchange are ones of conditioned positive–positive sanctions means that under certain conditions any actor *should* have an interest in transmitting positive sanctions to others of the network. As we have seen, being imbedded in a modern capitalist system has the effect to a greater or lesser degree of reducing the size of these systems and the frequency of these transmissions.

C. Visiting and the Insulation of Mutual Benefit Systems

Because their sanctions are positive—positive and not negative—positive, mutual benefit systems have no haggling and no bargaining. The rules of such systems could be roughly termed "ethical" in contrast to the "expedient" rules of larger capitalist systems.

But mutual benefit systems existing as they do in the larger system need to maintain their boundaries so that they do not become simply smaller versions of the larger structure. This seems to require continual reaffirmation of the nature of the group's relationships in their full complexity. This is one of the conditions that maintain the extensive relations of visiting seen in the systems discussed in the previous two chapters. These systems are small islands in a large sea of capitalism.

There are definite limits to the expansion of person-centered networks in the two communities. Take the case of visiting among friends and neighbors. The size of a's network is determined by the number of actors with whom a has visiting relationships. a may choose to attempt to expand this network following the proper etiquette. Visiting with others may be modeled as a reception of positive symbolics for a. Nevertheless, visiting and resulting exchanges demand much time and energy of a and this eventually stops a from further expanding the network. Assume that the time and resources that a can devote to visiting remain constant. The persons at the outer edge of a's network, the new friends, might want to establish a close relationship with a; however, if this happens then a's network expands. Actor a then runs the risk of offending older friends because of the demands of the new friends. Hence people will proceed with caution when they enter into new, close relationships. The larger community network can be seen as a set of partly overlapping *regions* of close relationships. For instance, a may have b and c as close associates, and b may be closely associated not only with c but also with d who is not part of a's close network. Actor a may do favors for d but they will have to be limited in nature and seen in the context of a's relationship to b. If d has an associate e who is interested in a favor from a but who has no close links to b or a, then mediation and sponsorship is needed before e can cross the network region boundary. In the small communities studied most members know something about the previous exchange performances of most other persons in the community: This knowledge makes sponsorship and mediation easy or difficult, as the case may be.

Visiting is the basis for needed information concerning plans, proposed activites, sources of supply, newly developed skills, opinions and so forth. In the case of Finn River, scores were kept on visiting. While this was an expression of the resident's sense of rightness, we should not loose sight of the fact that *by minimizing duplicate visits and maximizing the spread of visits all persons in the network were kept maximally informed for the time spent.*

But visiting may not be the only way to maintain such systems. Visiting is very time consuming. Given the time limits imposed by modern economic systems, those of us who are concerned about the destruction of systems of mutual benefit should think again about how material benefits might be maintained under a less time-consuming information system. Consider the following example. Imagine a fairly large group of persons that exchange services like baby-sitting, car tune-ups and the like. Each transaction is entered into a computer that has also been programmed with agreed-upon equivalence rules for services (for instance, one car tune-up equals four hours of baby-sitting). When contemplating a new transaction each member could then go to the computer and get all the relevant information about his or her own current exchange balance and about the past exchange performances of the relevant others. The computer would be the social control agent in this system; a person could be excluded from services until a negative exchange balance was made up.

D. Normative Control in Embedded Systems

The problem of normative control in embedded systems was broached in Chapter 1, formulated in Chapter 3 and is discussed further in Chapter 8. Thus this discussion can be short. Consider first shunning and expulsion. The effectiveness of either of these control procedures depends first of all upon the extent benefits are gained in the system of exchange as compared to other systems possible for the actor. In the case of mutual benefit systems the level of benefits is necessarily less than that found, for example, in tribal systems. Thus the costs to the "deviant" of shunning and expulsion are less than for systems not embedded in larger structures. Escape from a mutual benefit system, though of variable cost to the actor, is always possible. If the actor can escape at little or no cost (and/or if the actor can escape to any other system of equal benefit) then these procedures will not be effective at all.

The mutual benefit systems reported in this volume are supported by normative systems that are still strong though possibly weaker than in the past. Their effectiveness is reflected in the fact that the hinting of negative convergence is generally sufficient to stop a person from committing or from the further commission of an act prohibited by it. This process of hinting can be modeled as the transmission of information from others in a network to an actor a regarding the beliefs held of its behavior and steps that will be taken by them to deal with it. The content of these communications to a will depend upon the extent of shared beliefs and the type of social control in the system.

Negative convergence also depends upon the effective circumscription of the actor. If escape can occur before convergence, then this procedure of control is not effective. More importantly, due to the rules of state systems (laws) actors in mutual benefit systems are effectively limited to the use of symbolic negatives for control. But the effects of symbolic sanctions in many cases will not be strong enough to maintain the actor's interest in transmitting positive–positive sanctions (see Chapter 8).

The foregoing points were particularly well illustrated in the case of Mads. Mads was able to escape from the mutual benefit system *with the benefits that he had acquired*. That escape was possible because of the property laws of the state and the lack of circumscriptive conditions. (Again see Chapter 8 for further discussion of these conditions.) We may sympathize with Mads's "enserfment" to the group—clearly some mutual benefit systems have rules that are less than "fair." But we should not lose sight of the relative weakness of that system as evidenced by his easy escape.

E. Personal and Impersonal Relationships

Mutual benefit systems break down under various conditions. Rank attainment in a larger system may become more important than the standing within the group. Most of a's time and other resources would be used to further the new rank through, for instance, consumption or service in outside groups. Also, the social control exerted through convergence becomes less effective as a pays more attention than before to the reactions of persons outside its old group. Loss of resources on the part of many members of the group and the loss of members may also contribute. A certain minimal "density" of exchanges is necessary to sustain a community as a mutual benefit system.

The social sciences in general and sociology in particular developed in response to the development of modern capitalism; they developed as an attempt to understand, and as a means of justification for, modern capitalism. Stated somewhat (but not entirely) differently, sociology developed in reaction to Marx's work. Early conceptualizations of social exchange (and mutual benefit systems) contained strong value biases. To Durkheim (1933) these systems were characterized by "mechanical solidarity," the sense of which was that primitives and others were simply too unenlightened to choose to deviate. This position was brilliantly critiqued by Malinowski in *Crime and Custom in Savage Society* (1959). Malinowski's reports on social exchange in that work are consistent with the formulations offered here—but Malinowski did not recognize the structure of normative control and the bifurcation of interest upon which it rests. Durkheim characterized social control as restitutive in modern "organic" systems and repressive in "mechanical" systems. The role of terror in modern societies and reports of restitutive social control in simpler systems clearly indicate that, if anything, Durkheim's characterization was exactly backward. Little better was Weber's treatment of traditional behavior as based on habit and at best nonrational. [See Weber (1947:115ff).] But Weber's treatment was reductionist. Simply because behavior has been repeated over time does not imply that such behavior was habit based. Any stable interest system that reproduces itself can produce similar behavior, over time, which is a consequence of the rational interest-based choices of its actors. Such a statement is as true of normatively controlled social exchange systems as bureaucracies. In fact no evidence whatsoever has been offered to indicate that habit-based acts are more or less frequent in the first as contrasted to the second of the abovementioned systems.

In reacting to Marx's materialism the social sciences have become excessively idealistic in their explanations of human behavior. Shared values, norms and beliefs have been seen as the source of order among those poor folk who insist on having noncapitalist relations among themselves. Of course only enlightened modern people such as ourselves can recognize our interests and act upon them. Thus in spite of the fact that systems of normative control and their social exchange networks have been reported time after time in ethnographic case studies, no anthropoligist or sociologist has up till now treated these as *structures* that contain people who are psychologically much like ourselves, and whose patterns of action differ precisely because they live in a different kind of social structure. The people in these systems know how their systems work. Is this but another case of social scientists being the last in town to learn the location of the local whorehouse?

At least this much should be said to balance the record. The impersonal relations that occur in large systems are inhuman relationships—human relations for all of their faults and virtues have, up till now, been found only in mutual benefit and other social exchange systems. Mutual benefit systems, not systems of exploitation and domination, will support *ethical* behavior. It is a simple exercise for the reader to derive that any actor in a fully effective mutual benefit system has an interest in acting by the "golden rule."

F. Final Comments

Until now the structures that we call normatively controlled social exchange systems have been idealistically interpreted in at least the following sense. The order of these systems has been seen as having its origin in the unthinking acceptance of ideas of right and wrong (norms). No attempt has been made to systematically account for those norms. Instead the aim has generally been to uncover the norms by examination of behavior (including verbal behavior in interviews) and then "explain" observed behavior by its relationship to the norms. This position is the current received view. Beyond being idealist, the received view is both empiricist and circular. We feel that the elementary theoretic interpretation offers certain clear advantages over the received view, not the least of which is the possibility of moving from macro- to microsystems and back again.

Until now it has not been possible to move systematically from micro- to macrosystems, not because theoretic formulations did not exist, but because theoretic formulations for large and small systems use differing and contradictory conceptions for the actors of the two system types. (In other words our conceptions of human nature varied by system type.) While actors in small systems have been seen as being reactive, mechanical, moral and so forth, large-system actors have been seen as expedient, amoral, calculative and so forth.

How has the present formulation avoided these problems? Roughly speaking, the problem has been avoided by treating small-system actors as initially like the calculative, expedient actors of large systems, but placing them in a system in which calculations would lead to an interest in "moral" behavior. But here an important disclaimer is in order. The foregoing treatment is not a complete statement of how the actors of either system could be treated. Instead of beginning with "expedient" actors—that is, actors with no reflexives and thus no "ethical system," we could begin with a formulation for actors with reflexives (an ethical system) the consequence of which in action would be consistent with the behavior thus far expected of expedient actors in fully effective normatively controlled social exchange systems. An array of valuations could be attributed to those actors such that some would never be "tempted" by expedient behavior (i.e., never be deviant), others tempted sometimes and others tempted only if very significant individual advantage could be gained. Nor would this formulation be excessively idealistic, for it could rest upon the idea that actors will to greater or lesser extents *internalize* preference systems and beliefs that are consistent with their conditions of existence. How would the actions of an ideal typical ethical actor then differ from the expedient actor? If the normatively controlled social exchange system were fully effective there would be no difference. But if it were possible to act on one's own interest, not on the interest of others, and not be subject to normative control, then the ethical actor would not do so and the expedient actor would so act.

Now turn to larger systems and consider the behavior of the ethical actor. If one such actor made no differentiations of systems and of social distance then that actor would be easily exploited by any other actor. (This point will not be demonstrated but can be derived by the reader in light of the basic concepts of the theory and the formulations of Chapter 9.) But consider a somewhat different social actor who is *realistically ethical* —who makes decisions concerning ethical behavior contingent upon any other actor's social distance. Assume that to be ethical toward those closest in the actor's network implies that the same actor must be increasingly expedient toward actors at greater social distance. For example, a working parent similar to the foregoing formulation would be highly manipulative toward any large system, not out of personal concerns and individual interests but out of ethical concerns for the well-being of the parent's children. The resulting behavior in the large system for this realistically ethical actor would exactly correspond to the expedient actor's acts. Observations of that behavior from the point of view of microeconomics would simply confirm the microeconomist's fixed conception of human nature. If the foregoing formulations have any correspondence to real cases—as we believe that they do—then it follows that at least certain types of large systems at least limit, and could in the long run destroy, ethical bases of behavior.

References

Durkheim, Emile
  1933   *The Division of Labor in Society* (tr. George Simpson). Glencoe, IL: The Free Press.

Malinowski, Bronislaw
  1959   *Crime and Custom in Savage Society.* Patterson, NJ: Littlefield, Adams and Co.

Snell, Bradford
  1976   American ground transportation, in Jerome Skolnick and Elliott Currie (eds.), *Crisis in American Institutions.* Boston: Little, Brown and Co.

Weber, Max
  1947   *The Theory of Social and Economic Organization* (tr. A.M. Henderson and T. Parsons). Glencoe, IL: The Free Press.

Now the focus moves from the relatively small systems of the last section to a concern with large systems and their structures. This movement from micro- to macrosystems is not only a change in size of system but also a change in system type. None of the systems to be examined here are ones of mutual benefit.

The section begins with Chapter 7 which extends certain formulations of the elementary theory. In order to avoid drawing *n* system states, algebraic interpretations for network attributed properties are introduced. Given their introduction it is much easier to deal with structures whose form can determine the processes and outcomes of social interactions. Strong and weak structures are differentiated and a quantitative formulation for resistance is developed so that solutions to interaction processes in weak structures can be derived.

The concern of Chapter 8 is the investigation of some of the relations between exchange and coercive relationships. In that chapter it is seen that exchange is by no means more "primary" than relations of other types, and that modern exchange systems are quite unthinkable without modern legal systems and the

MACROSYSTEMS

rights that they enforce. One result of this investigation is a much clearer idea of the meaning of exchange and of resources held by actors.

Of course both Marx and Weber recognized the relationship between property and exchange. Chapter 8 departs from certain ideas of both scholars but develops its argument in light of the elementary theory. As a consequence the connections between coercion as a basis of property and economic exchange is made especially clear.

The concern of Chapter 9 is the theoretical investigation of certain types of centralized structures which are here called strong structures. The aim is to clarify the relation between type of structure and its reproduction over time. The place of structure in the reproduction of systems is implied in Marx. In Chapter 9 this relationship is explicitly drawn out for certain theoretically simple systems. Rates of exploitation in both exchange and coercive relationships are treated. These formulations are implicit in Marx. However, the extension of these formulations to hierarchy is new.

Chapter 10 on political brokerage is an application of the elementary theory to one political system that concentrates upon certain unofficial networks. These unofficial networks are seen as strong structures that are supportive of the reproduction and thus the maintenance of the Mexican political system.

The high levels of political participation in Mexico might give the impression that the system was democratic, even egalitarian. This impression, however, ignores the fact that a stable and steep system of stratification has been reproduced over time. That reproduction leads us to look for strong structures in the political network system. A number of such structures are identified.

Chapter 11 reports upon some of the experimental research that has been carried out under the theory. The systems studied have small numbers of subjects, but the aim of the experimental work is to investigate, in a controlled setting, structures that are typical of macrosystems. The chapter takes its style from that recommended by the American Psychological Association.

These experimental systems are artificial if compared to any ongoing social structure. This artificiality makes generalization from the systems studied to ongoing systems impossible. However, with the elementary theory we have no interest in generalization among any empirical cases. Instead the interest is to derive from the theory a set of model types, each with its own implied dynamics. These model types can then be investigated in a number of settings. These settings include institutional, historical and experimental research. Thus from the point of view of the elementary theory the aim always is to relate the results of experimental (and all other) research back to the theory through the models for the cases studied. If two empirical cases are compared and are said to be similar, it is exclusively because the models for the two cases are similar. It is through abstractive connection to models, not empirical generalization, that general knowledge is gained in any science.

Too often sociological discussions of exchange give the impression that the process of exchange consists of two or more actors mechanically grinding out offers and counteroffers according to preset rules. The fact that some interactions seem to have such a character does not imply that all exchange can be so viewed.

In ongoing systems, any exchange that can occur is a consequence of a great many rules. At times, as in modern economic exchange, these rules are widely known within and even between societies. However, as pointed out in Chapter 12, it is often the case that the rules for exchange can be specific to particular groups. How then can exchange occur among members of different groups with different context specific rules? To answer that question fully also requires that the idea of group boundary be formulated.

If the term ''group'' is to have a meaning then there must be a way of theoretically comprehending the group as a bounded unit. (Similar statements could be made concerning associatons and organizations.) This is not a new problem. Weber referred to status groups in his substantive work and drew their boundaries in relation to commensal and connubial relationships. The relations between the drawing of national boundaries and the development of the modern languages of Europe drew his attention.

In order to construct a model for any system, boundaries must be introduced for its potential network. The term potential network was first introduced in this volume as a theoretic device. Its limits were the limits of interest of the theorist for a given purpose. But by this point it is evident that boundaries have a phenomenological meaning which must be taken into account by the theorist. For example, a major fault of exchange theory up until now has been the (implicit) presumption that there is an impermeable boundary between exchange and coercive relationships. But in previous chapters we have seen that view is unsound, and that an adequate understanding of exchange systems requires that the boundaries be extended to include relevant relationships of coercion.

The development of social boundaries is connected to both symbolic and power processes. This chapter then represents a beginning point of our research toward an understanding of these interconnected issues.

Specialists may find that the papers of this section that concentrate on areas of their specialization offer few "new" or "surprising" facts. For example, Marxists will immediately recognize the place of the reserve army in Chapter 7 and in the reported experimental systems and elements of the treatment of property in Chapter 8. Latin Americanists will recognize certain of the structures identified in Chapter 10. In fact, there are new ideas in each of these and in the other chapters. However, the aim of any theory is not simply to present new ideas but to integrate the widest possible number of ideas in the most precise way possible. Our pursuit of that aim is best seen by the range of cases here considered and by comparing these studies with those of Section I.

7

David Willer

QUANTITY AND
NETWORK STRUCTURE

A. Introduction

The idea of quantity as a property of sanctions and thus of actors, their meanings and resources was mentioned in Chapter 1 and used in Section I. The procedures for a quantitative interpretation will now be introduced in this chapter. Let us consider some reasons for that introduction.

One important restriction of the theoretical procedures discussed up till now is the number of system states that can be drawn for any potential network. But merely thinking of a sanction flow as quantitative is not a general solution to that restriction, for we are left with the following problem: Consider an actor in an exchange system in which exchange rates can vary quantitatively. There will be n system states, but n can be a very large number. Would any theorist have time to draw the n system states and order them for each of m actors so that preference systems can be represented?

How can we avoid drawing n system states and ordering them for m actors? The solution to this problem lies in the introduction of an algebraic function which can be used to stand for the ordered system states of the actor's preference system in the following way: If sanction flows are quantitative we know that any flow either to or from an actor in which the sign of the flow is positive will alter the actor's preference state in a positive direction. Any flow either to or from an actor with a negative sign for that actor will alter the preference state in a negative direction. Thus the preference state alteration of an actor can be expressed as a function of amounts of the flows and their valuations. For any system, a given range of solutions for this function will be possible. The limits of that range are the actor's preference alterations for the most- and least-preferred system states. The points between these limits are the actor's preference alterations for the remaining (ordered) system states that can occur for the system.

This function is the first law. Like the formulations for actors introduced up till now it can be subject to a wide variety of interpretations depending upon the actor and system conditions to be represented. Thus the preference system of an actor can be defined by the law and by the range of preference state alterations possible for the actor for the system in which action is to occur.

With the quantitative interpretation of sanction flow, other terms already introduced such as "interest" and "cost of confrontation" can be given quantitative interpretaton. The relations between exchange rate and network structure will be theoretically investigated. For some networks, called strong structures, the network structure (together with other initial conditions) determines the rate of exchange as an outcome (or final condition) of the interaction. (See also Chapter 9.) The concept of resistance is introduced to determine the rates of exchange (and coercion) in other (weak) structures.

Abstract quantities of abstract units will be used in calculating interaction models. But what are abstract quantities and what are abstract units? Here it should be no surprise that operationalists have this issue backward. What counts as mass in physical theory is first of all a theoretic question. Expressions such as "point mass" obviously could not be determined through empirical operations. On the contrary, measurement operations simply follow from the empirical realization of a theoretic model constructed for measurement.

Physical units such as grams and meters always have two separable meanings: first as properties of an abstract system and only secondly and empirically as consequences of theoretically guided measurement operations. An abstract value of n meters is not the same as an empirically measured length of n "meters." Thus when the examples of the next section refer to units of money or of particular commodities the referent is to abstract properties and not to the empirical objects in people's wallets and the things they consume.

In light of the foregoing points I will take the following position: A quantitative interpretation of networks will be introduced for purposes of interpretation and explanation. That introduction is not based on an operational definition of the quantitative terms and will not be limited by already developed measurement procedures. In fact no *general* procedures for quantitative measurement have been worked out at this point. However, as the theory is applied in a number of cases in later chapters, procedures particular to those applications are used which are consistent with (and consequent upon) the formulations of the theory. Perhaps at a later time (and in another work) the problems of measurement can be fully unpacked and general procedures developed. At this point we must proceed step by step.

B. The First Law

Let x be the quantity of any sanction flow, v the valuation of the flow by the receiving (or transmitting) actor and p the preference state alteration of the flow for the actor. For any one sanction flow, if p is a function of x and v, then for any actor a either receiving or transmitting one sanction flow,

$$p_a = f(v,x)$$

and the simplest expression of that function for our purposes would be

$$p_a = vx.$$

In a number of theoretically important systems each actor can transmit one type of sanction flow and can receive one type of sanction flow. When the preference state alteration of transmissions and receptions is independent, and when the subscripts t and r represent transmission and reception, then the first law can be stated as

$$L_1: \qquad p_a = v_{t_a} x_{t_a} + v_{r_a} x_{r_a},$$

and by removing the restriction on numbers of flows, when all preference alterations are independent, T is the index set of sanctions transmitted and R is the index set of sanctions received,

$$L_1: \qquad p_a = \sum_{i \in T} v_i x_i + \sum_{j \in R} v_j x_j.$$

Since the examples that follow in the next section are confined to systems in which any actor can transmit one type of sanction and receive one (other) type of sanction the first expression for the first law will be used. In those examples, the quantitative value of the v term will be treated as a constant for the range of x quantities considered. However, as discussed below, these expressions can be given a more general interpretation with the introduction of parametric equations relating variations in the value of v to variations in x.

In the interpretation of the first law, the x terms are always either zero or positive. The sign of the v terms is the sign of the sanction for the actor a. For example, if an actor a transmits a negative–positive sanction then the sign of that actor's v_t is negative. If the actor receives a negative–positive sanction the sign of that actor's v_r is positive and so forth. The procedures for determination of values for v and p terms in light of certain initial system conditions will be presented in the next section. In this section the meaning of the first law in use will be discussed.

Let an economic exchange system be defined as containing negative–positive sanctions.[1] Thus any transmission for any actor is a negative preference state

---

[1] More precisely, the sanctions of the exchange relations are negative–positive sanctions; however, the system of economic exchange can, and (but for certain limiting cases) must contain certain negative sanctions. See especially Chapter 8 and also Chapters 2 and 4.

alteration (i.e., a "loss"). In light of the first principle, no actor in an economic exchange would transmit any sanction *unless* the actor believed that a sanction reception (i.e., a "gain") were contingent upon that transmission. Thus the occasion of rules such as offers, and system rules such as prices in economic exchange systems.

Now consider how the first law would be used in the interpretation of a bilateral monopoly. Each actor would have its own v values for transmission and reception and its own p values as a result of those flows. A quantity transmitted by actor a would have the value of x_{t_a}. This value is a number of units of flow to b. This number of units when received by b is x_{r_b}. Thus the numerical values of x_{t_a} and x_{rb} will be equal. The value of x_{t_b}, the quantity of sanction transmitted by b, and x_{r_a}, the quantity of sanction received by a, are also equal. (These statements assume that there is no loss "in transit" of the sanction, a loss that could be modeled by extension were that a need in a particular application.) For example, for an economic exchange, a quantity of money is transmitted by a and received by b. The amount of preference state alteration for each actor consequent upon that flow will depend upon the value of the actor's v term. Of course the direction of the preference alteration for any one sanction flow of the a–b economic exchange will be negative for a the transmitting actor and positive for b the receiving actor. (More generally, for economic exchange v_t is always negative and v_r is always positive.)

For the dyadic exchange system L_1 will be used twice, once for a and once for b. With the introduction of the initial conditions, the v terms for each actor can be determined. Then it will be possible to solve L_1 for p given any flow possible for the system. A flow from a to b and a second flow from b to a can be represented as an exchange rate for the system. These same two flows will determine the value of the x terms for both actors. Thus using L_1 first for one and then for the other actor, p_a and p_b are calculated. Thus for any rate of exchange a value for preference state alteration can be calculated for each actor. Exchange rate and p_a and p_b are the central parameters for expression of each system state.

The problem then is to determine the exchange rate predicted for the system. The solution to the problem is guided by application of the first principle to the first law. Actors decide among potential lines of action based on calculations of their own and other's preference state alterations with the first law. As will be seen the procedure for this determination differs with the structure of the system.

For systems larger than two actors, L_1 is applied to determine the preference state alteration of each (type of) actor. The application may be to an economic exchange system, a social exchange system (which is defined as containing positive–positive sanctions) or to coercive or conflict systems. Following its meaning as introduced above, any coercive relationship will contain one positive and one negative sanction. Thus v_r for one actor will be positive and v_r will be negative for the second. (For coercion the transmission signs can vary by system conditions.) In fact the procedures for the quantitative treatment of coercion are very similar to those introduced for exchange below.

L_1 can be given a more general interpretation by the introduction of parametric equations such that v can vary by the value of x. In this way, "declining marginal utility" and/or "satiation" can be introduced when and if such ideas are needed. Here three points are relevant. First, when the first law is applied to economic systems as defined above, there will be a standard for exchange against which all other sanctions can be exchanged. Since that standard is not necessarily "consumed" by the actors, it is not itself necessarily subject to either satiation or declining utility. Second, even given the operation of such ideas as marginal utility, for most economic exchange systems, no actor with an adequate potential network and adequate system information would exchange significantly into the declining portion of its utility function—a point that can be derived as you become familiar with the applications of the first law. Third, unlike the derivations of economic theory, for the elementary theory, rates of exchange for a variety of systems are not determined by utility functions, but by the first and second laws, and *by the structure of the network in which the exchange occurs*. Thus the statement of L_1, wherein the v terms are treated as constants, is more general than it might seem at the outset.

C. Some Initial Calculations for Two Exchange Systems

The first step in the determination of the exchange rate for a system of economic exchange is the determination of the negotiation set. The negotiation set is the range of exchange rates potential for the system. This will be illustrated by reference to the system of Figure I. In that system there are two actors of central interest, a and b, and two further actors, c and d. For this system, a has a commodity, a car, and b has money resources, wherein money is the commensurable quantity of the system. Figure I is a potential network for the system which indicates that (1) a can exchange with c at a fixed rate of $1000 for the car, or can exchange with b at an exchange rate to be determined, and (2) b can exchange with d for a commodity identical to a's at the fixed rate of $1500 for the car or can exchange with a at a rate to be determined. Let it be taken as an initial condition that the network of Figure I, as interpreted, is exhaustive of the alternatives of the two actors. Further let it be taken that a and b will exchange

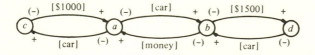

FIGURE I. The network determination of the negotiation set for a dyadic economic exchange.

with c and d respectively if the $a-b$ exchange does not occur. Thus the alternative exchanges are the baseline from which the negotiation set of a and b can be derived.

It follows from principle one that if a and b are to act in the $a-b$ exchange relationship, then each must induce the other to act. Let the minimal inducement for any actor in the system (or *just noticeable difference*) j be set equal to \$1.00. It follows, then, *by inspection*, that the range of potential exchange rates (the negotiation set) for the system is from \$1001 to \$1499.

In an exchange, when there is a disagreement between the actors concerning the rate of exchange, a confrontation occurs and the exchange does not occur. Relative to the baseline, at confrontation there has been no alteration of preference state for either actor. Thus, p_{con} the preference alteration at confrontation is

$p_{con} = 0.$

Applying the first principle, it follows that, for any actor,

$p_{min} = p_{con} + j$

and for this system for a and b

$p_{min} = p_{con} + j = 0 + 1 = 1.$

Thus for the system, for both actors, the worst of all possible system states is confrontation, the state of no exchange in which there is no preference state alteration. Also there is a system state in which the preference alteration of a is p_{min} and a distinct system state in which the preference alteration of b is p_{min}.

If $p_a = p_{a_{min}}$, then a has received the minimum price for the car which is \$1001. Thus, if $p_a = p_{a_{min}}$, then $x_{r_a} = 1001$. Also, if $p_a = p_{a_{max}}$, then a has received the maximum rate for the car and $x_{r_a} = 1499$. Turning to the actor b, we know that $p_{b_{max}}$ will occur at the same system state as $p_{a_{min}}$ —that is, when the price is \$1001. Thus, if $p_b = p_{b_{max}}$, then $x_{r_a} = x_{t_b} = 1001$. Further, we know that $p_{b_{min}}$ will occur at the same system state as $p_{a_{max}}$ —that is, when the price is \$1499. Thus if $p_b = p_{b_{min}}$, then $x_{r_a} = x_{t_b} = 1499$.

Now let us determine the *relative* values for the v terms for each of the actors beginning with a. (All that we will need to know for any actor is the value of one of the v terms *relative to* the other.) Since a is receiving the money, let us set $v_{r_a} = 1$. Since the commodity to be transmitted is a single unit, set $x_{t_a} = 1$. Remember that when $p_a = p_{a_{min}}$, $x_{r_a} = 1001$, and that $p_{a_{min}} = 1$, then since

$p_a = v_{t_a} x_{t_a} + v_{r_a} x_{r_a}$
$p_{a_{min}} = v_{t_a} (1) + (1) 1001 = 1$
$v_{t_a} = -1000.$

Now $p_{a_{max}}$, a's best of all possible preference alterations, can be determined. At $p_{a_{max}}$, $x_{r_a} = 1499$. Thus

$p_{a_{max}} = -1000 (1) + (1) 1499 = 499.$

Now let the corresponding values be determined for b. Since b is transmitting the money, set $v_{t_b} = -1$. Since the quantity to be received is a single unit, set $x_{r_b} = 1$. Remember when $p_b = p_{b\min}$, that $x_{t_b} = 1499$, and that $p_{b\min} = 1$, then since

$$p_b = v_{t_b} x_{t_b} + v_{r_b} x_{r_b}$$
$$p_{b\min} = (-1) 1499 + v_{r_b} (1) = 1$$
$$v_{r_b} = 1500.$$

Now $p_{b\max}$, b's best of all possible preference state alterations can be determined. At $p_{b\max}$, $x_{t_b} = 1001$. Thus

$$p_{b\max} = -1001 + 1500 = 499.$$

Let us review the characteristics of this exchange system. Since $j = 1$, and the range of possible exchanges is from \$1001 to \$1499, there are 499 possible system states in which an agreement to exchange can occur. There is, in addition, the system state of disagreement. Taken together, there are, for this exchange system, 500 system states (thus the need for quantitative interpretation). For each system state, a value can now be assigned for the preference alteration of a and a value can be assigned for the preference alteration of b. (For example, what are the preference alterations for a and b at the price of \$1350?) Before proceeding, let us introduce a second system for purposes of comparison.

A laboratory system was constructed for the experimental study of systems of exchange. For that system two types of positions were constructed, f and g, which differed by the scoring of their transmission and reception of counters. Given that points scored were valued (for subjects were paid by point score), this scoring system, together with the resources assigned to each position, can be used to model the theoretic actors, f and g, who occupy their corresponding positions. The issue of the correspondence between the behavior of the theoretic actors as modeled here and experimental subjects' behavior will be discussed in Chapter 11.

The system to be modeled is a bilateral monopoly—that is, a system in which each actor had only the other as a member of its potential network. Let us call the initial sanctioning resources of the actors, x_i. Initially, f held 11 counters. Thus $x_{i_f} = 11$. Initially, g held one counter. Thus $x_{i_g} = 1$. Any counter retained by the f position was worth one point. Thus $v_{t_f} = -1$. A counter received by the f position was worth ten points. Thus $v_{r_f} = 10$. Any counter retained by the g position was worth no points. Thus $v_{t_g} = 0$. Any counter received by the g position was worth one point. Thus $v_{r_g} = 1$. The counters were indivisable—thus $j = 1$. In summary, then, for the two theoretic actors of the system,

$$v_{t_f} = -1 \qquad v_{t_g} = 0$$
$$v_{r_f} = 10 \qquad v_{r_g} = 1$$
$$x_{i_f} = 11 \qquad x_{i_g} = 1.$$

This is an economic exchange of a limiting type. [The resources of the actor g are valueless to g. Thus the (negative) sign of v_{t_g} is lost as its value goes to zero.] The sanction of f is a negative–positive sanction as can be seen by the values of v_{t_f} and v_{r_g}. Given these initial conditions, the range of exchanges possible for the system, the negotiation set, can be determined by using L_1. We know that if an exchange is to occur, then the sanction of g will be transmitted. Thus $x_{t_g} = x_{r_f} = 1$ for any exchange. Further,

$$p_f = v_{t_f} x_{t_f} + v_{r_f} x_{r_f},$$

and

$$p_{f_{min}} = 1 = (-1) x_{t_f} + 10.$$

thus

$$x_{t_f} = 9.$$

Thus the maximum number of sanctions which f would transmit would be 9 and for that system state the preference alteration of f is minimal at one. The preference alteration of g is maximal at that system state and its value is

$$p_{g_{max}} = (0)1 + (1)9 = 9.$$

The minimal preference alteration of g is one. Thus the minimum number of sanctions which would be received by g (and transmitted by f) is determined by

$$p_{g_{min}} = 1 = (0)1 + x_{r_g}$$
$$x_{r_g} = 1.$$

Thus the minimum number of sanctions which f would transmit is one. At that system state, the reader can determine that the preference alteration of f is maximal and equal to nine ($p_{f_{max}} = 9$).

As in the first system modeled in this section, within the negotiation set the preference alterations of the two actors are inversely related. In this instance, at the system state in which f transmitted one sanction and g one sanction, the preference alteration of f is maximal (and equal to 9) and the preference alteration of g is minimal (and equal to 1). At the other extreme, at the system state in which f transmitted nine sanctions and g one sanction, f's preference alteration is minimal (and equal to 1) and g's preference alteration is maximal (and equal to 9). Thus *within the negotiation set* the interests of the actors, as in the first instance, are *opposed*. However, both prefer any exchange within that set to no exchange. Thus insofar as the *act of exchange* is concerned, their interests are *complementary*.

For this system there are ten system states, nine in which exchange can occur, plus the system state of confrontation. It will be convenient to define the term exchange rate (E) so that the system states of this and certain other similar systems can be clearly referenced. An exchange rate is a ratio of sanction flows. Since there are two possible flows, there are two possible ratios. For this system let us take the ratio of f to g's sanction (the appropriate term being $E_{f/g}$) whose range is

$$1 \leq E_{f/g} \leq 9.$$

For the condition of no exchange, exchange rate is undefined. (When one of the sanctions of the system is money, the exchange rate can be expressed as a price per unit as in the previous example.)

D. Modeling Some Strong Structures

Now let us introduce the first mental experiment wherein the process of interaction and rate of exchange will be determined. Figure II represents a variation upon the system of Figure I. The actor a is now an "auctioneer" with a car to sell to any one of the actors, b_1, b_2, b_3 or b_4. The actor a knows that the car can be "wholesaled" to c at \$1000 and, since $j = 1$, will set a reserve price of \$1001 for the auction. The bidder b_1 is similar to the actor b of the Figure I in that b_1 has the alternative of exchanging with d_1 for an identical car for \$1500 and thus will not bid beyond \$1499. The actors b_2, b_3 and b_4 also have alternative exchanges which are, however, more favorable than b_1's. Consequently their maximal offers will be lower than b_1's and will also be determined jointly by j and their alternative exchange. Thus the maximal offer of b_2 (the next highest bidder) will be \$1479, of b_3 will be \$1399 and of b_4 will be \$1299.

FIGURE II. A potential network for an auction.

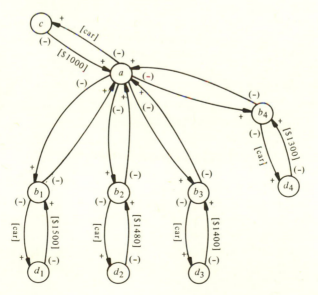

Let the system begin with no actor knowing the maximal bids of any other, but with the reserve price of \$1001 set by a known to all actors. Let all offers (rules) which are transmitted to a be received by all actors. Let the settlement be to the highest bidder.

The *process* of interaction is as follows. Any b actor has an interest in making an offer equal to the reserve price. Let the first offer be made by b_1. Then b_2, b_3 and b_4 have an interest in making an offer better than b_1's. Thus any actor of that set will offer the price of \$1002. Of course, all others now have an interest in making a bid better than the last and one will do so. The bidding then will continue at the j increments (unless we were to specify larger, more realistic, increments) with all b actors bidding against each other until the price of \$1300 is reached, at which point b_4 drops out of the bidding. There are now only three bs in a's potential network. However, the bidding continues past \$1399 at which point b_3 drops out. Now a's potential network is two, and b_1 and b_2 continue to bid against one another until the price of \$1480 is reached. At b_1's bid of \$1480, b_2 drops out and the car is sold to b_1 at that price.

This is a system in which the process of interaction as well as its outcome is determined by its structure. Consider any other system in which one commodity is to be sold to one of a set of n actors when $n > 1$, in which all have an interest in the exchange, and in which all actors of that set act independently. A set of offers would be expected with actors dropping out of the central actors' potential network as the system state corresponding to p_{min} for that actor was transcended. Bidding would continue until there is only one actor remaining in a's network at which point an agreement would be reached and the exchange completed.

Now consider the system of Figure III. This system has been constructed by connecting a set of relationships of the $f-g$ type at the f point such that f now has a set of n g points with whom exchange is possible. Thus the size of f's potential network (N_p) is n. Let f have an interest in exchanging with a maximum of only m of the g points wherein $m < n$. The maximum number of points with which an actor has an interest in relating is called the maximum possible network N_m. The size of N_m is m. Let the initial resources of each g actor be as modeled before and

FIGURE III. A potential network for the $f-g_n$ exchange system.

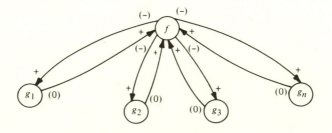

the initial resources of f be equal to or greater than $x_{i_f}m$. Finally let all of the g actors act independently — i.e., no g actor colludes with any other g actor.

Let the actor f initially transmit a (tentative) rule to any g actor which contains an exchange rate favorable to that actor. Let that rule be accepted. (The meaning of a favorable offer will be unpacked as the concept of resistance is introduced in the next section.) Now let f turn to any other actor with the same rule, which is again accepted, and again to another actor and so forth until m actors have accepted tentative offers from f. Now f has no interest in making or receiving further (tentative) offers at that rate. The actor f has now filled its maximum possible network. Thus f has an interest in making or receiving offers only if the offers have as their referent a system state preferred by f to that referenced in the first set of offers. (If, up to this point, the tentative offers corresponded to $E_{f/g} = 7$, then further offers by f would correspond to $E_{f/g} = 6$.) Furthermore, the g actors not yet included would have an interest in making that more favorable offer to f (if the offer was $E_{f/g} \geq 1$). As in the auction the offers (or bidding) continue with (in this case) the exchange rate falling as a consequence of the process. For this system, the g actors have identical worst exchange rates ($E_{f/g} = 1$). Thus no g actor drops out of f's potential network until agreements are reached. Instead, the process continues until the offers correspond to f's most preferred system state ($E_{f/g} = 1$). At that point, the first m of the g actors who agree to that rate are included in f's actual exchange network and the remaining $n-m$ actors are *excluded*.

The processes and outcomes outlined for these two examples are typical of processes and outcomes for strong structures. For strong exchange structures of this type, the potential network of the central actor is larger than its maximum possible network. As a consequence, the cost of confrontation for the central actor with any $n-m$ actors is zero, while the cost of confrontation for any one of the g actors is exclusion from the system. In other words, *the structure of the system had the consequence of differentially allocating the costs of confrontation and, as a result, the central actor was able to gain its most preferred system state*.

Two terms will now be introduced, which will be useful in characterizing strong exchange structures. First, the process of interaction will be termed *iteration*. Thus, in the mental experiments, the a actor in one system and the f actor in the other iterated the remaining actors in their respective networks. Second, the process of iteration is conditioned by the comparative values of C_a, the centrality index of any actor a. C_a is determined by the equation

$C_a = n_a/m_a$.

In the $f-g$ exchanges, $C_f = n/m > 1$, whereas for any g actor $C_g = 1$. For that system both were constant for the duration of the interaction. Since the centrality index of f was larger than the centrality indices of the g actors, some confrontations were costless to f. Thus f gained its most preferred exchange rate, and the g actors that were not excluded gained their worst possible exchange rates. In the auction system, the centrality index of the a actor changed as the offers ongoing in the system changed. However, as long as the centrality index of a was greater than that of the b actors the process of iteration continued.

Consider a simple capitalist system in which workers are separated from their means of production and have only their labor time as sanctioning resources. These resources would have no value to workers—thus their value of transmission can be treated (for a first approximation) as zero. Let it be specified that there are n workers and only m jobs (where $n>m$). This system exhibits structural similarities to the system of Figure III. For that system $n-m$ is the size of the "reserve industrial army."[2] In the absence of collusion (i.e., organization of unions among the g actors or workers), wages would always go to subsistence—though the process of iteration might be less obvious and of longer duration in the "real" case than might have been implied in the model. Subsistence would then correspond to the worst of all possible exchange rates for the set of g actors.

As an exercise, the reader is encouraged to construct more realistic capitalist–labor exchange systems, beginning with a system of two and then n capitalists. As will be seen from the mental experiments following from these constructions, as long as the set of jobs offered by the capitalists is smaller than the set of workers (i.e., the combined maximum possible networks being smaller than the combined potential networks), the exchange rate of the workers will, in each case, go to subsistence. On the other hand, for any system of $n \geq 2$ capitalists, if the capitalists' combined maximum possible networks are greater than their potential networks, wages go to the maximum for the system. By expansion of the mental experiment the reader will see that capitalists have an interest in "welfare" if welfare keeps workers from starving and thus reducing the size of the capitalists' potential networks; but capitalists also have an interest in welfare being a highly undesirable world so that wages can be low. The correspondence between these mental experiments and conditions typical of capitalist systems implies that (1) those conditions are by no means accidental and (2) there is a correspondence between even this simple derivation and some ongoing social events.

The auction and laboratory exchange systems discussed in this section are strong structures. Exchange structures that are not strong include the dyadic exchange systems introduced at the beginning of this section. Consider the $a-b$ exchange system. For that system we determined the range of exchanges possible. Using L_1, preference alterations can be attributed to each of the actors which correspond to each of the system states which can occur in the relationship. However, no process of iteration would be expected for these systems. Instead, we would expect a sequence of offers and counteroffers—that

---

[2] For the concept of the reserve industrial army and its place in wage determination, see Marx (1967:637). For a more general elementary theoretic treatment of this type of strong structure, see Chapter 9 of this volume.

is, a bargaining process. We know that the bargaining process will be conditioned by the range of exchange rates possible as they are known by the actors and by the ''costs of confrontation'' for the actors—that is, by the actors' opposed but complementary interests. In the next section procedures will be introduced to account for the bargaining process and its outcome.

E. Resistance, the Second Law and the Second Principle

The concern of this section is economic exchange in bilateral monopoly—that is, a system in which the size of potential networks of each of the two actors can be treated as one. Relative, not total, isolation from larger networks is the condition for bilateral monopoly. For example, a system of exchange of two actors can be relatively isolated if there is an opportunity cost entailed in the extension of the network of both of the actors. The extent of that isolation, then, is a function of the size of that cost as it is compared to the ''stakes'' involved in the relationship of exchange itself. That is, when the stakes of an exchange are very small, as in purchasing an inexpensive commodity, the costs, at least to the buyer, of network extension can be larger than the total cost of the purchase itself. (For a *bi*lateral monopoly, however, it is important that these costs be conditions for both of the actors.) Further, any given actor can, over a given period of time, be engaged in a large number of exchanges, as, for example, in the purchase of a variety of distinct commodities, and yet any of these exchanges could be bilateral monopolies.

We have already characterized the position of actors in economic exchange relations (following Weber) as one of opposed but complementary interests. That idea will now be examined from the point of view of the actor engaged in the system and formulated under the concept of resistance. Once formulated, the concept of resistance will be used in a manner similar to (but broader than) Weber's use of that term.

Any actor a in a bilateral monopoly has two interests.[3] Consider the first of these interests. For that actor there is a most preferred rate of exchange, and a set of less preferred rates of exchange which are possible given the conditions for the system. The *difference* between the preference alteration of the most preferred exchange $P_{a_{max}}$ and the preference alteration of any other exchange p_a is I_b, the interest of that actor in gaining a *better* exchange rate. Thus

$$I_{b_a} = p_{a_{max}} - p_a,$$

where p_a is any preference alteration for a for the system. For example, assume that an actor received an offer which was its best of all possible offers. Then $p_a = p_{a_{max}}$, the difference goes to zero, and the actor has no (zero) interest in gaining a better rate of exchange (and also no interest in receiving a better offer). Assume that the actor received the worst offer possible for the system. Then $p_a = p_{a_{min}}$

---

[3] The formulations of the resistance equation, I_b and I_c were developed by Douglas Heckathorn.

and I_b is maximal—that is, the actor's interest in gaining a better offer is now as large as is possible for the system. In general, for a set of offers, I_b can vary between (and inclusive of) these extremes such that as offers become more favorable to the actor, I_b (its interest in gaining a better offer) declines.

Now consider the second interest. We know that when an actor has an interest in exchange its worst of all possible system states is no exchange, that is, p_a is minimal at $p_{a_{con}}$. The actor's interest in *avoiding* $p_{a_{con}}$ also varies with the exchange rate and with its consequent preference state alteration. For example, if an actor is offered its worst possible exchange rate, then $p_a = p_{a_{min}}$ which is very close to the value of $p_{a_{con}}$ (i.e., differing only by j). At that point that actor will have a minimal interest in agreeing to exchange, for its interest in avoiding the confrontation is minimal. But, if $p_a = p_{a_{max}}$, then the actor has a maximal interest in avoiding the confrontation. Designating the interest in avoiding the confrontation as I_c, then for any actor a,

$$I_{c_a} = p_a - p_{a_{con}}.$$

As offers become more favorable to a, the value of p_a increases and the actor's interest in avoiding the confrontation I_c also increases. As offers become less favorable I_c decreases.

Any actor in a bilateral monopoly will be modeled as recognizing and acting on both of these interests. Let the combination of these two interests be called R_a, the resistance of the actor a. If resistance is to be a quantitative term, then, for any system, an actor's resistance to a preferred exchange should be lower than to any less preferred exchange. The simplest expression satisfying that and certain further conditions discussed below is

$$R_a = I_{b_a} / I_{c_a}.$$

Expanding that expression we have the second law of the elementary theory which is

$$\text{L}_2: \quad R_a = \frac{p_{a_{max}} - p_a}{p_a - p_{a_{con}}}.$$

First consider the interpretation of the equation for any actor in a given system. As p_a approaches $p_{a_{max}}$, the numerator of the equation approaches zero while the denominator approaches its largest possible value. As a consequence the value of R_a rapidly becomes smaller, approaching zero as the best of all possible system states for that actor is realized. As p_a approaches $p_{a_{min}}$, the numerator approaches its maximal value while the value of the denominator declines. As a consequence the value of R_a increases rapidly as the least preferred system state is approached.

Now consider the variation of R for the "economic" bilateral monopoly. We know that as an offer becomes more favorable to one of the actors it will become less favorable to the other. *Thus, as the resistance of the first actor decreases (because the offer is more favorable), the resistance of the second actor increases (because the offer is less favorable).*

In Figure IV are drawn a pair of typical resistance curves for a bilateral monopoly. These curves were taken from calculations from the $a-b$ exchange system of the last section. It will be remembered that in that system the actor a had a car and b had money. As can be seen by reference to the figure, as the amount of money received by a increases, a's resistance decreases while b's resistance increases. Stated in terms of rules, as offers move from less to more money to be paid by b, b's resistance increases and a's resistance decreases.

Now let the concept of resistance be used to interpret the bargaining process. Let the $a-b$ exchange be a full information system. Let it be given for the $a-b$ exchange system that a begins the bargaining process at its zero resistance offer, an exchange of the car for $1499. Let it be further given that b opens the other end of the bargaining with its zero resistance offer of $1001. We know, if bargaining is to occur, that each actor will now adjust its offer to one more favorable to the other. How can that first adjustment be accounted for? Consider a first. The actor a knows that for b, I_{c_b} is very small for a's first offer. How can a reduce b's resistance so that b might accept an offer? For this system a has only one option—to make an offer more favorable to b. This more favorable offer both increases b's interest in avoiding confrontation and decreases b's interest in a better offer. Thus, to avoid the confrontation, a has an interest in making an offer more favorable to b, which we can interpret as reducing b's resistance.

FIGURE IV. Resistance curves

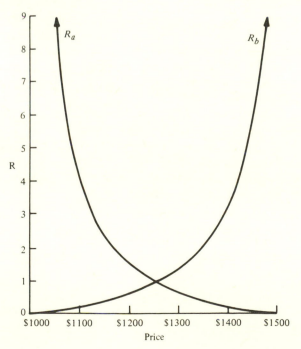

What kind of offer will that be? The first criterion for that offer was that it reduce b's resistance. A second criterion is that the offer be an expression of a's resistance to offers that are unfavorable to it. The increment of a's second offer below its first can be seen as an interaction of I_{b_a} and I_{c_a} and a's attribution of I_{b_b} and I_{c_b}. Let the system be interpreted as if the actors' offers were conditioned by their own changes in I_b and I_c and their attributed changes in I_b and I_c for the other actor(s) (i.e., actors' acts are guided by those changes, not necessarily by their calculations of changes in R). If the theoretic actors are differentiated only by the resources of their positions and have full information, then a's attributions of consequences of its second offer for b for I_{b_b} and I_{c_b} are similar to b's own calculations for that offer and vice versa. More generally, the results of a's calculations for itself and b, if multiplied by any positive constant, give the same values as b's calculations for itself and a. What then are the implications of this information for b's second offer?

Since b has an interest in increasing a's interest in avoiding a confrontation and decreasing a's interest in a better offer (this being an expression of b's interest in avoiding a confrontation), b will, like a, have an interest in making a second offer more favorable to the other. How, then, will the incremental change of that offer compare to the incremental change of a's second offer? The actor b has interpreted the incremental changes of its own and attributed I_b and I_c from a's first to a's second offer and can compare those changes to any increments between its own first and second offer. To avoid confrontation, b has an interest in making a second offer, the changes of which are incrementally no less than the changes consequent upon a's for the I terms. On the other hand, given b's interest in the best possible exchange rate, b has an interest in making an offer which is incrementally no larger than the change consequent upon a's for the I terms. Thus b has an interest in making a second offer which reduces a's resistance by a value identical to the reduction of b's resistance by a's second offer.

Furthermore, for a sequence of offers that are conditioned as above (if bargaining is either costless or "equally costly" to the two actors), a point will be reached at which the two actors make the same offer to each other, and given that rule, the exchange will occur. It also follows that the point of exchange will be the point at which the resistance curves cross, the point of *equiresistance*. Thus the second principle of the elementary theory is

P₂   COMPROMISE OCCURS AT THE POINT OF EQUIRESISTANCE FOR
     UNDIFFERENTIATED ACTORS IN A FULL INFORMATION SYSTEM.

In the theoretic and empirical interpretation of P₂, at least the following points must be kept in mind:

1. If one or the other actor (or both) have not accurately inferred the negotiation set, then the point of compromise can be affected in a number of ways. For example, if a attributed that b's best of all possible system states was to pay

$1200, and if that was b's belief, then the effective resistance curves would shift accordingly and a distinct compromise point would be reached. If a believed that its best system state was to receive $1200 and b had full and accurate information, but believed that a could receive further information during the bargaining process, then b would have an interest in accepting a's first offer.

2. Actors can be differentiated by their ability to communicate and thus affect the beliefs of the other. Any actor can infer that condition and act on it, and if that is a condition of the system, give false information which if believed affects the beliefs of the other. The result is to move the compromise to a point more favorable to that actor. (These effects can only occur for differentiated actors in less than full information systems.) This phenomena is called *influence*.

3. If bargaining is costless, bargaining increments are j. However, the costs of bargaining can vary among actors affecting the point of compromise. In general, any increase in bargaining costs for an actor will increase the bargaining increments for that actor, and thus can move the point of compromise from equiresistance.

4. The shapes of resistance curves are not necessarily mirror images of each other (as they were in the $a-b$ system). If they are, any two offers at a given point in the sequence which reduce resistance by identical amounts will be offers of equal increments insofar as change of exchange rate is concerned. If the shapes of the curves differ, equal resistance concessions are not equal concessions insofar as exchange rate is concerned but instead vary by the shapes of the curves.

5. Actors need not act on conditions as received initially. If an actor can increase the cost of confrontation for the other, any increment of that change will result in a more favorable compromise point for that actor. At the extreme, exchange and coercion can be combined, such that an actor combining an offer and a threat ("The offer you can't refuse.") can so increase the cost of confrontation for the other that the resistance of the other is *dissolved*. The addition of coercive elements can not only alter the compromise point within the original negotiation set but also can alter the limits of that set in a direction favorable to the coercer.

6. Not all systems are compromise systems. For example, strong structures such as the auction and "wage labor" system of the last section were not compromise systems, were not characterized by hard bargaining and did not result in agreement and exchanges at the point of equiresistance.

7. The iteration process of a strong structure, however, can be interpreted from the point of view of the resistance equation. Consider an exchange system in which the centrally placed actor a has a centrality index larger than one, and other (b) actors have a centrality index equal to one. Let it be assumed that tentative agreements have been negotiated between a and a number of b actors

large enough to fill a's maximum possible network. At that point in the iteration process the cost of confrontation for a (in relation to the remaining b actors) is no longer no exchange, but exchange at that agreement. This increases the resistance of a. Furthermore, $p_{b_{max}}$ has, for the excluded actors, changed from its original value to a value j smaller than the given offer. Thus the resistance of the b actors decreases at that point and at further points in the process. As can be seen, the structure of a system of interaction can heighten the resistance of some actors and dissolve the resistance of others.

8. Not all centralized systems are strong structures. If, for example, there is a system of four actors such that one actor has an interest in exchanging with all three other actors (and has the resources, including time, for those exchanges), and only with those three actors, and the remaining three actors each have an interest and resources only for exchanges with the first actor, then the centrality index of the first actor is $C_x = 3/3 = 1$ and for each of the remaining actors is $C_x = 1/1 = 1$ and the system is *not* a strong structure. For that system, if the resources of the *centrally placed* actor are not overloaded by the set of exchanges, then each exchange can be treated as if it were a bilateral monopoly of the type discussed above. Systems of this type can be treated as if they were compounds made up of dyads connected at the centrally placed point. Compound systems, unlike differential centrality systems, are bargaining process systems and thus are treated under the concept of resistance by simple elaboration of the analysis offered for the bilateral monopoly dyad above.

Space considerations have not allowed the presentation of a set of calculations for resistance curves. However, the reader has been given the basic information needed to construct hypothetical (or interpret real) cases, make the calculations and apply the concept of resistance.[4]

F. Final Remarks

Strong and weak structures can be distinguished in a number of ways. Consider the issue of the costs of confrontation. In weak structures the costs of

---

[4] The second law is not independent of the first law, nor is the second principle independent of the first, for both the first law and principle were used above in the development of the second law and principle. It is the author's intuition that, with the addition of certain appropriate assumptions, a formal derivation could be carried out. While that derivation would establish the (conditions of) consistency between the laws and principles, space limits of this volume have precluded that exercise here. The second law and second principle have been presented (somewhat) independently because their primary focus of application is to systems (such as bilateral monopolies and their "compounds") that cannot be simply and easily solved by application of the first law and principle. The author, is of course, aware of the "established" theories for bargaining, such as Nash (1953) and Smorodinsky and Kalai (1975). Since the first priority of this volume is to present a new social theory and demonstrate some of its applications, space will not be taken at this time for an analysis of scope of agreement and disagreement between those theories and the application of the elementary theory to the bargaining problem. Instead, this issue will be the subject of a future publication.

confrontation are constant over time. If, as in the cases discussed in this chapter, those costs are significant for all actors, a process of bargaining results. In strong structures the costs of confrontation for the central actor vary over time, a variation that is related to the iteration process. For any iteration, the costs of confrontation for the central actor are the costs of agreement with other actor(s). As a consequence the central actor's costs are very low, and its resistance is very high and remains high as the process continues. In contrast the resistance of peripheral actors is continually dissolved throughout the iteration process.

Why are orders given by some people and accepted by others? Should this phenomenon be interpreted psychologically? Is it an indication of individual differences of people? Or should it be interpreted sociologically? If so, how?

Consider any system in which the resistance of one actor is dissolved and the resistance of another related actor is very large. It follows that the second can generate rules that will be accepted by the first. These rules are orders. If orders are found in any ongoing system, the first question to be considered would be, "Is the structure strong?"

The formulations for strong and weak structures and their associated processes will aid in the analysis of macrosystems. The analysis of macrosystems is furthered through the development of formulations for mixed systems, particularly mixed exchange– coercive systems. These formulations for mixed systems lead immediately to the investigation of the meaning of property. However, these two kinds of formulations are only a beginning point for the elementary theoretic investigation of macrosystems.

There are only three pure types of dyadic relationships. That limitation suggests that there may be a limited number of fundamental types of social structures or, more precisely, there may be a limited number of first-order models for social structure that can be drawn from the elementary theory. A variety of models that compound different first order models can be conceived. Second-order variations upon fundamental and compounded structures could be developed.

How general would these formulations be? General enough to use in broad gauge historical investigations? Only further work will tell.

References

Marx, Karl
   1967   *Capital* (Vol. 1). New York: International Publishers.

Nash, J.F.
   1953   Two person cooperative games, *Econometrica,* 21:128– 140.

Smorodinsky, M. and E. Kalai
   1975   "Other Solutions to Nash's Bargaining Problems," Technical Report No. 11, Department of Statistics, University of Tel Aviv.

8

Steven A. Gilham

STATE, LAW AND
MODERN ECONOMIC EXCHANGE

A. Introduction

Economic exchanges are not merely exchanges of things but are social relations among people. The social relations central to understanding economic exchange are property relations, and different forms of social organization are accompanied by different forms of property relations. No economic exchange, therefore, is a purely economic relation. These points recur persistently in the works of social theorists such as Marx and Weber. What they might mean in a rigorous theoretical formulation, however, has remained unclear. In what follows I shall undertake to give formal theoretic content to those points and to clarify the social relations involved in certain economic exchanges by examining the rights that underlie such transactions and the ways in which such rights are ensured, particularly by the legal institutions of political states. The overarching question with which we are concerned has been posed with stark clarity by Weber (1954:29–30): "Can it be said that a stable private economic system of the modern type would be 'unthinkable' without legal guaranties?"

On the way toward answering that question it will be helpful to review briefly the way in which exchange relations have been treated by social exchange theorists and economists. The relation upon which those exchange theorists[1] have focused is extremely simple to model, particularly in its dyadic form. The potential network of such an exchange and the two system states of its actual

---

[1] Throughout this essay the term "exchange theorists" refers to both social exchange theorists and economists. I include not only theoreticians per se but also those researchers—e.g., sociologists, anthropologists and historians—who have been concerned with economic relations in their investigations. Although I recognize the substantial differences among the approaches taken toward their subject matter by scholars in these various fields, those differences are less important than their shared assumptions and do not alter the argument made here.

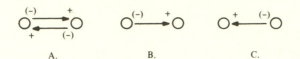

FIGURE I. Normal exchange: A. potential network, B. $SS_1(t_0)$, C. $SS_2(t_1)$.

network are shown in Figure I. But, whereas most exchanges are actually transacted between only two actors, few if any occur among actors who are not connected to larger networks. Any simple dyadic exchange may thus be seen as only the actual network from a much larger potential network such as, for example, the one represented in Figure II.

Exchange theorists share a number of assumptions about the requisite conditions for economic exchange and about actors' interests within those transactions. First they assume that human actors have a common interest in appropriating "objects" to their own use (hence, "utilities") and in maximizing both the "return" on their "expenditures" and the absolute quantity of their utilities. They recognize, however, that an interest in exchange as the means to obtain utilities does not follow automatically from those assumptions alone. Rather, exchange theorists derive the interest in exchange from the conditions of a social division of labor—the second major assumption.

As usually employed, the term division of labor implies minimally the following two conditions: (1) each actor holds resources in some form(s), only a limited quantity (or none) of which can be "consumed" by that actor; conversely, (2) no individual actor holds resources in forms or quantities sufficient to satisfy all of its needs or desires at any given time. These two conditions are assumed to hold in all economic exchange systems; other conditions may be added to accommodate and to distinguish different types of systems.[2] In any case each actor is presumed to have at least some resources that are of little direct utility—that is, of less utility than those held by others—to that actor.

Given those conditions exchange is expected to occur when (1) the "value" or "utility" of what each actor expects to receive is some increment greater for both actors than (a) the costs of what each is to give up, (b) the utility that would be realized by keeping whatever is to be relinquished and (c) the values potentially realizable in other exchanges that would be foregone such that (2) there is no other outcome preferred by both actors. Each actor's choice of an exchange counterpart among several possible ones (where such alternatives exist) is thus

---

[2] Historically at least two significant conditions have been added to these "fundamental" requisites for exchange: 1) at least some of actors' resources exist in a form that cannot be directly consumed by anyone but which is useful only for exchange (i.e., "money"); 2) actors hold resources that are "incomplete factors of production" (e.g., land or labor) which become "useful" only when brought together through market exchanges.

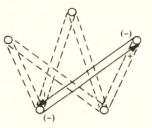

FIGURE II. Potential exchange network (actual network included).

presumed to be conditioned by the relative values of the utilities held by others and by the relative rates of exchange possible within each potential transaction.

Even granted that the foregoing conditions are features of a particular type of exchange, taken together they are not sufficient conditions for the occurrence of exchange. That they are insufficient can be seen in light of the following point. No utility-maximizing actor would have an interest in acting to produce or otherwise acquire low (in contrast to high) utility resources *unless* the actor knew that the low utility resources could be exchanged for higher utility resources *and* that the exchange would result in a higher net utility than any other possible means of acquisition.

Exchange theorists' failure to see that dilemma rests on two major implicit assumptions. First, preexisting distributions of resources—whatever they may be in particular cases—are taken as given. This assumption consists of two subsidiary ones—first, that all actors "have" some resources of which they can dispose and, second, that all remaining resources (i.e., those which any actor does not already have), which any actor has an interest in acquiring or using, are held by others. That step permits exchange theorists to ignore the ways in which distributions of particular types of resources occur, to consider all resources in the abstract as theoretically undifferentiated exchangable utilities[3] and to disregard the costs incurred by actors in producing or acquiring the resources attributed to them.[4] Consequently exchange theorists do not regard it as paradoxical that utility-maximizing actors have resources—which they have produced or otherwise acquired—of low utility to them when compared with other possible resources. Rather than examining how actors come to have resources in the first place, exchange theorists attend primarily to actors' calculations of the relative costs and benefits of relinquishing (or not receiving) and receiving (or not relinquishing) utilities. Second, and fundamental to the issues to be dealt with here, the foregoing conditions assume that actors would "naturally" exchange with one another instead of selecting some other method of acquiring the resources they desire. In short the existence of actors with an

---

[3] We will consider later the theoretical liabilities of the failure to make crucial distinctions among types of resources

[4] See pages 140–142, for a discussion of the "givenness" of resources.

interest in exchange presupposes that an exchange system exists, is known by the actors to exist and is a condition of their productive or acquisitive behavior.

Let us grant for now those assumptions. Now consider two alternative methods of acquiring resources held by others—acquisition by stealth and by coercion. For both instances there is a prospect that the resources of others could be acquired with effectively no cost and particularly *without transmission of the actor's own utilities*. It follows that if a utility-maximizing actor could expect either method of acquisition to be successful, then it would be preferred to exchange. It is crucial, therefore, to ask what conditions would make such alternatives less preferred (or less "natural") than exchange.

A fully general theory of social relationships must recognize that there are alternatives to exchange and, since there are, that exchange is conditioned by the elimination or restriction of those alternatives. This recognition implies the need to model systems which include a variety of social relationships. But that is not the path chosen by exchange theorists. Instead they have implicitly presupposed as universal a relationship that I shall call normal exchange.

By *normal exchange* I mean an exchange relationship in which each party gives some good or service and receives a good or service in return. The central idea of normal exchange is that any transmission of a positive sanction by *a* to *b* is *necessarily* followed by transmission of a contingent positive sanction from *b* to *a*. (The quantities of these transmissions are determined by the conditions mentioned earlier.) Different theorists attribute different reasons to the necessity for this universal give-and-take assumption. All of them, however, find the origin of that necessity in the potential networks of exchange relations and *not* in relations of another type.

Since they consider only exchange networks as theoretically significant potential networks, exchange theorists have been little interested in examining other types of relations, especially as those relations condition exchange. Homans (1967:46) for example, has effectively claimed that exchange is virtually exhaustive of social relations. Although others such as Blau (1964) and Gouldner (1960) take somewhat less extreme positions, they also usually treat both conflict and coercion as either variations on exchange or as derived from it.[5] For example, where these theorists have been concerned with social power they treat it as based on monopolies of resources. If they employ the term coercion at all in such discussions, they treat it as a threat by one party to withhold (monopolized) goods from others. Coercion by negative sanctions has been either ignored or seen as an empirically rare and relatively ineffective means of controlling the behavior of others and, therefore, as theoretically uninteresting.[6]

---

[5] Conflict, for example, is treated by both Homans and Blau as an *exchange* of negative sanctions. Even the few exceptions to this general blindness are more enlightening for what they ignore than for what they tell us. For example, Blau mentions *physical* coercion (a questionable term in itself) no more than four times and never develops a formal analysis of it nor even shows any theoretic interest in such relations. See Blau (1964).

[6] See, for example, Homans (1961), Blau (1964:224–226) and Chapter 1 of this volume.

Because the transactions of normal exchange are completed without the *apparent* presence of negative sanctions—that is, without their actual transmission (unless one regards conflict as exchanges of negative sanctions, as both Homans and Blau clearly do)—social exchange theorists have come to regard coercion as not only distinct from exchange but unrelated to it. Economists—who for their part restrict their investigations to market transactions and the ''choice behavior'' of producers, investors, sellers and consumers—have not been interested in coercion at all.[7]

The failure to grasp the relation between coercion and economic exchange has had unfortunate consequences for the study of economic exchange. First, given the preoccupation with normal exchange, all sorts of exchanges appear formally similar. Economic exchange has thus been seen as a special case of the ''universal'' phenomenon of social exchange. But that view misconstrues the social conditions that create an interest in economic exchange in the first place. Second, the special character of the state as a creator and guarantor of rights has not been understood. Consequently economic exchange within the context of political states has been seen as not significantly different from any other economic exchange, and the state's role in such exchanges has been wrongly viewed, in Durkheimian fashion, as an extension of the community's. Where exchange theorists have been concerned with the state's role in ''things economic'' they have focused on the impact of state ''regulation''—for example, taxation, tariffs or operating restrictions—on the calculations of actors already engaged in ongoing economic exchange.[8]

Exchange theory rests on an assumptive world in which the conditions for exchange have remained unarticulated. Despite the claim that economic exchange is only a subspecies of social exchange (or because of it in the case of economists), many exchange theorists have actually appropriated the assumptions of economic theory to the study of nonmarket phenomena. Attempts to employ those assumptions universally (i.e., to all societal configurations) without regard to crucial differences in the rights and enforcement structures of various social networks has led to some curious conceptions of the historical development of markets and nation states.[9] In order to overcome the consequences of those theoretical shortcomings we must do at least three things here: (1) establish the relation between coercion and economic exchange, (2) show the differences between normative control and legal (state) coercion, and (3) show precisely how legal coercion informs economic exchange relations by articulating the conditions it creates as rights and by showing how those conditions *transform* an interest in appropriating utilities into an interest in entering exchange relations.

[7] Indeed, Weber argued that economists quite properly ignore the mechanisms by which rights are enforced. See Weber (1954:28–29).

[8] See, for example, Joseph Spengler (1947:123–143).

[9] For an articulate commentary on the view of history produced by such assumptions see Karl Polanyi's chapter, Societies and economic systems, in Polanyi (1957:43–55).

B. Exchange and Coercion

Clearly, given the assumptions of exchange theory, any actor (as a maximizer of utilities) may have an interest in appropriating objects without relinquishing any. But no actor has an interest in relinquishing objects without receiving something at least "roughly equivalent" [to borrow Homans' (1951:285) phrase] —indeed something of greater utility—in return. We would not expect any actor acting on an "economic" interest, then, to relinquish an object to another without both an expectation of receiving something in return and *some means of ensuring the validity of that expectation*. Thus a condition for economic exchange is a's belief in a right to demand reciprocation from b and some means of enforcing that right against b.

According to exchange theorists such as Blau (1964), Homans (1951) and Gouldner (1960) the enforcing mechanism for that right in exchange transactions is a "norm of reciprocity" which dictates that an actor has a duty to reciprocate any good or service received and a right to expect reciprocation for any given.[10] The sense in which that norm is actually an enforcing *mechanism,* however, is imprecise at best. If the norm of reciprocity is an "internal" characteristic of social actors (rather than a network contingency), then exchange theorists must assume that the norm is universal. But no exchange theorist has offered either sufficient reason why we should believe the norm is universal or supportive evidence for any such claim.

Indeed exchange theorists have not conclusively shown that enforcement of reciprocity is normative at all. Their analyses rarely go further in addressing such prospects than to suppose that violators will be excluded from future exchanges. Although exclusion from exchange networks may be an effective enforcing mechanism under certain circumstances, it is by no means established that it is either universally employed or universally effective. We would do well to consider the conditions upon which normative enforcement depends.

Stable, ongoing exchange systems cannot operate in the absence of potential coercion from sources external to any particular exchange. This claim is counter to the orthodoxy of exchange theory. Its development thus demands an explication of the sense in which coercion is necessary. Southard's paper in this volume demonstrates how shunning and, ultimately, expulsion operate to enforce *social* exchange rules, but it also clearly makes two points crucial to us here. First, normative control by members of an exchange network is contingent on four minimal network conditions: (1) a bifurcation of interest with respect to particular acts, (2) a full information network, (3) an approximately equal distribution of both sanctioning resources and opportunities to violate the norm among members, and (4) an excess of costs of confrontation for potential violators over the absolute value of their interest in the violative act. Second, and

---

[10] Blau, however, finds it necessary to correct Gouldner's view of how the norm "works" (Blau 1964:92–97).

more immediately important, the possibility of shunning and expulsion rests ultimately on the availability of negative sanctions to members of the network and, therefore, on the collective coercion we call negative convergence. Without negative sanctions no group could ensure that an actor excluded from its exchange network or expelled from the community would not "reenter" the group and/or resort to alternative means of acquiring members' resources.

Now consider the interaction of normative and state systems. At least some rules regulating exchange—particularly "reciprocity" rules—are based on bifurcation of interest. That is, despite any actors' interest in nonreciprocation, all actors engaged in ongoing exchanges have an interest in other actors' reciprocations. But since "legal coercion by violence is the monopoly of the state" (Weber, 1954:14), the state centralizes control of negative sanctions *outside* all exchange networks within its jurisdiction (except those to which agencies of the state are party) and at the same time dissipates (or imposes high potential costs of confrontation on the use of) the negative sanctioning resources available to "private" individuals.

By itself this concentration of potential negative sanctions in the overall network, whatever the remaining equality of the state's subjects,[11] weakens normative control and can render it impossible.[12] But, in addition, the scope of the market networks "unified" by state controls and the market conditions enforced by the state may further undermine normative control by (1) precluding full information in any exchange network and/or (2) reducing the costs of shunning or expulsion by (a) providing readily available alternative networks for rule violators or (b) centralizing most material positive sanctions in sources outside networks of *social* exchange. By weakening normative control, the state's legal coercion creates its own necessity and reproduces itself.[13]

A convenient device for clarifying the role of state coercion in economic exchange is to examine what would be, from the standpoint of exchange theory, an abnormal or deviant case of exchange. Let us take any of the following hypothetical examples of "economic" exchange involving money, all of which can be modeled identically and have corresponding "social" exchange counterparts (where some good or service other than money is stipulated as repayment): a agrees to rent b a's lawnmower; b uses and returns it but does not pay for its use; a agrees to sell b a's car, b takes the car but does not subsequently pay for it; a agrees to lend b $1000 at 6% simple interest, b takes

[11] Cf., Weber (1958:226): "The most decisive thing here [i.e., in democratic equality before the law] . . . is the *leveling of the governed* in opposition to the ruling . . . group, which . . . may occupy a quite autocratic position, both in fact and in form."

[12] Compare this argument to Hobbes's famous statement of the relation of the state to the "naturall condition of Mankind" in *Leviathan*.

[13] It might be argued that legal coercion does not preclude normative control but has only replaced it historically as communities became incapable, for other reasons, of effectively exercising the latter. For a fuller treatment of that question than is possible here see Stanley Diamond (1974:225—280).

FIGURE III. Incomplete exchange: A. SS_1 (t_o),   B. SS_2 (t_1).

the money and subsequently repays only the principal. If modeled as isolated transactions all three cases would look like Figure III. In that figure the incomplete exchange is represented by two system states, one occurring at time zero, which indicates the flow of a positive sanction from a to b and the second (vacuous) system state occurring at a later time one, which indicates the absence of a transmission from b to a.

In order to understand the relation between legal coercion and exchange and to clarify the way in which legal coercion weakens normative control, however, we must introduce several of the initial conditions alluded to earlier and alter the model correspondingly. Briefly summarized, those conditions are as follows: (1) each actor a and b has connections to other social networks; (2) all actors derive most of their "income" from transactions with a market m; (3) there is a state s in which negative material sanctions are legally concentrated, so that (4) members of each network have both material and symbolic positive sanctioning resources but only symbolic negative sanctioning resources that they may legally employ.

If we take those conditions into account in a model of the potential networks for these examples we get the networks shown in Figure IV, in which the "deviant" relation is indicated by the darkened sanction arc. We can animate that model to indicate what would happen if (1) members of one potential network excluded b (Figure V A), (2) members of that network attempted to converge on b symbolically (Figure VB_i) and materially (Figure VB_{ii}), and (3) a resorted to legal sanctions against b (Figure VC).

We do not have space here for a detailed discussion of the empirical possibilities in each case, but we should note that in Figures VA and VB_i actor b retains exchange relations with several other actors and with m. In order to overcome the absolute value of b's interest in violating the exchange agreement

FIGURE IV. Incomplete exchange within a potential exchange network.

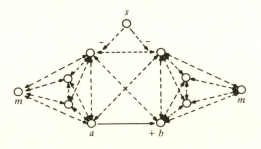

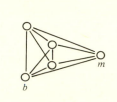

A.

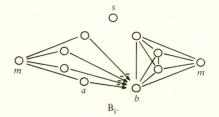

B$_i$.

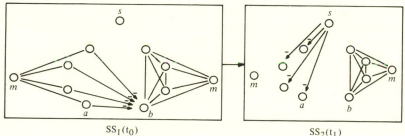

SS$_1$(t$_0$)   SS$_2$(t$_1$)

B$_{ii}$.

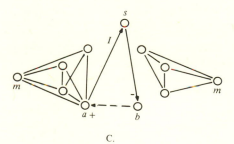

C.

FIGURE V. Alternate enforcement contingencies for nonreciprocation: A. exclusion, B$_i$. symbolic negative convergence, B$_{ii}$. material negative convergence, C. legal (state) coercion.

then the future potential utilities lost from exclusion (and the costs of confrontation in Figure VB$_i$) would have to exceed the sum of the utility gained from violation and the utilities available through future exchanges in the remaining network. Where those conditions cannot be met a will not get compliance (or restitution) even though normative mechanisms have actually been employed.

Interpretation of the remaining possible network configurations shown in Figures VB$_{ii}$ and VC shows how the state maintains its monopoly of material negative sanctions. We shall not discuss all the possible system states implicit in the two configurations but shall focus on only the actual network that would occur in each, given the conditions we have stipulated. Should the limited normative controls available to a fail to overcome b's interest in nonreciprocation (or, alternatively, fail to create for b an interest in reciprocation greater than that in nonreciprocation), a is left with effectively only two possible worlds from which to choose: transmit no information to the state, transmit a negative material sanction to b, receive a negative material sanction from the state, and receive no positive sanction from b; or transmit information to agencies of the state (invoking the state's threatened transmission of a negative material sanction to b), receive no negative sanction from the state, and receive a positive material sanction from b. Clearly a's preference order would be for the second over the first. In either case the choices for b would be the same—transmit no positive to a, receive a negative (from either a or the state); or transmit a positive and receive no negative—both of which would be ranked below b's most preferred world of a null relation.

I have purposely preserved the possibility that b could transmit a negative material sanction to a for separate discussion. Given that condition we should consider the possibility that an attempt by a to coerce b's compliance would turn into conflict. That would clearly be the result if the costs of conflict were lower than b's interest in nonreciprocation. We should recognize, however, that while any attempt at material coercion by a exposes a to potential legal coercion, conflict would expose both a and b to potential legal coercion. In either case the potential costs of confrontation for a exceed the costs to a of invoking legal sanctions. It is thus no accident that a has a greater interest in invoking legal sanctions than in "taking the law into its own hands."

A word of caution is needed here. The presence of negative sanctions and related network contingencies does not guarantee compliance with either norms or legal rules in the sense that no violations can or will occur when such contingencies exist or that particular violations will be transformed into actual compliance with exchange agreements (or, in legal language, performance of contractual obligations). Given such contingencies, it is obvious that actors have an interest in violating rules if they believe they can avoid detection, if they believe that the sanctions will not (for whatever reasons) actually be transmitted, or if the absolute value of that interest exceeds the actual costs of confrontation. More to the point, however, coercion may be employed to create an interest in compliance without actually stipulating it. In practice, legal institutions relatively rarely transmit negative sanctions directly to "lawbreakers." Instead, legal coercion, like normative control, consists of a variety of mechanisms that may be employed prior to actual negative sanctioning. For example, instead of being sanctioned directly for a violation, an actor can be ordered—under ultimate threat of a negative material sanction should it fail to comply—to perform the contractual obligation, to pay restitution (to return the "injured party" to its condition prior to the agreement and subsequent violation), or to pay a fine or provide some service to "the community." The first two of those prospects are shown in the potential network in Figure VIA; the remaining one in Figure VIB. Only one of these options nets the expected return for actor *a*, and the legal determination of whether any of the examples with which we began here are "theft by deception" (criminal), "conversion" (tort), or "breach of contract" (contractual violation) rests not on an actor's expectations or on the violative act itself but on the enforceability of those expectations and the legal remedy sought by the complainant/plaintiff. Indeed, from the state's point of view, there is no violation until it is reported and no "guilt" until the case is adjudicated. Thus although legal enforcement does not ensure *reciprocity*, *a*'s *right* to reciprocation is presumed to be protected by the impact of potential legal contingencies upon *b*'s interest in appropriation.

While we have established that coercive relations are crucial for exchange and that legal coercion is significantly different from normative control, we have not shown that legal coercion is indispensible for exchange. It remains true, as exchange theorists have noted, that actors may comply with exchange agreements out of consideration of their interest in continuing exchanges within networks and of the utilities that would be lost if excluded from those networks. And where coercion were required it might be exercised collectively, even to a

FIGURE VI. Coerced remedies for nonreciprocation (potential networks only): A. "performance" or restitution, B. fine.

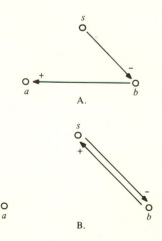

considerable extent "outside" the legal system of a political state. We shall see, however, that those contingencies are insufficient to ensure the stability of modern economic systems.

C. Property and Legal (State) Coercion

Any actor enters a potential exchange situation with some resources that can be relinquished in exchange for others. Exchange theories and all of our discussion up to this point take as given that actors have such resources; yet it is the very "givenness" of resources that is most problematic for exchange theory. Some "resources" (e.g., a capacity to labor or "labor power") are given in that they are "natural" attributes of actors. It may be true that some such resources cost actors nothing to *acquire*; but, tied as they are to the biological life of actors and consequently to resources in the physical environment, even those resources cost actors something to *maintain* (and, in the case of skills, to develop). And the sense in which actors "have" resources external to them is by no means "natural." We cannot, therefore, ignore the variety of ways in which actors may have (access to) external resources.

Unless some means exist by which actors can conditionally exclude others from resources they claim as their own, there is no social basis for exchange. Consider the following example. There is among a group of actors one mortar and pestle x used for grinding grain. Actor a is using it when actor b asks to use it. Actor a has "possession" but relinquishes x to b. Whether that act is the first system state of a normal exchange (i.e., transmission of a positive sanction) depends entirely upon the proprietary status of x or the rights a and b have in the object. If both a and b had rights of access to x (i.e., if x were "common" property) then a would have a *duty* to relinquish x to b (for a's failure to do so would be a violation of b's right to x) and no right to demand contingent reciprocation as a condition of b's access to it. If, on the other hand, only a had a right of access to x (i.e., if x were "private" property) then a would have no duty to relinquish x and a right to demand contingent reciprocation of a positive sanction as a condition of b's access. Similarly, while b would have no right to x except upon condition of exchange, b's control of some other resources would also have to be assured. *The basis of the right to reciprocation is thus the right to exclude.*

Exchange, therefore, does not constitute the mere transfer of objects from one actor to another. More precisely, the sanctions transmitted in exchange are not objects.[14] Rather, exchange amounts to each party's relinquishment of the "*right*

---

[14] Otherwise our "deviant" examples of loan and rental above would not have been deviant. These examples also raise some interesting theoretical problems in value and equivalency of exchange for economists who treat money as a measure of value, which they presume in turn is determined by utility. For example, why is it that the money price of a commodity is presumed to be equal to the value of the commodity whereas the repayment of a money loan obviously is not equal to the money value of the loan itself? Attempts to explain away such problems by reference to the utility of the loan obviously assumes a distribution of property not accounted for by economic theory.

of disposition over the goods concerned'' (Weber, 1954:29, emphasis added) to another, contingent on an expectation of reciprocation. In this section we shall undertake to articulate precisely what rights of disposition—exclusionary proprietary rights—mean in terms of our theory.

It will be helpful in this regard if we unpack the exchange relation to include objects and to show the relations between actors and objects. A normal exchange, then, looks like Figure VII, where the relation between actor and object is treated not as a sanction but as a unit relation, and a particular object is treated as a part of the stock of resources *r*. These are the conditions presupposed by exchange theorists. We can get behind that assumptive world most easily by eliminating the boundary around *r* and treating objects temporarily as unrelated to or disconnected from individuals. Empirically, of

FIGURE VII. Normal exchange (with sanctioning resources shown).

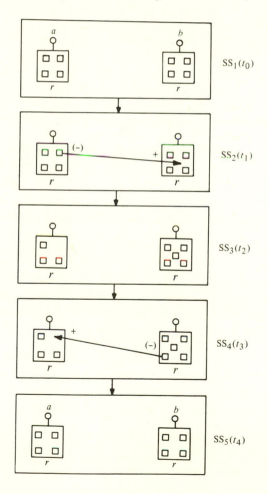

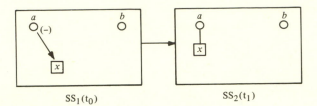

FIGURE VIII. Proprietary appropriation (completed).

course, objects are physically distinct from individuals, but a graphic representation emphasizing that condition will help us to illuminate the nature of the *social* relation of ownership.

Suppose, then, that two actors *a* and *b* have an interest in obtaining an object *x* and that *a*, by some effort directed toward the object (which "costs" *a* an expenditure of labor), appropriates it. Under what circumstances could we regard that appropriation as completed? Should we envision a series of transactions following the appropriation in which *b* appropriates *x* from *a*, then *a* from *b*, then *b* from *a*, and so on indefinitely (and in which conflict could ensue as a consequence of each party's attempt to defend its claim by coercion)?[15] In fact, we sense that no such series of transactions would follow. Rather we sense that *a*'s appropriation would be followed by no action toward *a* from *b* as shown in Figure VIII, but that sense is founded on an assumption of an effective proprietary right.

We might argue that *a*, by virtue of chronological primacy and the effort expended in acquiring *x* has made a claim to possession of the object and has thereby acquired a "moral" right to its ownership.[16] But no presumption of moral right makes clear why *b*'s interest in appropriating *x* should be expected to vanish or dissipate or why *a*'s claim to *x* would be secure against *b*'s future appropriation by stealth or coercion.

If *a*'s claim to the object is to be secure, *a* must be able to exclude *b* or any other actor from unconditional access to it, and, as with any other right, the claim must be enforceable. We might interpret a "moral" right to mean that the right would be normatively enforced, but in contrast a legally enforced proprietary right would look graphically like the sequence of system states shown in Figure IX. (Note, in this figure, *I* is an information flow. For the treatment of *I* arcs, see Chapter 2.) These conditions would hold irrespective of how *a* came to acquire the object, but we should repeat that acquisition by exchange would not occur unless these conditions were guaranteed in the first place. Under such conditions if *b* retains an interest in acquiring *x* it will be, presumably, less costly to enter an exchange with *a* than to take the object by stealth or coercion.

[15] That is precisely, of course, what Hobbes warned his contemporaries would happen in the absence of an effective state.
[16] This example, by the way, is theoretically identical to those invoked by Locke in his articulation of a labor theory of property. See Locke (1965:327–338).

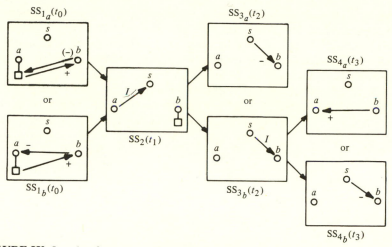

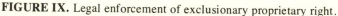

FIGURE IX. Legal enforcement of exclusionary proprietary right.

D. Property in an Historic Context

It is a relatively rare occurrence, of course, for actors in market societies to acquire proprietary rights in objects by straightforward appropriation. Far more frequently they are acquired by gift, inheritance or purchase—all of which presuppose property and/or exchange. (Even where people produce objects for themselves they typically acquire tools and raw materials through market exchanges.) Thus the example drawn in Figure VIII corresponds to a small range of cases in modern economic systems; however, its application is not as limited as it might appear. It corresponds quite closely to some historical cases, a brief investigation of which points up the fallacy of assuming normal exchange, and it is quite suggestive of the way in which at least some markets developed historically.

Let us take as an example early English property in land. English feudal landed property included large areas of land on which all peasants of their respective vills were free to graze livestock and gather fuel. Such land and its attachments were "common" property in the sense that all had rights of "free" access to it and none had a right to exclude others of their vill. Peasants did, however, acquire "private" proprietary (i.e., exclusionary) rights in such goods as they appropriated from the commons by their own labor. If we take actor *a* to represent a peasant and *b* the lord of a manor within the vill, then, such appropriation would look like that in Figure VIII, and the legal protection of the peasants' "private" proprietary rights (in the king's courts) like Figure IX.[17]

---

[17] However much a lord might "charge" his tenants in labor services or "fees" (purportedly in exchange for his protection of their rights of seisin or for the use of his mill or ovens), he had no warrant to take any personal property from them by coercion unless they had themselves committed crimes.

Enclosure of common land, however, created a quite different situation. By enclosing commons, feudal lords claimed that land and its attachments as private property, and future appropriation by peasants from the same land became theft. (Although we have not space to treat the following condition formally, we must note that such enclosures were technically illegal in England until at least the 17th century. But the king needed the continued support of the nobility; thus, prior to the 17th century, the state rarely coerced compliance with antienclosure laws.[18]) Since such cases of theft from nobles were tried in manor courts, nobles could, with the aid of shire reeves (who were themselves vassals who held a "fee" in exchange for state services), enforce their claims in their own courts and jails. The lords' newly acquired proprietary right against peasants is represented in Figure X.

The peasants' costs of confrontation for violation of that right created an interest in seeking other, less costly means of acquiring the goods (or substitutes for those goods) they had "lost" to enclosures. For many that meant increasing their own production in order to trade in the marketplace, whereas for others it meant flight to the towns to sell their labor services. In any event, *peasants found themselves engaging in exchanges in order to acquire what had once been "free."*[19]

This example helps us to understand why the centralized legal coercion of a state is essential to "modern" economic exchange systems in which land, raw materials and labor services are treated as marketable goods little different from finished products. In the case of dispossessed peasants we have no warrant for assuming that they had an interest in selling labor services for money prior to enclosures. They clearly had no "need" to do so prior to enclosures or until some were actually disseised—also "illegally"—of the land they held "privately" by copy of court role (or by "custom"). Rather, peasants had an interest—for which they fought in the uprisings of the late 14th century (Hilton, 1973)—in gaining more secure—indeed, free—rights in land. For those who ultimately sold their labor power, the interest in wage–labor exchanges was a consequence of extreme (and coercively enforceable) feudal dues and/or forceful exclusion from access to land and raw materials sufficient to maintain themselves.

More generally, no community capable of normative control would *normatively* enforce a system of rights that granted monopolies of productive resources to some and deprived most others of them. That condition would be precluded by

[18] On those rare occasions when the state did intervene against enclosures the usual remedy was a nominal fine.
[19] To a limited extent the history of enclosures in England parallels the development of the colonies and frontier territories in the United States with a new cast of characters—settlers instead of nobles; Indians instead of serfs. If we are to understand either case, however, there is no safe generalization for them or from the former to the latter. We would have to model the networks of social relations and delineate the network conditions for each case independently in order to appreciate the crucial and substantial differences between them.

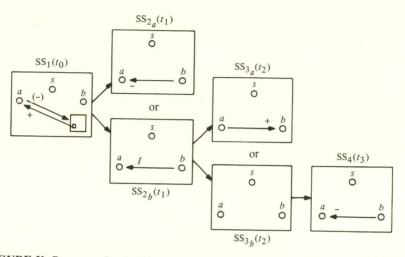

FIGURE X. Property after land enclosures.

the bifurcation of interest in proprietary rights—an interest on the one hand in acquiring as much "property" as one wanted but on the other hand in restricting others to such limits as would leave, in Locke's (1965:329) words, "enough and as good left . . . for others"—and by the normative control processes that would coerce actors to act on their interest in the behavior of others. That does not imply that a normative system cannot tolerate private property—even in land or raw materials. It does mean that in order to create and enforce monopolized property (which may be a monopoly shared by some segment of the community's population) negative sanctioning resources must be centered in a social organization that will enforce proprietary rules based on actors' interest in their own behavior rather than in the behavior of others. Thus the institution of modern property systems could not be supported by a normative system. Instead they had to be instituted by the centralized coercive power of political states and even against the resistance of local normative groups.

On the other hand, with the institutionalization of modern property systems under general rules and the weakening of normative systems, property rules appear to rely on a normative base. In particular, anyone with any resources whatsoever has an interest in preventing others from exercising unconditioned access to their use. With the state as the only actor capable of effectively validating that right, it would seem that all would have an interest in the state's enforcement of property rights. And, by enforcing proprietary and market rules, political states do restrict the ways in which the resources of others are acquired to those legally allowed—to wit, exchange, gift and inheritance. Modern states and their markets, however, do not make distinctions among the *forms* of property that may be thus acquired (except insofar as some objects are excluded from legal markets altogether). Neither do they restrict effectively the amount of property that individuals may amass so long as it is acquired by legal means. Thus land and other basic resources can be monopolized *legally but contrary to majority interests*.

But if exclusionary proprietary rights create interests in exchange, they are not sufficient to ensure that any particular exchange can occur. It is further necessary that actors have the right to *relinquish* control over the resources they hold, in exchange for control over resources held by others. To the extent that any actor cannot *alienate property* the actor's control over disposition of resources is limited.

E. Alienability and Legal Coercion

The normal exchange posited by exchange theorists is possible only when individuals can alienate goods without coercive intervention from their communities or from the state. The right to alienate in a legal system, however, is more than the absence of state coercion. As with other rights it extends to a protection against attempts by others coercively to restrict such action. Legal protection of alienability rights can be easily represented as in the very simple example in Figure XI. In that figure, actors b and c have an interest in exchange, and in particular b has an interest in alienation of the material resources to be transmitted to c. Actor a has an interest in b not alienating the resources to c, but

FIGURE XI. Legal protection of alienability.

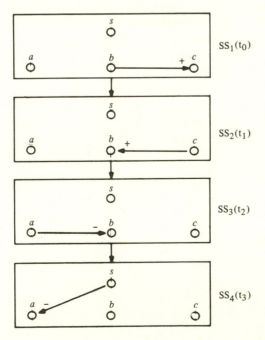

the legal system of the political state s supports b's interest and not a's. Thus after the exchange occurs in SS_1 and SS_2, s transmits to b a negative in SS_3 and receives from s a negative sanction in SS_4.

The issue of alienability as a right and the "necessity" for its legal protection as such obviously would not arise under conditions where no one had an interest in restricting it. But such interests have obtained historically, and political states themselves place some restrictions on alienability. For example, numerous goods are defined as illegal in modern markets. That is, either their ownership or their sale is legally prohibited. Some such restrictions apply only to particular categories of persons (e.g., felons may not legally purchase or possess firearms), others apply to particular goods (e.g., no one may legally possess, sell or purchase a switchblade knife), and still others to both goods and persons (e.g., some drugs may be purchased only from licensed pharmacists by prescription).

Such restrictions do occlude some exchanges which, if not prevented, are at least restricted to the subterranean world of "black" markets (See Chapter 4). But the marketability of some goods may be proscribed and still leave an extensive legally protected market intact. In fact alienation of some goods may be proscribed precisely to protect the interest of "legal" producers, sellers or consumers. A general restriction on alienability would be fatal to exchange *systems*, but limited restrictions on alienability of certain key goods can alter dramatically the entire character of an exchange system.

One of Marx's great contributions to the study of economic systems was to show that the "free" markets we now know depend on the alienability of only a few fundamental "objects" — in particular land, raw materials and labor services (or capital and labor power) as opposed to objects *produced* for exchange. We know that neither land nor labor have always been marketable as commodities and, since we have just reviewed their development as private property, we would do well to see what it meant for them to become legally alienable. Once again English feudal arrangements provide a convenient and fairly clear case for illustration.

For much of the period under Norman and Angevin rule in England neither land nor labor were freely alienable. Nobles' use of land rights as a "payment" for feudal services gave them a strong interest in retaining control of land, while the fact that serfs' labor provided the "income" from land created an interest in retaining an adequate population of enserfed laborers on that land. At the same time, at least some nobles had an interest—on which some of them acted—in reducing or avoiding feudal dues. There were two common devices for doing so: One was a gift of land to the church (*mortmain*); the other, *subinfeudation* for a nominal return such as a "rose at midsummer" or a set of silver spurs annually. Both reduced "income" received by the grantor's overlord since the grantor claimed reduced obligations based on a reduced ability to perform (as a consequence of the smaller enfeoffment) and the grantee's dues went to the grantor rather than to the overlord. The church, in fact, was free of any obligations to any lord beyond spiritual services such as prayers. Similarly, as we have seen, serfs acquired interests in leaving their enserfment (when they lost free access to commons and/or when feudal dues were increased) in order to seek their subsistence in the "employment" of either another noble or an urban craftsman. While remedies against such violations of feudal contracts had existed for nobles in the manor courts for some time, all such alienations were statutorily prohibited by 1290 in the case of land and by 1349 for labor. Nobles were not free to alienate land and serfs, their labor, because the good was not legally theirs to give. It either "belonged" or was "owed" to another.[20]

A simple model of the state's prohibition of these alienations is shown in Figure XII. In contrast to the transactions modeled in Figure XI, the (threat of) negative sanction from the state is directed toward b rather than a, since the legal system supports a's interest in b not alienating resources to c rather than b's interest in alienation. Such prohibitions were ultimately lifted—indeed transformed into "free" rights—first by the emancipation of serfs; then by Henry VIII's sale of royal (previously monastic) lands; and finally, by the Long Parliament's abolition of military land tenure. The new rights to alienate look graphically very much like the representation in Figure XI. It is noteworthy that transactions in the latter cases—the "free" sale of land and labor services—look incomplete or deviant from the standpoint of the earlier rights represented in Figure XII.

F. Concluding Remarks

Each of the rights we have discussed—reciprocation, exclusion and alienation—correspond to what Weber (1954:99) called, respectively, prescriptive, prohibitory and permissive rights. Even where all three are present, of course, there is no guarantee of "free trade" for there are numerous additional ways in which states can intervene in markets. Today, for example, a host of legally enforced restrictions limit the ways in which we use our dwelling places, tools (certainly weapons!), vehicles and even our bodies. There are restrictions on commodity prices, rents, interest, wages and collective bargaining. These are the kinds of legal intervention in market arrangements with which economists concern themselves, but all such restrictions presuppose exchange and its fundamental prerequisites. While all three rights must be guaranteed by some enforcement mechanisms in order that stable ongoing exchange take place, it is clear that the latter two must be ensured before the question of reciprocation is meaningful. And as Polanyi (1957:68–76) has argued, additional controls such as those suggested above may be necessary to the smooth functioning of "free" markets.

To their credit, exchange theorists recognize that where actors are more or less

[20]Note that alienability of labor power was similarly restricted for bondsmen and slaves—again under very different conditions—in the United States. For one brief discussion of the English statutes of 1290 and 1349, see Lyon (1960:457–463, 555, 630). More generally, see Bloch (1961) and Hilton (1973).

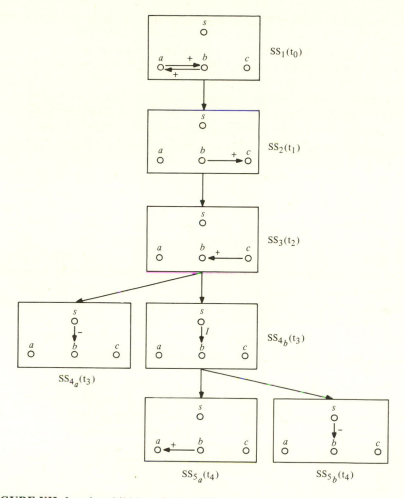

FIGURE XII. Legal prohibition of alienability.

free to make exchange agreements there is no assurance that they are equally free within those exchanges. Weber, for example, was at his best when he wrote that

> [t]he possibility of entering with others into contractual relations . . . determined by individual agreement . . . has . . . been immensely extended in modern law. . . . However, the extent to which this trend has brought about an actual increase in the individual's freedom . . . cannot be determined simply by studying the development of formal legal institutions. The great variety of contractual schemata . . . by no means makes sure that these formal possibilities will in fact be available to all and everyone. Such availability is prevented above all by the differences in the distribution of property as guaranteed by law. (Weber, 1954:188)

Where modern exchange theorists deal with such inequalities they fail to show as much insight as Weber. Typical of modern orthodoxy is Blau's (1964:205) claim that the *ultimate* source of power in modern labor contracts is the employer's monopoly of resources and employees' dependence on them. He is wrong. As we have shown the ultimate source of such power is the legal coercion that protects monopolized property (or oligopolies if we borrow the term of economists), enforces market rules, and prevents the formation of normative economic communities. Modern exchange theorists' treatment of economic exchange and social exchange as theoretically equivalent would not be possible unless they assumed, without investigation, existing distributions of resources and the marketability of labor. Never, otherwise, would they be able to conclude that an exchange of labor services or some "favor" for other labor services or favors differed from a labor–money exchange only in its meaning to the participants and the specificity of the agreement. Nor would they have been able to relegate coercion to a dark closet of social theory.

If coercion recedes into the background in normal economic exchanges and shows itself only on those comparatively rare occasions of labor strikes and in the "noneconomic" phenomena of criminal law enforcement, it is nonetheless present as a potential. If the conditions maintained and the rights enforced by legal coercion make its actual use less apparent, we should not be misled into the Durkheimian position that restitutive sanctions have largely replaced retributive ones; for the restitutive sanctions (which are after all not imposed but coercively extracted) would not be possible without the ultimate threat of negative sanctions. Nor should we stop at Weber's (1954:30) claim that "forcible legal guarantee, especially where exercised by the state, is not a matter of indifference." Rather, in answer to his own question—"Can it be said that a stable private economic system of the modern type would be 'unthinkable' without legal guaranties?"—our answer must be "Yes."

References

Blau, Peter
    1964   *Exchange and Power in Social Life*. New York: John Wiley and Sons.

Bloch, Marc
    1961   *Feudal Society* (L.A. Manyon, tr.). Chicago: University of Chicago Press.

Boulding, Kenneth
    1955   *Economic Analysis* (3d Edition). New York: Harper.

Diamond, Stanley
    1974   The rule of law versus the order of custom, in S. Diamond (ed.), *In Search of the Primitive*. New Brunswick, N.J.: Transaction Books.

Gouldner, Alvin
    1960   The norm of reciprocity: A preliminary statement. *American Sociological Review*, 25(2):161–178.

Hilton, Rodney
   1973   *Bond Men Made Free*. New York: Viking.

Hobbes, Thomas
   1968   *Leviathan* (C. B. MacPherson, ed.). London: Penguin.

Homans, George
   1951   *The Human Group*. London: Routledge and Kegan Paul.
   1961   *Social Behavior: Its Elementary Forms*. New York: Harcourt, Brace and World.
   1967   Fundamental social processes, in Neil Smelser (ed.), *Sociology: An Introduction*. New York: John Wiley and Sons.

Locke, John
   1965   *Two Treatises of Government* (Peter Laslett, ed.). New York: New American Library.

Lyon, Bryce
   1960   *A Constitutional and Legal History of Medieval England*. New York: Harper and Row.

Polanyi, Karl
   1957   *The Great Transformation*. Boston: Beacon Press.

Spengler, Joseph J.
   1947   The role of the state in shaping things economic. *Journal of Economic History*, Supplement VIII (September), pp. 123– 143.

Weber, Max
   1954   *On Law in Economy and Society* (Edward Shils and Max Rheinstein, tr.; Max Rheinstein, ed.). Cambridge: Harvard University Press.
   1958   *From Max Weber: Essays in Sociology* (H.H. Gerth and C.W. Mills, tr. and ed.). New York: Oxford.

9

David Willer

STRUCTURALLY DETERMINED NETWORKS

A. Introduction

The concepts of exploitation and domination are, respectively, at the core of Marxian and Weberian theory. To the extent that these two traditions are commensurable, it is reasonable to ask how systems of domination are structurally reproduced through exploitation. The issue investigated in this chapter is the role of social structure in that reproductive process. The focus of concern will be upon the theoretic properties of strong structures.

Instead of exploitation and domination, social exchange theory has limited its concern to power. Typically power has been seen as a consequence of resource control, with the implication that differences of social power are due to resources as physically given facts. The core image of that view is one of an oil well or manufacturing organization as a "money mine" which gives off resources somehow ending up in the hands of selected social actors. This view is compounded by unfortunate statements about social power such as, "To use it (power) is to *lose* it" (Emerson, 1972:67). However, as is seen in the chapter by Gilham in this volume, the *control* of resources is itself a *social* phenomenon which is evidenced at some points in history as property rights, themselves based upon a network of *coercive* relations. Of course, all social systems must be seen as energy systems that are powered by their relations to the biophysical world, and, since they are, the social control of resources is important. It is the contention of this chapter, however, that the *social structure* of the system can be fundamental to its reproduction.

By social structure, I mean the kind and arrangement of potential and actual social relationships. Since the point of departure is social structure and *not* the division of labor or the beliefs of the actors, this treatment will differ from Marx's and Weber's.

B. Exploitation

Sanction flows have two components, v (valuations per unit) and x (units). For reasons that will become clear as the exposition proceeds, only the x terms and the sign of the sanction are relevant to the discussion. Furthermore, only material sanctions will be considered. The discussion will begin with consideration of a coercive system which can be compared to slave organizations, and an exchange system which can be compared to capitalist organizations, these being selected specifically for their contrasting *modes* of domination. The decision as to whether the discussions of the coercive and exchange systems are adequate first-order models for any slave or capitalist organization must be left to the reader's judgment in light of his/her historical studies.

In order to concentrate attention upon certain crucial sanction flows, the following important elements of the systems in question will be subject only to brief comment. First, neither the coercive nor the exchange system could exist in the isolation in which each are modeled. It is the class of masters that circumscribes and dominates the slaves. It is the class of capitalists that dominates the workers and separates them from the means of production. These conditions are assumed but are not included in any of the models drawn. Second, for any particular organization to reproduce itself, the productive process of the whole society must have reached a minimal level of effectiveness such that the actors of the system can subsist. It is self-evident that, as the level of productive effectiveness increases beyond that point, higher and higher rates of exploitation are possible, and thus there is the possibility of a more "powerful" reproductive process (see below). This discussion will not investigate either the physical or social sources of productive effectiveness, although selected issues related to the "costs of administration of domination" will be treated tangentially. Third, organizations do not necessarily produce the actual "material things" that are the means of subsistence for their actors. For example, some of the flows to be considered within the exchange organization are money flows, which are generated by selling the produced commodity in a market and which are, in turn, used by actors in exchange in other markets for subsistence. It is immediately evident that the rate of exploitation possible for any capitalist organization is a function of its productive effectiveness, the advantage or disadvantage of its market position (both in sales and purchasing), the costs of commodities to workers, levels of taxation and so forth. Note that all but the first of these are concerned with rates of exchange and coercion outside the organization to be modeled, not biophysical or social conditions of production. Again, having noted their importance, models for these further systems will not be an element of the discussion. Fourth, the origin of any system to be discussed here rests upon financial and/or coercive "investment" (that is, prior exploitation) by the dominant actor and its class.[1] While the discussion of reproduction may have a

---

[1] It is perhaps self-evident that that investment is typically based on prior exploitive relations.

number of implications for the understanding of the origin of each system, origins will not be explicitly discussed. In general the reader should compare these limitations and elements of the discussion that follow to Marx (1967: Chapter IX).[2]

In Figure I are models for the two systems, each containing only two actors. The purpose of these models is to represent the points and flows that will be central to the discussion. In later models, which contain more actors, the need for clarity of representation will require that even these representations be simplified. The models are intended to frame the question, "What does exploitation mean?"

The coercive model contains three points: the m point of the "master," the s of the "slave" and the f point representing the biophysical field of productive action of the slave. The arc from f to m represents the (positively valued) product of the s which is appropriated by m—the quantity of that flow is x_w. Two transmissions from the m to the s point are possible: (1) a negative sanction and (2) a positive sanction—the quantity of the positive sanction flow is x_y. The s point has no sanctions but is engaged in a reflexive relationship with f. The transmission to f represents the labor of the s point that is negatively valued by s. The size of the flow from s to f is x_v. It is assumed that the s point cannot escape from the domain of m.

The internal relations of the system are as follows. The flow from s to f is the labor of the slave, which together with the "fixed" conditions of production generates the $f-m$ flow of valued units produced. The $f-m$ flow is the resource base for the threatened (or transmitted) negative sanctions and for the $m-s$ flow (the latter being the subsistence for the s). Clearly the value of x_y must have a minimum below which the s cannot survive. Beyond that minimum there can be any number of possible relationships between the size of x_y and x_v. Furthermore, as x_v increases, x_w will increase, at least up to a point depending upon the quantity of the means of production that are treated as "fixed."

The exchange model also contains three points: the c point (the capitalist actor), the l point (the laborer) and the f point representing the biophysical field of productive action of the l. The arc from f to c represents the (positively valued) product of the l which is appropriated by the c—the quantity of that flow is x_w. The positive sanction from the c to the l (the quantity of which is x_y) is the payment by c for l's labor. The $l-f$ flow is l's labor—the quantity of the labor is x_v.

The internal relations of the system are as follows. The flow from l to f together with the "fixed" conditions for production generates the $f-c$ flow of

---

[2] The parallels between this discussion and certain formulations by Marx are not accidental. However, certain differences should be noted, particularly the use of the modeling procedure. (It is hoped that its use here will be a guide to those Marx scholars interested in using modeling procedures in extending and codifying Marxist theory.) The reader should note that the term "exploitation" is used more broadly here than in Marx's work and includes both exchange- and coercion-based types.

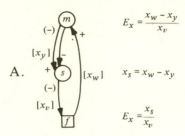

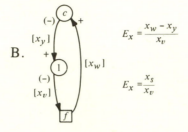

FIGURE I. Two actor models for systems of exploitation: A. Simple slave organization, B. simple capitalist organization.

valued units produced. That flow in turn is the resource base for the payment of the laborer, the $c-l$ flow. As in the slave system there is a minimum size for this flow, which is subsistence. There can be any number of possible relations between the size of x_y and x_v and between x_v and x_w.

Now consider some of the meanings of the ratios of the labeled flows for either system. The ratio of x_w to x_v is the rate of productivity of work. The ratio of x_y to x_v is the rate of payment to the dominated actor for its labor. The difference between x_w and x_y is the quantity retained by the dominant actor (surplus) and will be called x_s. Then E_x, the rate of exploitation, is defined as the ratio of x_s to x_v. That is,

$$E_x = \frac{x_s}{x_v}.$$

For the remainder of the discussion certain further conditions will be introduced. Let it be a condition that the productivity of work is high enough that significant variations of the specified terms can occur. Let it also be a condition that the relation between x_v and x_w is direct and linear—that is, that work is not subject to declining marginal productivity. Thus any increase in x_v increases x_w such that either x_s or x_y would increase (and conversely). Now let us turn to the modeling of the actors and their consequent interests.

C. Reflective Actors and Their Interests

A reflective actor may be defined as an actor whose preference system contains only material flows ordered in accordance with their quantity and in light of the sign of their valuations of transmission and reception, and who has full information of the system as modeled. (The concept of reflective actor is a useful theoretic tool because, having modeled the system of relationships, we then derive the preference system of the actor. The belief system of the actor is given by the system of the relations and the preferences derived for the other actors. Thus separate formulations for preferences and beliefs can be avoided.) The idea of a reflective actor follows from the Marxian conception of reflection. Needless to say, reflective actors have only (informed) *material interests*. Here the idea of material interest is used in a manner similar to its use in Marxian and Weberian theory.

Let all of the actors of Figure I be reflective actors. Now certain of the material interests of these actors can be derived. The m actor has an interest in the maximization of x_w and a minimization of x_y. (Given the assumed relationship between x_v and x_w this means that m has an interest in a maximization of x_v.) Stated somewhat differently, the system of domination, if it is to function in the interest of the m actor, will first of all maximize x_v and then, for any resultant value of x_v, will maximize E_x. The interests of the s actor are exactly opposed to the m. That is, the s has an interest in minimization of x_v and minimization of E_x, such that for any x_v, the value of x_y will be maximal and thus E_x minimal. Using the terms as defined above, the interests of the c actor are identical to the m, and the l are identical to the s.

D. Strong Structure, Domination and the Rate of Exploitation for the Coercive System

There are two fundamentally different modes of domination possible for the coercive system modeled in Figure I. First, the negative sanction of the m could be used only to circumscribe the modeled s (and any other s actors of the system) so that an "economy" relating the $s(s)$ and the m could be established. The $s(s)$ would be isolated from any economic relations outside the system. Having eliminated other alternatives, the m would then establish a relationship between x_v and x_y, the purpose of which would be to maximize x_v while keeping x_y as small as possible. Because the dynamics of this system are similar in certain regards to those of the exchange system yet to be discussed, we shall turn to the second mode of domination possible for the system.

In the second mode, x_y is fixed at a minimal level, that level being determined by the minimal biophysical needs of the s. The work of the s, (x_v) is then extracted by threat of transmission of the negative sanction. The general character of the threat is

$$\left[(x_v \geqslant x_{v_1}) \; \rightarrow \; \sim T_n \right] \& \left[(x_v < x_{v_1}) \; \rightarrow \; T_n \right]$$

where x_{v_1} is a quantity of labor chosen by m and T_n is the transmission of m's negative sanction.

In order to continue the exposition it will be necessary to turn our attention to a coercive system with $n + n' + 1$ points as in Figure II. For purposes of clarity the system of relationships has been packed (see Chapter 2). This packing rests on the linrear relation of x_v and x_w, and on x_y being fixed. Thus in Figure II the flow from any s to the m can be treated as x_v, which in turn is proportional to x_s. The potential flow from m to any s is of course the negative sanction. The subsystem contains one m and n s points. Outside the subsystem is a further set of potential s points of size n'—any of which could be brought into the subsystem by m at a cost of x_c.

Let it be given that no s position develops any joint rule with any other s position. Since the cost of transmission of negative sanctions is relatively low, let it be given that the negative chosen by m has a value such that all s points prefer to transmit $x_v = x_{v_{\max}}$ (where $x_{v_{\max}}$ is the maximum work possible for any s point) than to receive the negative sanction from m. However, this does not imply that all s actors will always work at a maximum for m, for all s actors also have an interest in minimizing x_v and reducing x_{v_1}, the rate of labor demanded. Whether the value of x_{v_1} can be smaller than $x_{v_{\max}}$ depends in turn on the interest position of m.

The actor m has an interest in receiving $x_{v_{\max}}$ from all s actors and can transmit the negative sanction to that end. But consider the possibility of resistance on the part of any subset of the n s points, the meaning of which is a demand to transmit any $x_v < x_{v_{\max}}$. If this demand implies disagreement, the confrontational act of the m would be the transmission of the negative sanction. Let it be given that any transmission of the negative sanction will reduce x_v for the receiving actor (i.e., the slave who is beaten can no longer work as effectively due to injury). Let it be given that q or more transmissions of the negative sanction eliminate any s as a social actor—that is, the s is killed by the m. Let q equal any "small number." Thus it follows that there is a cost of confrontation for the m actor, which is determined by (1) the immediate loss of x_v and (2) the prospective loss of all future productive labor by the s who has received q negative sanctions. However, the latter cost is conditioned further by the size of the set of actors who can be brought into the system and by x_c, their individual cost. As x_c decreases and n'

FIGURE II. Coercive system of $n + 1$ points.

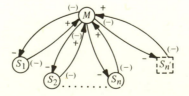

increases, the cost of confrontation for m decreases. Conversely, as x_c increases and n' decreases, the cost of confrontation for m increases.

Let it be given that the cost of confrontation for m is small and that $x_v < x_{v_{max}}$. Then m has an interest in adopting the rule that *a proper subset of s transmitting the smallest x_v will receive at least one negative sanction.* Let the size of that set be one. The m actor has an interest in adopting that rule not only because the costs of confrontation are low but also because of its consequences upon the calculation of interest by the s actors.

Consider the interest of any s, given m's rule. The s has an interest in minimizing x_v. However, the s has an interest in avoiding $x_{v_{min}}$ where $x_{v_{min}}$ is the lowest amount of work for the set of s actors. But all other s actors have the identical interest. Thus all s actors will act to avoid $x_{v_{min}}$ because of the contingency relating $x_{v_{min}}$ to the reception of the negative from m. Thus x_v will approach $x_{v_{max}}$ for all nonnegatively sanctioned s points.

Now consider the coercive system in which the costs of confrontation for the m is high (relative to x_s). Under that condition the m point could still adopt the same rule as above; however, the costs of its adoption are high even if the result is a maximization of x_v. But the adoption of any other rule would be less effective and would not result in the maximization of x_v.

In the extreme case, the set of potential s actors is empty, no s eliminated by reception of the negative can be replaced and m's rule becomes irrational. Of course, a quantity of x_v could still be "extracted" by threat, that quantity being determined by the point of equiresistance. However, maximal levels of exploitation would not be possible.

When the s points can be replaced at little cost to the m, a structural condition is generated. The system of domination–exploitation possible under that condition opposes the interests of all s points to one another—each having an interest in not being the least productive. The mode of domination consists of the policy of transmission of at least one negative sanction to the least productive s and the replacement of occupants of the s positions as needed. This generates a process of iteration in which the resistance of the s actors is dissolved while the resistance of the m is increased. During this process x_v approaches $x_{v_{max}}$. This is the first *strong structure* discussed in this chapter.

E. Strong Structure, Domination and the Rate of Exploitation for the Exchange System

The exchange system of Figure III has been subjected to packing analogous to that of the previous example. The flow x_w is taken to be proportional to x_v; thus the vector from any l to any c point represents the work of the l as it has been transformed in the field of biophysical action into the x_w, while the vector from any c to any l is x_y. For the figure there are p c points and q l points. The average size of the maximum possible network for the c points is r. Let the c actors have an unambiguous interest in filling their maximum possible networks. Thus the

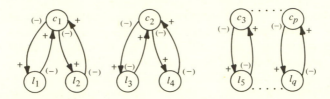

FIGURE III. Simplified capitalist–labor system.

number of "jobs" in the system is r times p. Let each l point have a maximum possible network of one "job." Let all actors be reflective actors and let the cost of replacement of any worker be zero and the cost of taking a new "job" be zero. Let there be no "welfare" for the l points and no "government subsidies" or alternative "labor markets" for the c points—that is, neither has an alternative network. Finally let it be given that no c point develops any joint rule with any other c point and no l point develops a joint rule with any other l point. That is, there are no conspiracies to depress wages, nor are there any unions. What then are the dynamics of the system?

As in the case considered in the last section, the dynamics of the system are a consequence of the structural distribution of the costs of confrontation for the two sets of actors. Here three cases are important: (1) when the number of l points exceeds the combined size of the maximum possible networks of the c points ($q > rp$), (2) when the number of l points equals the combined size of the maximum possible networks of the c points ($q = rp$), and (3) when the number of l points is smaller than the combined maximum possible networks of the c points ($q < rp$). The first case will be considered in detail, the remaining two more briefly.

Let $x_{y_{min}}$ be subsistence. Let any relationship in which $x_y \geq x_{y_{min}}$ be preferred to no relationship by any l. Let x_y initially be any value substantially above $x_{y_{min}}$ and no larger than $x_{y_{max}}$. There is a set of l actors of size $q - rp$ that do not exchange with any c, but who have an interest in exchanging. Furthermore, any c has an interest in exchanging with any of that set if and only if the member of that set will accept a value of x_y smaller than the present rate. But all l have that interest. Thus any l actor now exchanging with any c will either accept a smaller value of x_y or that actor will be displaced. Since this is a reflective system any l actor exchanging with any c will accept the smaller x_y. Using the concept of resistance, all c actors will be infinitely resistant to any but incrementally smaller values of x_y and all l actors will have zero resistance to any incrementally smaller x_y if the smaller $x_y \geq x_{y_{min}}$.

It is clear that the specified system is a strong structure. Since it contains reflective actors the actions within it will be structurally determined. In application to any real case this model has an important further implication. If the $q > rp$ is known to be a stable condition of the system, the set of c actors will have an interest in transmitting to the l actors at least the minimum information needed to act reflectively; for it is evident that, if the l actors had certain types of distinct systems of meaning, action would not be structurally determined. (It also follows that although the set of c actors has no interest in collusive generation of joint contingencies, the set of l actors has that interest, if it would result in reversal of the process of iteration and thus increase x_y).

In this system, domination–exploitation rests again upon the unequal distribution of the costs of confrontation. Any disagreement concerning x_y is resolved in favor of the c actor(s). Therefore, as the process continues, x_y would approach $x_{y_{min}}$, and (though it has been neglected up to this point) x_v would approach its maximum.

Now briefly consider the condition in which q is less than rp. For that condition it is immediately evident that the differential allocation of the costs of confrontation has been reversed relative to the previous example. Now the resistance of the c, and not the l, actors is dissolved. Thus x_y will go to its maximum and x_v to its minimum. (In other words, if there are more jobs than laborers, wages will be very high and will be earned with a minimum of labor.) That this condition has not been found in historical cases is *exclusively* due to prevailing (initial) conditions of historic systems, a point that will be considered briefly below.

The structural condition of $q = rp$, if considered in isolation, would be subject to analysis from the point of view of bargaining, for unlike the two cases discussed above, this sytem is not a strong structure. Thus, neither c nor l actors are subject to successive reductions or increases of resistance. Thus the system will support bargaining that is settled at the point of equiresistance. By monopolizing access to jobs in any capitalist organization, a union can set $q = rp$ and thus can bargain. In the United States, so called "right to work" laws make that monopolization impossible, thus either weakening or eliminating the bargaining position of the l actors. In the absence of a union that acts to maintain that equality, the condition of $q = rp$ is a limiting one. As a limiting (boundary) condition it is *bounded* by $q < rp$ and $q > rp$, both of which are structurally determined systems, and, since only a small change away from the equality results in powerful structural effects, the role of resistance will be small. This follows because any reflective actor in a $q = rp$ system will negotiate not only in light of resistance but also in light of the prospects of changes in q, r and p.[3]

---

[3] This discussion is similar to certain points made by Marx [see especially Marx (1967:637)], but an important difference should be noted. In the theoretically pure system as modeled in this paper, if there is a "reserve industrial army" of any (even minimal) size, wages go rapidly to their minimum and work demanded (and received) goes rapidly to its maximum. These changes are consequent upon the iteration process. The speed and end point of the iteration process is a function of a number of factors especially information and the presence or absence of any organization among the l points. A result of elaboration of the model to include these last two factors is the following points: First, assume that the proportion of l actors in the reserve industrial army is related to the proportional amount of information on relevant system conditions available to all the actors. Then the rate of iteration will be proportional to the amount that q is larger than rp. Given that formulation, for short time periods there would be, as Marx noted, an inverse relation between wages and the size of the reserve industrial army, [even though in the long run

The foregoing analysis has certain further implications that are a consequence of prevailing historical conditions and of the boundary conditions of the systems discussed. Let it be a condition of any capitalist–labor system that technological change is ongoing. Let one consequence of that change be a change in the means of production, which can successively increase x_w / x_v. Let the adoption of new means of production reduce r. Let any c not have an interest in adopting any new means of production if $x_v = x_{v_{\max}}$ and $x_y = x_{y_{\min}}$. Let any c have an increasing interest in adopting any new means of production as either of the foregoing values departs from its specified limit. It follows then that as $q > rp$ approaches $q = rp$, any reflective c actor will adopt the new means of production in order to reduce the size of its r. It thus follows that q will always be greater than rp if the new means of production can be adopted. It is through these dynamics that the separation of workers from the means of production has its results in prevailing wage rates.

Of course any l actor has an interest in joining with other l actors in order to monopolize jobs and generate joint contingencies. More precisely, any l actor has that interest if and only if joining others is either costless or results in an increase in preference state. If not, then any l actor has an interest in all *other* l actors acting in accordance with that interest. The analysis of the consequences of this latter condition can be seen by combining the foregoing analysis with the models for normative systems, as discussed in Chapters 3 through 6.

The analysis of the interest situation of an actor, if it is to be complete, must take into account changes which that actor (or other actors) can make in the network. Clearly, any c actor has an interest in maintaining the $q > rp$ condition. It may be that further l actors can be brought into the system, or that the relational system itself can be moved to a different network in which large numbers of potential l actors are present. Both of these possibilities can be found in contemporary societies.

F. A Note on Reproduction and Initial Conditions

There can be a problem of correspondence between the idea of initial conditions and the reality of ongoing systems. Any modeling enterprise with the elementary theory begins with a set of *initial conditions* such that a model for the structure

(i.e., at "equilibrium") wages would be minimal if there were *any* reserve industrial army]. Second, if there were an organization among l actors, then they could jointly develop rules. One aim of that organization would be to monopolize the available jobs. Were that to occur, the iteration process would end and wages would be determined by resistence factors as in the case of $q = rp$. Assume that the effectiveness of any l actor organization is inversely proportional to the size of the reserve industrial army. Then wages would, even in the long run, be inversely related to the proportion of l actors in the reserve industrial army, as suggested by Marx. Thus the relationship between wages and size of the reserve industrial army proposed by Marx, although it does not hold for the simplest possible system as modeled in this paper, would be expected to hold at least approximately for any real case involving either of the two discussed conditional factors. For further relevant points see the results of the experimental study of Chapter 11.

and dynamics of the system can be constructed. When the theory is used in experimental work, corresponding to these theoretic initial conditions are the conditions of the system being constructed in the laboratory. An experimental run can begin with these initial conditions and can generate certain interactional dynamics and outcomes, which are then compared to the interactional dynamics and outcomes that are theoretically expected.

In the case of historical systems the situation is quite different. Historical systems normally do not have distinct beginning and end points. Facts may be available for later but not for earlier periods. The situation is similar in ethnographic research. The researcher typically enters an ongoing system and leaves it still ongoing. Is there a lack of correspondence between the idea of initial conditions, consequent dynamics and outcomes, on the one hand, and the reality of ongoing systems, on the other?

This problem is dealt with by use of the idea of reproduction. Consider any system over the time period t. Let the conditions of the system at t_0 (the initial conditions) be C_0. *If the conditions of the system at $t_1 = t_0 + t$ are C_1, and if $C_1 = C_0$, then the system has reproduced itself.*

Now consider the coercive and exchange systems under the following conditions: the coercive system in which any number of $s(s)$ can be (cheaply) replaced and the exchange system in which $q > rp$. In both cases the flows of material sanctions are particularly favorable to the dominant position as a consequence of the strong structure. Given these flows, at the end of any time period, all resources (beyond those currently used for subsistence by the dominated) will be held by the dominant actor(s). The concentration of these resources, taken together with other relevant conditions, can be then be treated as the initial conditions for a new sequence of interaction, which has a similar result and so forth. Thus the system reproduces itself.

Here two brief historical notes are relevant. It was Weber's contention (1963:339ff) that the decline of ancient civilization was a consequence of the increasing lack of availability of new slaves which followed from the stabilization of the boundaries of Rome. The model for the coercive system given above is consistent with Weber's position. The high rate of coercive exploitation possible in the strong structure was dependent upon the replaceability of the s actors. When s actors could no longer be replaced, the rate of exploitation would decrease and reproduction would end. Instead of reproduction, a transformation of system type would be expected.

Marx pointed out that, in capitalism, the wage rate is related to the "size of the reserve industrial army." However, the reproduction of capitalist systems, as he well knew, was not dependent upon the continual expansion of the labor force, but was importantly conditioned, as discussed above, by the introduction of technological change in the means of production. Given this technological change, modern capitalism is not subject to the same kinds of limits as was ancient civilization. All of the foregoing points are, of course, consistent with the analysis of the systems as modeled above.

G. Hierarchy

All but the smallest systems of domination contain an administrative hierarchy in which a set of hierarchically arranged actors stands between the dominant actor and the dominated. If the actors in the administrative hierarchy act in the interest of the dominant actor, they will take orders from that actor and transmit them and enforce them on the actors at the "bottom" of the system. The effectiveness of an administrative hierarchy *as a system of domination* rests on at least two conditions. First, the system of communications from top to bottom must be so arranged that the interest of the dominant actor can be realized in the particular orders given by any superordinate to any subordinate. Any hierarchical system of communication can be maximally vulnerable to errors in communication in the following sense. If any actor in the hierarchy receives inaccurate information (or misreceives accurate information), all actors under that actor will receive inaccurate information. The *extent* of this vulnerability is a function of the rank of the actor first transmitting inaccurate information.

This discussion will concentrate upon obedience, the second condition of effectiveness of an administrative hierarchy. Let the following two conditions be given. First, that any disobedient actor will transmit and enforce orders that are not maximally in the interests of the dominant actor. Second, that all actors "under" that actor will, if they are maximally obedient, transmit the orders of that actor. Thus the effects of any disobedience will cascade. Systems of this type are maximally vulnerable to disobedience. The extent of that vulnerability is a function of the rank of the disobedient actor. Moreover, when the system administered by the hierarchy has a set of interdependent tasks, the cascading disobedience of one part of the hierarchy can ramify, affecting task completion in all other parts of the system.

It follows theoretically (for any system conforming to the foregoing conditions) that a necessary condition for the effective domination of those at the "bottom" of the system is maximal obedience of all actors in the hierarchy. If the actors of the hierarchy are maximally obedient, there will be no immediate cascading or ramifying consequences even for maximally vulnerable systems. In fact, very high levels of obedience are typical for hierarchical systems. It was Weber's position (1947: Section III) that this obedience rested upon the legitimacy of the system. If a system is legitimate, the *ideal* interests of the actors in the hierarchy are brought into correspondence with the material interest of the dominant actor. If obedience is to follow from legitimacy alone, the members of the hierarchy must act only upon the aforementioned ideal interests.

But why did Weber resort to ideal interests? It is evident that Weber saw the actors of administrative hierarchies as very highly obedient, but could not account for that obedience without resort to ideal interests. [See Weber (1954:322ff).] However, Weber did not have at his disposal the idea of strong structure. If hierarchies are strong structures, the resistance of the actors in the hierarchy will be dissolved, and all will act to transmit and enforce orders that are in the interest of the dominant actor. What then are the conditions for strong structure and thus for the dissolution of resistance in administrative hierarchies?

Consider a hierarchical system with the following conditions:

1. The system has n levels between the dominant and dominated actors.
2. The remuneration of any administrative (a) actor is a direct function of level occupied (and the gradient between levels is salient to the a actors).
3. Both upward and downward mobility occur in the system contingent upon the relative obedience of the a actors.
4. The interests of any a actor are confined to remuneration in the system (i.e., office and personal life are separated).
5. The dominant actor has full information for application of the mobility contingency, and its application is costless to the dominant actor.

Now compare this type of hierarchical system to the model for the exchange system previously discussed. For that system, there were two statuses: employed and not employed. When q is larger than rp, all l actors could be said to have an interest in maximal obedience with the rules of the dominant actor. That obedience rested upon the prospects of "mobility" into or out of the actual exchange system. By extension it can be seen that any hierarchy contains a succession of $q > rp$ conditions in the following sense. Consider any level in the hierarchy which has below it a further administrative level. q is the number of actors at both levels, p is one, and r is the number of actors at the higher level. All actors in that lower level have an interest in moving to the higher level. No actor at the higher level has an interest in moving to the lower level. Given the obedience contingency rule, any actor at either level has either an *interest* in greater obedience than any other actor or (if greater obedience is impossible) maximal obedience. Thus obedience will be maximal solely through the relation of obedience to hierarchy and mobility and even in the absence of dismissal. But any administrative hierarchy contains $n - 1$ pairs of levels, each pair of which has this structural effect. Thus obedience is maximal for the system as a whole.

It is immediately evident that hierarchies are "stronger" structures than the coercive and exchange systems discussed earlier. Thus it is not at all surprising that obedience in such systems is not normally seen as problematic. But in ancient civilization a hierarcy of drivers (themselves slaves) administered the estate of the master in his interest; in modern capitalist systems propertyless bureaucrats administer large capitalist organizations in the interest of directors (and/or shareholders). These facts do need to be explained. One possible explanation lies in the application of the idea of strong structure.

H. Final Comments

In this chapter the theoretic properties of exchange, coercive and hierarchical strong structures were investigated. If a strong structure contains only reflective actors, it will be a structurally determined system. One implication of structural determination is that the dominant actor is very highly resistant to any but maximally preferred rules, while the dominated are minimally resistant to these rules. Thus any of the structurally determined systems would be characterized by a set of system rules such as orders, rules and laws that are in the interest of the dominant actor. A second implication of structural determination was that sanction flow rates consequent upon the structure would favor the reproduction of the system.

In some two-level exchange systems, structural determination at one level can importantly condition the processes and interactions at the other. Normative systems can coexist with strong structures and may either oppose or support the domination depending upon conditions initial to normative group formation. More than one kind of strong structure can be present in a given system. Thus, beginning with the systems discussed, a wide variety of complex models could be constructed and compared to historical and contemporary systems.

A more complete discussion would include a consideration of the results of the experimental research that has been begun. However, due to space limitations, only one set of experiments on strong and weak structures is discussed in this volume (see Chapter 10). The results of other experimental work, although consistent with the discussions of this chapter, must be published at a later time.

In this chapter no attempt was made to interpret systematically any of the models for historical or contemporary cases. Yet the discussion does have possible implications for the empirical study of systems of domination and exploitation. Are all (or most or any) historical and contemporary systems of domination and exploitation reproduced through strong structures? While this chapter cannot suggest an answer, at least the question can now be posed in a comprehensible manner.

References

Emerson, Richard M.
  1972   Exchange theory, Part II: Exchange relations and network structures, in Joseph Berger, Morris Zelditch, Jr. and Bo Anderson (eds.), *Sociological Theories in Progress* (Vol. 2). New York: Houghton Mifflin.

Marx, Karl
  1967   *Capital* (Vol. I). New York: International Publishers.

Weber, Max
  1947   *The Theory of Social and Economic Organization* (tr. A.M. Henderson and Talcott Parsons). Glencoe IL: The Free Press.
  1954   *Max Weber on Law in Economy and Society* (tr. Edward Shills, and ed. Max Rheinstein). Cambridge: Harvard University Press.
  1963   The social causes of decay of ancient civilization, in Russell Kahl (ed.) *Studies in Explanation*. Englewood Cliffs NJ: Prentice-Hall.

10

Manuel L. Carlos

Bo Anderson

POLITICAL BROKERAGE AND
NETWORK POLITICS IN MEXICO
The Case of a Dominance System

A. Introduction

When the dynamics of the Mexican political system are being considered, the structure and processes of the system's networks for political exchange must occupy the foreground of the discussion (Grindle, 1977). It is necessary to examine how the flow of demands for goods, services and expressions of loyalty are mobilized and negotiated through systems of political networks and brokers. To estimate the effectiveness of this system it is also important to determine the nature of regime responsiveness to articulated demands.

This chapter has two parts. The first part is an organized description of the structure and dynamics of political networks in Mexico. This is based on interpretive formulations derived from a variety of studies. In the second part, crucial aspects of this organized description are interpreted from the point of view of the elementary theory. The purpose of that interpretation is not to formulate a general model for brokerage systems of this type, but to uncover the structural bases of reproduction of one particular system in light of general conclusions from the theory.

B. The Mexican Political System in Perspective

In general, authors attempting to give an overview of the Mexican political system tend to vacillate between outlines of the formal organization charts of national, state and local governments and political parties [e.g. (Scott, 1964)] and analyses of the events within or outside of these formal structures [e.g. (Brandenburg, 1964)]. Since the available empirical data base about governmental processes and political behavior on the state and national level is sparse or difficult to assess and evaluate, the tendency toward speculation on these matters is understandable; yet, the discrepancy between authors on many important points concerning political relationships makes it clear that much of what is said about both formal and informal political behavior in organizations is guesswork.

Thus, while Scott assumes that the formal ''charter rules'' of government are followed, Brandenburg asserts that they are continually flaunted by those in power, political position being merely a tool for economic advancement. Padgett takes a position between these two extremes, pointing out that although power rests in the hands of a few, there have been some economic reforms since the Revolution of 1910, and at least the middle classes have benefitted from the present political system (Padgett, 1976:123).

The fundamental relationship between the state and its citizens is coercive. In a modern state such as Mexico there is a large and complex bureaucracy to implement coercive policies of capital formation (extracting surplus value) and to regulate economic activities that require official sanctioning through licensing and inspection procedures (Eckstein, 1976). Furthermore, the state exercises control over a number of resources, particularly water and farming credits which if withheld from any user would seriously jeopardize agricultural productivity. Nor are the resources collected through taxation fully used up in the costs of administration, for some are redistributed to selected communities, individuals and groups. It follows that there is an interest on the part of any citizen in receiving certain redistributed goods and services or rights in the form of licenses and access to scarce resources. The system of political networks and brokerage is an important condition for distributing these advantages.

It is notable that a system of nationwide political networks is not mentioned by any of the authors attempting to deal with a general picture of Mexican politics. This is remarkable on at least two counts. First, virtually every community case study that deals with political activity and center–periphery ties between the state and the community demonstrates the presence of local sociopolitical networks that are the primary mechanism for making demands and the foundations of political power in the community itself. [Good examples are Friedrich (1965), Torres-Trueba (1969) and Schryer (1976).] Studies reveal that network politics is not limited to peasant villages, as has been suggested by some authors (Wolf, 1956; Powell, 1972), but is also found in urban Mexico (Cornelius, 1973, 1975, Graham, 1968). Second, the conceptions that knowledgeable Mexicans have of their own system emphasize network links: the person who wants to get something done spends a good deal of effort cultivating network ties (Lominitz, 1977).

C. The Role of Political Networks

Studies showing the importance of networks on the local level point out that local networks are linked to networks on the state and national levels. Unfortunately, no detailed analysis of this linkage structure or of political network activity on either the state or the national level has been seriously attempted. Possible exceptions to this statement are Brandenburg's concept of the "revolutionary family" (Brandenburg, 1964), which is primarily conceptual and only sketchily illustrated, and Wolf's ideas of local–national network linkage, which similarly suffer from lack of empirical documentation and analysis (Wolf, 1956).

General political network models have been developed for and applied to a variety of locations; however, none of these models is easily applicable to the Mexican system and, indeed, some are seriously inadequate (Schmidt et al., 1977). Weingrod's analysis of Italian patronage systems, for example, shows a sharp delineation and opposition between patron–client relationships and party patronage (Weingrod, 1968). Essentially, he argues that patron–client relationships are based on kinship and traditional landlord–tenant ties and limited to traditional agrarian societies with little national integration. Party patronage or institutional patron–client ties, on the other hand, are based on developmental, economic goals and are found in developing and urban industrial societies (Weingrod, 1968:382–385). However, studies of Mexico's social networks show that they penetrate institutional ties and that they are *both* kinship-oriented *and* the bases of pragmatic endeavors, economic advancement *and*, inevitably, politically oriented activities in urban and rural environments and in isolated and integrated agrarian communities (Gonzalez-Casanova, 1970:35; Graham, 1968:43; Cornelius, 1975:248; Friedrich, 1965:193–197).

Although Powell's study of clientelist politics has more applicability to Mexico, the limitations of his approach are also very evident. For example, he argues that patronage ties must always be between nonequals. This is not true for Mexico. As shown by Graham (1968), Capriata (1972), and Smith (1979) political networks among political elites and the upper classes, of which Brandenburg's "revolutionary family" is a good example at the national level, are extremely important in Mexico. These networks, like those of the urban poor (Cornelius, 1975, Lominitz, 1977), involve ties based on reciprocal exchanges between persons of equal social and economic status. Another problem with Powell's analysis is the limitation of his discussion to peasant communities. In Mexico, political networks can be found in all sectors of society, although there are subpopulations that appear to be excluded from or very weakly connected to any but the most local networks (Fagan and Tuohy, 1972; Schryer, 1976). This phenomenon of political marginality will be commented on later in this paper.

Nevertheless, Powell's analysis, like Wolf's, is important for the development of a working understanding of the brokerage and network aspects of Mexico's political system. His concept of the clientelist state, a variant of the patrimonial state in which followers are bound to their patrons by access to material goods, is eminently applicable to Mexico. Similarly, his concept of political brokerage (*clientelas* or constituencies aggregated into networks, and linked to the vertical patronage structures in the political system) is applicable to the Mexican case and central to our analysis. In addition, Powell's assertion that political patronage systems are successful in the selected distribution of state-controlled resources

and in avoiding governmental overthrows from political extremes bears examination, explication and analysis, given Mexico's relative political stability since
the 1910 Revolution.

D. Social and Political Networks

In general, interpersonal relationships and exchange networks in Mexico may be
social or political or both (Lominitz, 1977). Often these relationships are based
on kinship or fictive kinship, with the *compadrazgo* or coparenthood system of
relations significantly adding to the number of possible relationships for any
individual (Carlos, 1973). These relationships involve the exchange of favors,
goods and services, and may be between equals or nonequals in socioeconomic
status. These relationships form complex and extended networks, Foster's
"dyadic contract" (Foster, 1961, 1963) being merely one kind of a two-person
exchange agreement and link within the larger social web. Individuals generally
will establish numerous direct and indirect exchange agreements and possess
both horizontal and vertical network links. In this context, a broker is a specialist
with vertical and horizontal ties who is at the vortex of many interpersonal
relationships: social, political or both.

Simply put, a collective political network is a structure for articulating,
exchanging and attending to expressed demands. Political networks, vertical and
horizontal, provide the means for the expression of demands for rights, favors,
goods and services directed to those in control of state resources, as well as
channels through which rights, favors, goods, services and demands for
compliant acts flow from these controllers to the demanders. The broker is a
person within this network who has the ear of those in control of state resources
as well as contact or access to those resources, with linkage to community- and
class-based groups with economic and political demands. The social network is
the social structure through which political transactions take place. To understand these aspects of Mexican society adequately, it is important to realize that
traditional kinship and social exchange ties have become incorporated into more
inclusive structures and political institutions (Gonzalez-Casanova, 1970:35;
Graham, 1968:43; Cornelius, 1975:240; Friedrich, 1965; 193–197; Smith,
1979:254–260).

Political networks, then, are part of the more widespread system of social
networks that comprises Mexican society in general. It is proposed here that
these political networks are a principal basis of political activity in Mexico, and
that they cut across political institutions and often act quite independently of
formal political organizations and structures. We further contend that political
networks and their constituency bases are to be found throughout Mexico and are
not limited to any region or to either rural or urban settings. Lastly, we submit
that they tie together community, regional and national levels, comprising a vast
web of interest groups with differential influence at each level. Within these
networks, political brokers with their respective constituencies (*clientelas*) are

the basic units of activity and analysis. In order to establish a realistic idea of the nature of Mexican politics, then, it will be necessary to develop a more precise understanding of the nature and dynamics of networks, brokers and constituencies in distinct settings.

E. The Broker and His Network

A political broker either has a specific political role, such as a political office, or he acts to attain goods and services from people with formal authority in the government or with control over political or social resources. He is the main agent in political brokerage. A political broker can either obstruct or facilitate the flow of demands, favors, goods and services to or from some constituency. In Mexico, the concept of political brokerage is culturally and linguistically acknowledged and clearly institutionalized as a sociopolitical phenomenon; there are terms for political brokerage in the language: *gestor* (petitioner) is one term, whereas *padrino politico* (political godfather) is used and has cultural referents that can be lauditory or derogatory, depending on the context and the speaker.

A *cacique* (political chief) is a political broker who is efficient enough in acquiring the goods and services for a majority of the politically active constituents in his area so as to maintain almost total monopoly over political power for many years (Goldkind, 1966; Barta et al.,1975). Even in areas where *caciques* hold sway, however, there are factions and opposition groups with their own brokers, who become politically marginalized as the result of not having effective power. It is well to note that the power of a *cacique* is based not only on his constituency's satisfaction but also on the pleasure of the regional and national level political brokers. Like any political broker a *cacique* must hold sway with those in control of resources. In addition, contrary to impressions that might be gained from some political case studies, the absence of a *cacique* in a community does not mean the absence of political brokers.

A political broker, say a peasant leader, party official, has his power base in at least one official constituency whose particular interests he articulates. Some brokers may represent more than one constituency. Political brokerage takes place horizontally as well as vertically within class, social and government levels. Thus, the system is organized on multiple levels: at the bottom are such units as local communities, *ejidos* or land grant villages, farmers' associations, etc. Their brokers are effective to the extent that they are linked to local, regional or national sources of state-controlled resources (Capriata, 1972; Carlos, 1974; Grindle, 1977). The brokers for the local or community-based-level *clientelas* form the *clientelas* of the regional brokers. The latter, in turn, are the clients of the brokers on the next higher level, for example, the state level or national level, depending on the brokerage path followed—and so on, until as in some instances brokerage paths and networks reach the top national brokers.

Some interesting questions can immediately be asked about this type of hierarchical political network. For instance, if persons on some level were to follow brokerage paths that skip brokers on the next higher level in order to approach directly brokers on an even higher level, then the power of the former could in time be undercut. We suspect that there are brokerage path mechanisms and political sanctions by which this is discouraged, and the hierarchical order in assessing state-controlled resources is maintained. On the other hand, it could be that it sometimes is in the interest of brokers on some level to ''get off the hook'' by having their clients go directly to an even higher level for help or favors. Also, it might be possible for some brokers, as in the case of peasant leaders, to operate on more than one level (Ronfeldt, 1973; Ugalde, 1973; Schryer, 1976). Formally, the levels of the Mexican system are organized in a structure that resembles a pyramid, an ancient image of Mexican politics (Paz, 1972). The number of brokers and constituents decreases as we move toward the top of the structure, but it has a very broad base. A basic rule of the system is that, as far as possible, all resources should travel only along paths (vertical or horizontal) within the pyramid and only to *clientelas* that are inside the structure (Purcell, 1975). It becomes virtually impossible for reform factions, or new poliitcal groups, to grow strong enough to challenge the system. This lends itself to a highly controlled system of negotiation, creating a conservative mood among those in the system and a radicalization of those outside it or marginal to it. What is seen to be repressive from the point of view of aspiring groups outside the structure is a relentless and single-minded application of this rule. It also leads to the charge that the system is highly authoritarian (Purcell, 1975; Reyna and Weinert, 1977).

In this network structure, a group on a given level will have effective control over resources only so long as it is tied in with an effective group on the next higher level. This applies to local and regional as well as national constituencies. Since brokers, regardless of level, attempt to maximize their control over the flow of resources, we expect that all brokers are strongly motivated to extend both vertical and horizontal ties to other brokers. For example, the efficacy of a village faction will depend to a great extent on the faction in power on the regional and national levels (Barta et al., 1975). If the broker for the village faction has the ear of the state-level broker, the village faction will be able to obtain goods and services. However, with a change in the power structure on higher levels, local power balances may also become disrupted. But a constituency and its broker that is cut off from power may not disappear, but go into a more-or-less temporary eclipse, often making public complaints through its broker about the vagaries of the faction in power (Ronfeldt, 1973:120; Friedrich, 1965:198). A broker on the national level must nurture the links connecting him to local-level constituencies. Without popular support, in the form of votes for him or for his government connections, his high-level brokerage power will be undermined (Graham, 1968:56; Adie, 1970:5). Like village brokers, state- and national-level brokers in eclipse may not disappear but merely wait for a more congenial political opportunity structure to come about in order to reclaim a role in the brokerage system.

While a broker is defined by his constituency, a constituency may have several brokers representing its different interests on vertical and horizontal levels (Powell, 1972:416). Other things being equal, the more brokers a constituency has, the more it has potential access to state-controlled resources. For example, under the *hacienda* system, the patron through state-sanctioned labor contracts was the sole broker for all aspects of the peon's life, and the peon's survival depended entirely on the benevolence of the *haciendado*. While *ejidatorios* (land grant recipients) under the *ejido* system are admittedly a group with comparatively little political clout (Barta et al., 1975), at least they are better off than their predecessors, having a wider choice of political brokers available to them in the form of the peasant's union, as well as the ejidal structure itself. These can intercede with the state on their behalf. More striking, however, is the ongoing discrepancy that exists between the efficiency of brokers available to private farmers through informal network structures (Scott, 1967:168; 1973). The latter have greater contact choices and more direct brokerage paths and consequently receive larger shares of state resources (Barta et al., 1975).

This process of demand articulation and delivery of goods and services can be either simple or complex, depending on the efficacy of the broker and directness of a brokerage path. If the broker has direct contact with the person in control of the desired resource, the broker will merely state the demands of his constituency to that person who in turn will procure the goods or services requested. More frequently, however, the broker must go through many such people, each of whom has the ear of a person somewhat closer in the network to the actual power holder. Other things being equal, the stating of demands becomes less efficient and subject to alteration with each intermediate broker it must go through. The shorter the brokerage path the better. This process of attenuation and transformation of demands is poorly, if at all, understood. The process begins with a broker with little overall influence and ends with the person in control of the required resources. This process, it is postulated, is the primary means of demand aggregation and articulation in Mexico. Although demands may be channeled through formal governmental agencies and party-affiliated groups, these in themselves are part of or related to a more widespread political brokerage path network which may deviate from formal lines of communication. In addition, there are informal networks that are quite often more effective mechanisms for demand making than the formal structures. It is this process and not only the formal structure that should be considered in analyzing the Mexican political system on any level. Having stated this omnibus hypothesis, let us emphasize that it needs a great deal of specification before we have an adequate picture of Mexican politics.

Political marginality may be defined as a lack of any access to those in control of state resources. Here it should be emphasized that all or nearly all of these resources come from the national government and its regional and local offices, as a result of the extreme centralization of power. Marginal groups are not linked through any path to those in the upper levels of the pyramid that control resources. Political marginality may indicate a lack of any vertical network connections in a constituency or the absence of an effective linkage of a group's local network to the vertical network system; that is, a network's broker or brokers are inoperative on the regional and hence on the national levels. Some politically marginalized groups may not be aware of this lack of access (Eckstein, 1976). This may be said of many Indian communities and of some urban core slums. These groups are the politically forgotten of Mexico, making no input of demands and receiving virtually no goods or services from the government.

Those groups that are aware of their absolute or relative political marginalization often organize public protests. These protests may take a variety of forms, from joining renegade unions such as the *Central Campesina Independiente* (CCI) in Baja California or the *Union General de Obreros of Campesinos Mexicanos* (UGOCM) in Sonora, to denunciations in the press, to public demonstrations (Adie, 1970). These groups protest, not against the government per se but against their lack of access to channels of influence within the government and their lack of access to political and, therefore, economic advantages. Although details of the dynamic process by which such groups are tamed or radicalized, coopted or kept marginal is little known, an interpretation of elements of the process will be offered later.

F. Regime Responsiveness and State Control

We now turn to the question of regime responsiveness to political inputs. The regime's responsiveness to constituencies varies from region to region and with each national-level administration. The state through the existing ruling regime responds to networks and not to formally organized groups such as the national political party or the government bureaucracy. Although formal groups may operate independently, networks within and outside political organizations are the effective means of political activity.

The nature of regime response to public demands of potentially dissident, marginalized groups in Mexico has been discussed by Anderson and Cockcroft (1969) who point out that there is a three-stage course of responsiveness to organized political demands. First, leaders of dissent groups are approached by leaders of *Partido Revolucionario Institucional* (PRI), the official political party, and offered minimal benefits and influence within the party network in return for incorporation into the party structure. If this approach fails, repressive measures are carried out against the group by government agencies: leaders are jailed, group headquarters ransacked, and the group "pacified." In the event that violence should erupt on the part of the dissidents and their demands are modest, however, some of their demands may be met by agencies of the government. A fuller understanding of Mexican political networks and their role in confrontations with the state will only be possible when we know more, not only about the shapes, extensions, densities, tie-ins and so on of networks, but also about the rules for exchange used by the brokers and other transactors.

Which faction holds power at any given time depends on numerous factors including economic stability of the constituencies, political connections of their respective brokers, as well as on who holds power on regional and national levels.

G. Analysis of Case Studies

The discussion turns now to an examination of case examples that illustrate in greater detail some of the traits of the political brokerage and network system. First, rural case studies are considered, followed by an analysis of urban examples. Finally, issues related to the operation of political networks and brokerage paths and systems to be found in these two environments will be discussed.

There are many studies done of rural political networks; these studies show without doubt the person-centered, kinship-based nature of networks as the primary source of political affiliation. They also note the existence of political brokers both within and without the government and party bureaucracies, as well as the importance of vertical networks for effective brokerage. Although no study makes a categorical connection between effective political brokerage and economic development resulting from state-allocated resources in a given area, it is plain from at least one such example that a connection is possible.

David Ronfeldt's study of Atencingo, an *ejido* or land grant village in the state of Puebla, shows the vertical brokerage contacts through its analysis of the rise to power of a political faction with a man named Porfirio Jaramillo as leader, or broker (Ronfeldt, 1973). An important part of Jaramillo's support was seen to come from the state government and the peasants' union, the *Confederacion Nacional Campesine* (CNC), along with its leaders in Mexico City. Jaramillo, at the outset of his career, placed loyal supporters of his constituency in positions over which he had power, showing that he understood the fact that constituency support and loyalty should be honored as a means of repaying past favors and of placing claims on future favors. Unfortunately, this is the only evidence in the report of the use of personalistic contacts and the mode of favor exchange in rural political networks; however, the fact remains that rather than selecting those he deemed most competent for the job in question, the leader, himself an elected ejidal official, gave posts under him to his friends.

It is important to note that the Jaramillo regime's support in the village came in part from contacts he had in state and national government agencies. While these vertical-network connections were still open, Jaramillo's opponents and their respective brokers were dispersed and had little political sway. However, with the advent of a new faction in power in the state government, Jaramillo's network contacts and power abruptly evaporated. At this juncture, all the opposing groups became "impressively organized" (Ronfeldt, 1973:89). With this new opposition coalition, those supporters Jaramillo had had in the popular sector promptly deserted him for the newly powerful faction, hoping to be part of what was apparently to be the next constituency in power. The Jaramillo regime, thus bereft of all its local, state and national support, was ousted as a result of a federal investigation that uncovered "dishonest" practices on the part of ejidal councils he had headed and named. Thus relegated to a position of powerlessness by the loss of power in higher levels, Jaramillo and his supporters were reduced to making public denunciations of the practices of the new ejidal leaders (Ronfeldt, 1973:67–97).

This case study illustrates the idea that vertical political networks and local constituencies are vital to effective brokerage and dominance patterns in the operation of rural village politics in the Mexican political system. In addition, it shows how networks help bring groups to power as well as how they are marginalized.

Another important rural case study was done by Juan Felipe Scott (Scott, 1967). Scott showed that *ejidatarios* in an area of Sonora were unable to work their lands because of lack of the necessary allocation of irrigation water. This water shortage was a result of ineffective brokerage on the part of officials in the CNC, as well as the lack of alternate brokers with effective, informal, political contacts. The private farmers in the same area, on the other hand, had enough water through an allocation from the local government agency to farm their lands. Scott describes how this was a result of effective political brokerage on the part of their informal, nongovernment brokers. The reaction on the part of the politically marginalized *ejidatarios* was to join the UGOCM, a nongovernment-affiliated labor federation with socialist leanings. Unfortunately, this gesture on the part of the *ejidatarios* was to be little more than a symbol of their disaffection with their excluded position, as the UGOCM had little political sway and contact with government officials.

Scott's information on a more prosperous neighboring *ejido* showed that the *ejidatarios*, having effective brokerage, being relatively well off and certainly satisfied with their position, participated only in the progovernment CNC, the official peasants' union. While private farmers in this area still were apparently better off than the second group *ejidatarios* as a result of more effective informal political networks, the *ejidatarios* had important network and brokerage contacts and were satisfied with their economic position as well as the level of access they had to government resources.

This study shows the relative importance of informal, extragovernmental political networks. In addition, it demonstrates, at least partially, the relationship between effective brokerage and economic development. Thus, in the village where the *ejidatarios'* brokers within the ejidal network were highly ineffective, the *ejidos* could not be worked because of lack of access to state-controlled resources. The result of this marginality was the symbolic protest involved in the high participation in the opposition union. The private farmers in the same area, however, had effective political brokerage, resulting in the acquisition of water and ensuing economic advancement on their part.

Another rural study done by Paul Friedrich on *caciquismo* in a Tarrascan village illustrates both the kinship-based nature of political networks and the necessity for vertical linkage with the higher governmental levels for effective brokerage and accessing state-controlled resources (Friedrich, 1965). Friedrich illustrates the existence of village-based "political families," which are held together by extended kinship and personal relationships. Each family aggregates, usually forming two opposing factions in the village. Each faction in turn has its main political broker who serves as leader or political boss (i.e., *cacique*). The rise and fall of factions and dominant *caciques* is shown to be a function of many complex occurrences, not the least of which is the effectiveness of a *cacique* in acquiring state-controlled goods and services. The latter as elsewhere must be obtained through political contacts in both state and national governments. These contacts, in turn, are available only as long as a certain state or national brokers and their factions are maintained in power much as was the case in the village of Atencingo studied by Ronfeldt.

It is unfortunate that there are no case studies of state and national governmental factions. While many studies indicate existence of state- and national-level networks, with their respective constituencies and brokers as perceived from the local level, there is as yet no systematic study of these higher-level political networks and their role in controlling state resources. Research that moves beyond identification of the possible composition of these networks (Smith, 1979) will be needed to round out the information available on political activity on regional and state levels.

In looking at case studies in urban areas of Mexico, it is obvious that the literature has, in general, been limited to discussing cliques of upper-class and lower-class political elites [e.g., Capriata (1972) and Eckstein (1976)]. The elites studied tend to form horizontal networks that link up their respective constituencies, yet there is a dearth of material on lower- and middle-class urban political networks, which seems to stem from an apparent assumption that these networks are mostly found in rural areas. Cornelius' recent work on urban *caciquismo*, or the practice of *cacique* (political boss) rule, has opened a whole new area of inquiry on this subject (Cornelius, 1973; 1975). Although limited to *caciquismo*, one of his studies shows political networks existing in fringe slums in Mexico City. The *caciques*, like political brokers found in rural Mexico, have face-to-face relationships with members of their respective communities or constituencies as well as with minor officials in the city and national governments. These officials, in turn, have contacts in higher echelons, thus participating in a vertical political network within the capital city itself. Like his rural counterpart, the urban *cacique's* power is based on his brokerage service and his effectiveness in acquiring needed state-controlled goods and services. While the latter differ from those desired by rural constituencies, the network structures are similar. In addition, the *cacique's* local support falls away as soon as he loses contact with individuals controlling resources. Unfortunately, Cornelius does not examine the problem of the network ties of marginalized groups in the urban lower class.

Returning to urban power elites, it can be shown that they form a horizontal political network at the top of the regional structure. Lawrence Graham's analysis of urban elites in the town of Saragoza shows that the elites comprise an internal communication and influence network based on close personal relationships (Graham, 1968). As a group, these competing elites are capable of impeding or supporting any local business and public enterprise, from the introduction of industry to the paving of certain streets, according to what was the most desirable outcome for them. This group, comprised mainly of economic elites or businessmen, and divided into factions, effectively controlled the political arena locally, as well as having important contacts in the state capital and in Mexico City to whom they could look for political and economic patronage.

As with rural communities, the political brokers in this study were also divided into different constituencies or factions. Like village *caciques* and constituencies, these factions rose and fell in power with changes in state and national administrations, again showing the similarities of network process, and reemphasizing the concept of vertical political networks in assessing and controlling the flow of state resources. Thus, whereas the politicoeconomic elites of Saragosa made up horizontal networks, each of these was, in turn, differentially linked to regional and national political networks.

With regard to the activities of marginalized groups, in this context, Graham gives a detailed account of state actions which led to the cooptation of constituencies, networks and brokers. The elites as a group, supported by the state governor, had decided to create a large boulevard in the city. In order to do this, a large tax was placed on the residents of the area. These people, but especially the middle classes, unable or unwilling to pay the tax and unable to reach the people in power because they had no political contacts or brokers, turned to public demonstrations. These included the formation of a formal group, the enlistment of one businessman whose property was threatened with demolition, and the cooperation on the part of a deputy of the opposition party. However, although these public protest actions had little effect, the moment violence broke out, the group was allowed to establish communication with the state and to meet with the governor, who promised to suspend the tax. The governor, in turn, lost political face for allowing the protest to reach the violent stage and for having to give in to the formerly politically marginalized and inactive group.

By way of comparison between rural and urban contexts, it is well to note that, although networks may follow distinct network paths in the state's power hierarchy and be composed of different types of individuals with different demands, the basic structure, function and process of political networks are similar in every context, with differential efficacy resulting from differing brokerage paths and especially from the different distances of constituencies and their brokers from those in control of resources. It is, of course, true that the demands of, say, *ejidatarios* and private farmers are qualitatively different from those of fringe slum dwellers. Farmers want good land, enough water to farm it, and credit to buy seeds and fertilizer. Slum dwellers, on the other hand, desire roads, utilities, jobs, transportation facilities and schools. However, the means by which these demands are heard and met are similar. In Mexico, brokerage is the only effective way for both elite and nonelite constituencies to acquire desired state resources.

An important difference between rural and urban contexts is the fact that most upper-class individuals tend to live in cities. Although there are some wealthy farmers, they often spend much time in the city, keeping up the political contacts that will ensure their continued prosperity. Since more successful and prosperous individuals tend to hold more political offices and political sway (Fagan and Tuohy, 1972:90– 92), obviously the more effective brokers are concentrated in the urban areas. This phenomenon is even more obvious in Mexico City, because of extreme government centralization in that city. Upper-class urbanites, such as those described in Graham's study, are the most successful in acquiring goods and services, whereas rural lower-class individuals, especially if geographically isolated, are the least effective.

This is not to say that there is a rigid rural–urban continuum, for there exist pockets of extremely marginalized groups within Mexico City itself (Eckstein, 1976); likewise there are effective constituencies in many rural areas. But, by and large, cities contain more effective brokerage and patronage structures as a result of centralization of power, and also because the most effective groups (the wealthy) inhabit cities. Even rural elites tend to congregate in the city of their region in order to communicate with each other and are then collective network resources.

H. Synthesis of Formal and Informal Network and Brokerage System Rules

As we have seen, the Mexican state and its official governmental system is supplemented and conditioned by a system of informal networks of political influence within and outside the political organizations that share its operation. Some elements of that conditioning can be expressed as follows: In Mexico, state laws are typically shorthand statements of actual political system rules. At times the complete statement of the system rule for accessing state resources and achieving political brokerage is a synthesis of the law and the rules of the informal network. For example, a law may prescribe that a license is required to pursue some economic activity; it may also prescribe the procedures for license application. A naive person following the official procedures of application would find that his/her application was somehow never processed, perhaps even lost. On the other hand the proper introduction to the official through one's broker can result in immediate consideration. For the less powerful members of the larger political community in an urban or rural setting, rights to act (or to avoid acting, as in the payment of certain taxes) can be obtained generally only if the connection with the relevant state agency can be made through the right broker.

Given the *entre* that would be needed, it is by no means surprising that there are no studies of brokerage and the management of brokerage at the individual power elite level. In the absence of direct evidence (Smith, 1979) inferences must be founded on what we generally know of the phenomena of informal power networks among elites. Unless Mexico is wholly unique, there is reason to infer that the informal traits of networks are dominant for the power elite in the following sense. If an elite member can make the proper network contacts, that person can utilize legally based power to pursue or support his/her desired activity unless the desired outcome is blatantly unlawful and public. Here one suspects that the fundamental control mechanism of elite behavior is not state power but normative control emanating from accepted rules.

I. State Dominance, the Brokerage System and State Control: Strong Structure and the Political System

The widespread participation of *clientelas* in the political process, and their connections to it through their brokers, the connections of brokers from local to national power levels, and their relations to political elites may give to the outsider an image of an open system, a kind of participatory democracy, which is different from Anglo-Saxon systems but no less effective at representing the interests of those who participate. But the apparent openness and authoritarianism of any system must always be seen against a background of its structure of relationships of domination and exploitation and the ongoing reproduction of those relationships in segments of society.

Having reason to suppose that brokerage networks have a role in the reproduction of political control in the Mexican system (Purcell, 1975; Eckstein, 1976) leads us to look for evidence of strong state political control in these networks. That evidence is highlighted in the following points:

1. Only some, not all, communities and individuals have access to state resources and are included in the national brokerage system network. But those included have relative advantages that are not available to those who are marginalized or not included in the system. In terms adopted from Marx, there is a "reserve marginal army" of communities and individuals who have an interest in taking the place of those now participating in the brokerage and state resource allocation systems. We know that local communities exchange political compliance, votes and acclaimations of party nominees, for advantages such as water rights, road repair, government relief and so forth (Schryer, 1976; Fagan and Tuohy, 1972; Barta et al., 1975). Yet, what would occur if a community made ever-increasing demands for advantages? Such a group could be excluded from access to certain resources in favor of a more marginal group willing to offer the same level of political support for fewer advantages. If, as is evident from some studies (Barta et al., 1975; Graham, 1968), this process of circulation into and out of the state-linked effective brokerage network is operative, then the system of brokerage and network relations at its first level is a strong

structure. If it is a durable structure, then the level of community demands that will be satisfied through the network would improve the community's position beyond that of marginals, but only to the degree needed to maintain preference for a network connection over marginality.

2. Relative to a *clientela* the position of the broker is an advantaged one, yet the costs of the exclusion of his group from the network are to him the loss of status as a broker and its advantages. Thus the costs of marginalization from the access process can be greater for the broker than the *clientela*, and, as a consequence, the expected obedience of brokers to state demands from above is greater. This state-control effect can be mediated if the broker can be replaced from within the group. The threat of exclusion from the broker position from below generates a base for power of the *clientela* over the broker, such that when such brokers are too obedient to demands from above (and do not transmit demands from below) they can be replaced, as happened in the case of Jaramillo, the *cacique* of Atencingo (Ronfeldt, 1973). Thus the replaceable broker faces an ongoing dilemma. If he is too forceful in making demands, the community is excluded; if not forceful enough, *he* is excluded. The long-term solution to this dilemma of how to protect his status is to monopolize his political contacts, thus eliminating his replaceability from below and further entrenching his political rule (Goldkind, 1966). *But this resolution has the effect of strengthening the strong state control structure.*

3. If, as there is reason to suppose, there is competition for services at all levels of the brokerage system (Grindle, 1977), and if marginality can occur at any level, then the system is also a hierarchical strong structure which will generate very high levels of obedience to elite demands. This inference is consistent with the already noted centrist and pyramid shape of the brokerage and state resource allocating system, and with movements in and out of the network with the rise and fall of particular factions.

As a strong structure, the system of political brokerage is supportive of the system of state control and centrist dominance. When taken together with Mexico's high rates of unemployment and other official incorporative and cooptive structural factors, the smooth continuity of the system can be understood.

J. Political Marginality, Bargaining and the Issue of Cooptation

Underlying the brokerage system and its relationship to political incorporation and marginality are a variety of coercive and conflict relations, often potential and occasionally actual, which deserve consideration. There is a typical process by which a marginal group can attempt to gain access to the brokerage network. That process begins with a local organization centered on the grievances of the community. For example, as was asked by peasants in the state of Hidalgo

(Barta et al., 1975), "Other communities . . . have water rights; why must we be dependent on rain alone? Others have roads so that their produce can be taken to market. Why not us?"

As the group organizes, leaders are sent to contact local officials. Coercive contingencies are generated — "We will fight at every level necessary if our demands are not met or if the demands of others take precedence over ours." If real and extensive, these threats will have the cost of public confrontation with local political office holders as happened in the town of Saragosa studied by Graham (1968). If room can be made in the network for the emergent group (perhaps by cycling out some least obedient community), and if the emergent group will accept the ongoing rate of "payoff" and offer obedience in return, then they can lose their marginal status. (Remember the rate of exchange offered is conditioned by structural factors discussed in the previous section.) This implies that future study of dissidence in the Mexican system should take into account not only the power and influence of the emergent group itself, but also the network resources of communities and groups that are present candidates for marginality. Needless to say the circulation of groups into and out of the network is a condition for the maintenance of hierarchical control and the beliefs that sustain the ongoing structure of the state monopoly over certain resources.

A second alternative line of action is the coercive repression of the emergent group: an investigative team, the army or the police can be sent in and the dissident village faction pacified. This has happened often (Adie, 1970). Given a standing army and teams of government technicians and elected officials, this is not a particularly costly act for the state—although it may be costly to the career of the local official. Furthermore, through that act further effects are generated within the system. Before there were two community statuses in and out of the political brokerage system. Now there is a third least preferred status, the "pacified" community.

If the community is to maintain its status in the brokerage system, it is the leader who must generate the consensus for obedience. Thus the leader takes on the role of a broker, offering obedience in exchange for advantages gained through the informal network. But the position of broker becomes an advantaged one, with the result that he has a greater interest in obedience than others of the community. This is the structural base of the broker's cooptation, the source of state control over local communities, and the basis of oligarchy within local villages and urban communities.

K. Conclusion

Mexico has evolved a highly effective system of centrist, state control and political representation, which we have labeled a system of political networks and brokerage. The system connects to the centrist government which has ruled the country since the revolution of 1910. Through a hierarchical system of brokerage and constituency representation involving numerous brokers, the state distributes resources that are desired by individual constituencies and communities. The network components of this system are imbedded in the country's social and political institutions and cut across formal political organizations, giving the state an extensive mechanism for directing informal political processes. Bargaining in the system is limited and cooptation practices widely spread. Groups can gain and maintain representation but only at the cost of submitting to certain rules and to supporting many elements in the status quo. The system works precisely because it has roots deep in the exchange mechanisms and social structures of interpersonal relations in Mexican society. It also works because it allows the state to trade off its resources for political obedience from specific constituencies at all levels of society.

Research into Mexico's political networks and the brokerage system that incorporates them is still in its early stages. Much research needs to be done at all levels of the political order to understand fully and document the processes we have analyzed. Our goal has been to identify and analyze major components in the network and brokerage structures and to find the common factors that influence how they operate. Although this complicates earlier, more formalistic and institutionally-derived models of Mexican politics, we believe it also leads to a better assessment of the system's dynamics at the informal and interpersonal level.

References

Adie, Robert F.
   1970   Cooperation, cooptation, and conflict in Mexican peasant organizations. *Inter-American Economic Affairs,* 24(3):3–25 (Winter).

Anderson, Bo, and James D. Cockcroft
   1969   Control and cooptation in Mexican politics. *International Journal of Comparative Sociology,* 7(1):16–22.

Barta, Roger, Eckart Boege, Pilar Calvo, Jorge Gutierrez, Vicor Raul Martinez Vazquez and Luisa Pare
   1975   *Caciquismo y poder politico en el Mexico rural.* Mexico D.F.: Siglo vienteuno.

Brandenburg, Frank R.
   1964   *The Making of Modern Mexico.* Englewood Cliffs, NJ: Prentice-Hall.

Capriata, Jorge Alberto
   1972   "The Political Culture of Marginal Elites: A Case Study of Regionalism in Mexican Politics," unpublished dissertation, Stanford University.

Carlos, Manual L.
   1973   Fictive kinship and modernization in Mexico: A comparative analysis. *Anthropological Quarterly,* 46(2):75–91.
   1974   *Politics and Development in Rural Mexico: A Study of Socio-Economic Modernization.* New York: Praeger.

Cornelius, Wayne A.
    1973   Contemporary Mexico: A structural analysis of urban *caciquismo,* pp.
            135–150 in Robert Kern (ed.), *The Caciques.* Albuquerque: University of
            New Mexico Press.
    1975   *Politics and the Migrant Poor in Mexico City.* Stanford, CA: Stanford
            University Press.

Eckstein, Susan
    1976   *The Poverty of Revolution: The State and the Urban Poor in Mexico.*
            Princeton: Princeton University Press.

Fagan, Richard R., and William S. Tuohy
    1972   *Politics and Privilege in a Mexican City.* Stanford, CA: Stanford University
            Press.

Foster, George M.
    1961   The dyadic contract: A model for the social structure of a Mexican peasant
            village. *American Anthropologist,* 63(6):1173–1192.
    1963   The dyadic contract in Tzintzuntzan, II: Patron–client relationship. *American
            Anthropologist,* 65(6):1280–1294.

Friedrich, Paul
    1965   A Mexican *cacicazgo. Ethnology,* 4(2):190–209.

Goldkind, Victor
    1966   Class conflict and *cacique* in Chan Kom. *Southwestern Journal of Anthropol-
            ogy,* 22(4):325–345.

Gonzalez-Casanova, Pablo
    1970   *Democracy in Mexico,* London: Oxford University.

Graham, Lawrence S.
    1968   *Politics in a Mexican Community.* University of Florida, Social Science
            Monographs, 35. Gainesville, FL: University of Florida Press.

Grindle, Merilee Serril
    1977   *Bureaucrats, Politicians, and Peasants in Mexico: A Case Study in Public
            Policy.* Berkeley: University of California Press.

Lemarchand, Rene and Keith Legg
    1972   Political clientelism and development: A preliminary analysis. *Comparative
            Politics,* 4(2): (January) 149–178.

Lominitz, Larissa
    1977   *Networks and Marginality, Life in a Mexican Shanty Town.* New
            York: Academic Press.

Padgett, L. Vincent
    1976   *The Mexican Political System,* 2nd edition. Boston: Houghton Mifflin.

Paz, Octavio
    1972   *The Other Mexico: Critique of the Pyramid.* New York: Grove Press.

Powell, John Duncan
    1972   Peasant society and clientelist politics. *American Political Science Review,*
            64(2):411–425.

Purcell, Susan Kaufman
  1975   *The Mexican Profit-Sharing Decisions, Politics in an Authoritarian Regime.*
         Berkeley: University of California Press.

Reyna, Jose Luis and Richards Weinert (eds.)
  1977   *Authoritarianism in Mexico.* Philadelphia Institute for the Study of Human
         Issues.

Ronfeldt, David
  1973   *Atencingo: The Politics of Agrarian Struggle in a Mexican Ejido.* Stanford,
         CA: Stanford University Press.

Schmidt, Steffen, James C. Scott, Carl Lande, and Laura Guasti
  1977   *Friends, Followers, and Factions: A Reader in Political Clientelism.* Ber-
         keley: University of California.

Schryer, Frans J.
  1976   "Faccionalismo y patronozgo del pri en un municipio de la huesteca
         hidalguense." Mexico, D.F. Centro de Estudios Sociologicos, El Colegio de
         Mexico. Cuadernos del CES:16.

Scott, Juan Felipe
  1967   Social change in two Mexican communities. *Sociologus* (Berlin), n.s.
         17(2):162–179.

Scott, Robert E.
  1964   *Mexican Government in Transition* 2nd edition. Urbana: University of Illinois
         Press.

Smith, Peter H.
  1979   *Labyrinths of Power, Political Recruitment in Twentieth Century Mexico.*
         Princeton: Princeton University Press.

Torres-Trueba, Henry E.
  1969   Factionalism in a Mexican municipio. *Sociologus* (Berlin), n.s. 19(2):134–
         152.

Ugalde, Antonio
  1970   *Power and Conflict in a Mexican Community.* Albuquerque: University of
         New Mexico Press.
  1973   Contemporary Mexico from hacienda to PRI: Political leadership in a
         Zapolec village, pp. 119–134 in Robert Kern and Ronald Dolkart (eds.), *The
         Caciques.* Albuquerque. University of New Mexico Press.

Weingrod, Alex
  1968   Patrons, patronage, and political parties. *Comparative Studies in Society and
         History, 10 (July):377–400.*

Wolf, Eric R.
  1956   Aspects of group relations in a complex society: Mexico. *American An-
         thropologist,* 58:1065–1078.

11

John S. Brennan

Research reported in this chapter was supported in part by Grant Number SOC 76-02753 from the National Science Foundation to David Willer.

SOME EXPERIMENTAL STRUCTURES

A. Introduction

Consider systems in which actors can increase their preference states by exchanging some resources in their possession for resources from other actors in the system. What conditions, according to the elementary theory, determine the exchange rates upon which actors will agree? *Centrality index* (see Section D, Chapter 7) is one such condition. This chapter reports an experimental investigation of the effect of centrality index upon exchange rates in economic exchange systems.[1] The investigation uses three different experimental situations, characterized by different values of the centrality indices of theoretically important actors. This chapter has three parts: (a) a presentation of experimental situations and elementary theoretic models, (b) a description of methods and results for the three experiments, and (c) a discussion section.

Let us begin with the features common to all three experimental situations: (a) Subjects occupy either an "f" position or a "g" position for a bargaining *session*. (See Chapter 7, Section C, for a discussion of similar f and g positions.) (b) Initial resources (i.e., counters) are given to f and g subjects for each session. (c) Subjects in f positions receive 33 "blue" counters, which are each worth one point to an f and one point to a g subject. (d) Subjects in g positions receive ten "white" counters, which are each worth one point to an f subject but worth zero points to a g subject. (e) A set of rules (see methods section below) govern bargaining and exchanges of counters. (f) The f and g subjects can exchange with each other; the g subjects can not exchange with other g subjects. (g) Subjects are

---

[1] These experiments were designed by David Willer and Douglas Heckathorn. The experiments were conducted under the supervision of David Willer.

paid according to the number of points (scored with counters) earned by exchanges in bargaining sessions; payment is made after the end of an experimental run. (h) A series of "periods," each containing four bargaining sessions, comprises an experimental run. (i) The subjects occupy one position for one period; after the conclusion of a period, subjects rotate to another position. (j) There are as many periods in an experiment as there are subjects (i.e., each subject gets a chance to occupy each position in the experimental situation). (k) There is only one f position in an experimental situation. (l) There are at least three g positions in an experimental situation. (m) There is a specific rule about the *maximum* number of g positions with which the f position is *allowed* to exchange in a bargaining session.

The following features differentiate Experiment 1 from Experiments 2 and 3. Experiment 1 involves *only* three g positions and allows the f position to exchange with all three g positions. This produces a value of one for the centrality index of the f position. That is, the f has a potential exchange network of three and a maximum possible network of three. How are Experiments 2 and 3 different from Experiment 1? (a) These experiments have *more* than three g positions and again allow f to exchange with a maximum of three g positions. (b) It follows that these experiments have f positions with centrality indices > 1.

The main difference among experimental situations is a different centrality index for the f position. In Experiment 1 the f position has $C_f = 1$. In Experiment 2 the f position has $C_f = 4/3$. In Experiment 3 the f position has $C_f = 5/3$. To create these differences it is necessary to have different numbers of subjects in the three experimental conditions. There are four positions (one f and three gs) in Experiment 1. There are five positions in Experiment 2 (caused by adding one g position); there are six positions (one f and five gs) in Experiment 3.

What does the elementary theory predict concerning the system exchange rate $E_{f/g}$ in Experiment 1, Experiment 2 and Experiment 3? In order to answer this question, we must model the structures created by the rules of each experimental condition; we must represent the white and blue counters as initial resource conditions in the models. We will model Experiment 1 first. Figure I presents the potential network for the f position and the three g positions in Experiment 1. The model represents the rules allowing f to exchange its blue counters for white counters from the g positions. The negative and zero valuations of transmissions of counters are indicated; the positive valuation of reception for f and for g is represented. To use this model to predict exchange rate, $E_{f/g}$, we need only to remember that the f actor has 33 blue counters for its initial resources and that each g actor has ten white counters for its initial resources.

Model for Experiment 1. The model for Experiment 1 is a variant of the bilateral monopoly system discussed in Chapter 7. Here we have a compound system; to predict the system exchange rate we need to perform a simple elaboration of the analysis of the bilateral monopoly carried out in Chapter 7. That analysis used the First Law of the elementary theory and considered

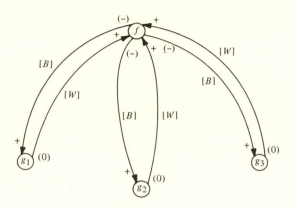

FIGURE I. *Model for Experiment 1.* Arcs labeled B indicate potential flow of blue counters from f, the F subject, to one of the g subjects. Arcs labeled W indicate potential flow of white counters from g to f. The white counters are valued zero by the g points and valued one by the f point. The blue counters have value one for all actors.

exchange between an f actor and a single g actor. The f actor has 11 initial counters and the g actor has a unit of ten initial counters. The following theoretic points were derived from the bilateral exchange model, with those initial conditions: (a) The maximum and minimum numbers of counters that f will transmit to g are nine and one, respectively. (b) The maximum preference state alterations for f and g are $p_{f_{max}} = 9$ and $p_{g_{max}} = 9$. (c) The costs of confrontation are $p_{f_{con}} = 0$ and $p_{g_{con}} = 0$. The reader now can calculate the resistance of f and of g to exchanges of ten white counters from g in return for one through nine blue counters from f. The second principle (see Section E, Chapter 7, on *resistance*) then can be used to predict an exchange of ten whites for five blues. In our (compound) model of Experiment 1, we arrive at a prediction of a total of 30 whites to f (ten from each g) in return for a total of 15 blues (five to each g).

We treated the structure of Experiment 1 as a compound of three bilateral monopoly systems with the f actor in common. There were 16 bargaining sessions in Experiment 1 and the elementary theory gives a prediction of 30 whites for 15 blues as the exchange rate to be expected in *each* of the 16 sessions.

Model for Experiment 2. Experiment 2 involves four g positions; let these positions be called g_1, g_2, g_3 and g_4. Following the line of argument developed in Chapter 7 about f–g systems, it can be seen that Experiment 2 will behave, from the point of view of the elementary theory, in a way quite unlike Experiment 1. The additional g actor, and the rule that f must decide which one of the four gs to *exclude* from exchange in a particular bargaining session, create a situation in which the exchange rate is expected to move over sessions to one most favorable for the f actor. This is unlike the predicted constant exchange rate in Experiment 1.

We expect to see an *iteration* process (see Chapter 9) during the course of the 20 bargaining sessions in Experiment 2. Imagine the following series of bargaining sessions, in our model for Experiment 2, between the f actor and the g actors.[2] (a) In session one, f exchanges five blues for ten whites with g_1, g_2 and g_3. (b) Actor g_4 gets excluded and realizes that f now has no interest in exchanging five blues for ten whites from g_4. (c) In a later session, g_4 offers to give ten whites to f in return for only four blues. (d) Actor f accepts this offer and accepts five for ten from g_1 and g_2. (e) Actor g_3 is excluded and now has an interest in offering f ten whites for four blues. (f) The iteration process continues in this fashion to a theoretic limiting exchange rate of ten whites from each g (only three gs can exchange) in return for one blue to each g from f.

The elementary theory predicts the following pattern of changes in system exchange rate over sessions for Experiment 2: There will be a "declining phase" like that described in the mental experiment above. An exchange rate will be reached that is most favorable to the f actor. Then the remaining sessions in Experiment 2 will continue at that rate; call this the "constant phase." Notice that all sessions of Experiment 1 can be seen as a constant phase with predicted exchange rates of 30 whites for 15 blues.

Model for Experiment 3. The model for Experiment 3 is similar to the model for Experiment 2; however, there is an additional g actor. This model also is a specific case of the $f-g$ system discussed in Chapter 7. We now have five g actors: g_1, g_2, g_3, g_4 and g_5. The rules for Experiment 3 require f to decide, for a specific bargaining session, which two gs to exclude from exchange. Perform the following mental experiment on our model: (a) Exchange, as in Experiments 1 and 2, begins at a rate of five blues from f for ten whites from a g. (b) Actor f exchanges with g_1, g_2 and g_3. (c) Actors g_4 and g_5 are excluded at this rate. (d) Hence, they have an interest in, and offer to f, a rate of four for ten. (e) Actor f accepts this offer and accepts an offer of five for ten from g_1. (f) Hence g_2 and g_3 are excluded. (g) Now f exchanges four for ten with g_2, g_3 and g_4; hence g_1 and g_5 are excluded. Our model for Experiment 3 also predicts movement, over sessions, of system exchange rate to one most favorable to f. Notice that the mental experiment on this model indicates the movement of exchange rate can be expected to occur *twice* as fast in Experiment 3 as in Experiment 2 (because two gs get excluded each session, as opposed to one g in Experiment 2).

We can summarize the elementary theoretic predictions derived from the above analyses in a single equation for system exchange rate:

$$E_{f/g} = .5 + k(C_{g\,2}\,C_f)s.$$
(1)

Where $E_{f/g}$ is the system exchange rate, k is a constant of proportionality (to be calculated from the data gathered in Experiment 2), C_g and C_f are the centrality

---

[2] This is a very simple interpretation of iteration. This model uses actors with a simple meaning system; the actors are modeled as unable to act according to a future farther away than that immediately before them. The model uses first-order actors.

indices of f and g, respectively, and s is the session number. Notice the following about Equation (1): (a) For Experiment 1 the two centrality indices are both equal to one, hence the equation becomes $E_{f/g} = .5$. (b) That correctly represents the prediction of a constant phase of exchange at 5/10. (c) For Experiment 2, $C_g = 1$ and $C_f = 4/3$. Hence Equation (1), for Experiment 2, simplifies to

$$E_{f/g} = .5 - (1/3)ks. \tag{2}$$

(d) Equation (2) represents system exchange rate, for Experiment 2, as a function of session number s and a constant that is yet to be determined. (e) For Experiment 3, $C_g = 1$ and $C_f = 5/3$; hence we have the following:

$$E_{f/g} = .5 - (2/3)ks. \tag{3}$$

(f) Equation (3) indicates that the exchange rate in Experiment 3 will decrease two times as fast over sessions as it will in Experiment 2. (g) The value of k can be estimated from data gathered in Experiment 2; this will allow a complete representation of exchange rate as a function of session number in Experiment 3.

Predictions for the Experiments. The elementary theory, with the above models, produces the following predictions: (a) Experiment 1 will yield a constant phase of exchanges at 5 for 10. (b) Experiment 2 will produce a declining phase in which exchange rate will move from an initial value of five for ten down to a minimum rate of one for ten. The number of sessions that will be required to reach the minimum is *not* predicted. (c) Experiment 3 will produce a declining phase; the system exchange rate will move from five for ten down to one for ten. (d) The declining phase of Experiment 3 will take half as many sessions as the declining phase of Experiment 2 (i.e., the exchange rate will decline twice as fast in Experiment 3).

B. Experiment 1

Method

Subjects

The subjects for Experiment 1 were undergraduates from the University of Kansas enrolled in sociology classes. A total of 16 subjects participated in this experiment, in four groups of four persons each. No attempt was made to control for age, sex, race or ethnicity, because these variables are not in the elementary theoretic models of the experiment (see Section A above). Subjects were told that they would earn a minimum of $2 per hour for the experiment. Subjects were also told (truthfully) that the average amount earned in the experiment, per subject, would be about $5.

Apparatus

The experimental situation for Experiment 1 consisted of four chairs; there was one "central chair" and there were three "peripheral chairs." Wooden barriers placed between adjacent pairs of peripheral chairs made eye contact among subjects occupying those chairs impossible. Each subject could hear all other subjects in the group of four. Chips were used as point counters (33 were colored blue; 30 were white).

Materials

Each subject was given a three-page set of instructions containing information about the experiment. The information was as follows:

1. General information about the experiment: (a) It will be an investigation of the influence of structure on negotiation and exchange. (b) The experiment will involve (i) beginning with initial counters (valued according to rules), (ii) having opportunities to negotiate with other subjects to agree on exchange rates, and (iii) then exchanging counters to score points. (c) "Get the best score you can" by "arranging exchanges most favorable to you." (d) "Gain the highest possible income from your participation." (e) There will be a F position allowed to exchange with three G positions.
2. Six "structural rules": (a) G positions may not bargain nor exchange with one another. (b) All bargaining and exchange will be between G positions individually and the F position. (c) All bargaining and exchange is public. "Please speak up so all participants can hear you." (d) Bargaining can be started by either the F or any G. Interruptions are allowed. (e) No communication among those in G positions should occur. (f) Each G shall make his or her own decision. "Do not attempt, if you are a G, to influence the decision of other Gs either directly or indirectly."
3. Instructions told subjects that there would be "periods" in which they would occupy F or G positions. Each subject would occupy the F position once. There were two sets of rules governing the sequence of bargaining in the experiment.
4. Sequential rules A: (a) Each period consits of four bargaining sessions of negotiation and exchange. (b) Old counters will be collected at the end of each bargaining session and a score for each participant for that session will be announced. (c) Each new bargaining session will begin with the distribution of new counters. (d) "You may bargain and exchange your counters at any time in the bargaining session."
5. Sequential rules B: (a) All exchange rates are determined by negotiations. (b) No exchange can occur until both people have agreed upon a mutually understood rate. (c) "You need not exchange unless you want to do so. That is, you may hold out at any point." (d) Exchange rates must be independently determined and agreed upon in each bargaining session.
6. There was a rule concerning negotiation that was emphasized in the instructions: "Bargain first, reach an agreement if you can, and then exchange." Subjects were reminded here that the exchange most favorable to them was one in which they gave up the least to get the most. Subjects were told that each point they scored was worth 2 ¢ . They were told the average amount earned was $5 and that they could earn more if they made successful exchanges.
7. Subjects were told about the value of counters and the scoring of points. "Under certain conditions the counters that you hold at the end of a bargaining session will each be worth one point (2 ¢). Under other conditions they will be worth nothing (0 ¢). These conditions follow the scoring rules below. Note: the scoring rules for F and G positions differ."
8. Scoring rules for F: (a) "For each bargaining session you will be given 33 counters." (b) "Each of these counters which you keep is worth *one* point to you." (c) "Each counter that you obtain from exchange with a G person is worth *one* point."
9. Scoring rules for G: (a) "For each bargaining session you will be given ten counters." (b) "Each of these counters that you keep is worth *no* points." (c) "Each of the counters that you obtain from exchange with the F person is worth *one* point."

Procedure

There were four different four-person groups for this experiment. Each group was subjected to the procedures described here. Upon arriving for their experiment, the subjects waited in a room, seated in face-to-face contact, until the full set of four subjects for an experimental run had arrived. Then instructions (see above) were handed out and each subject was allowed to read the entire set of instructions. The experimenter ensured that each subject understood all instructions. When all subjects indicated that they understood the rules, the experimenter lead the group of four subjects to the experimental room. Before arriving at the experimental room, one of the four subjects was picked at random to be the first occupant of the F position.

The first F subject and the remaining three G subjects were seated in their respective chairs. The experimenter distributed "initial counters" (i.e., 33 blues to F and ten whites to each G). The first bargaining session then began; this involved negotiation and exchange according to the rules presented above. The experimenter remained in the experimental room to keep the G subjects from interacting among themselves. What determined the end of a bargaining session? The session was over when the F subject had made agreed upon exchanges with three G subjects. If a situation arose where the F and a G agreed *not* to exchange counters, this agreement was considered like an exchange for purposes of determining the end of the session. In other words, the bargaining session was over when none of the four subjects would (or could) bargain for any further exchanges.

At the end of the first bargaining session, the experimenter collected counters from each subject, tallied points earned, and made a public announcement of points earned by all subjects. The intent here was to keep the subjects interested in earning points in later bargaining sessions. Then the experimenter again distributed initial counters to all subjects. The second bargaining session began; it was conducted like the first session. After the second session, counters were collected, points were tallied and announced. Another distribution of initial counters and a third session followed. Then points were calculated and announced a third time. A fourth session was conducted.

After the announcement of points for the fourth session, the "first period" was considered to be over. The four subjects rotated counterclockwise to the adjacent chair. That is, the F subject took the first G chair, two Gs shifted and the third G became the F. When all subjects were seated once again, the experimenter distributed initial counters again. A second period of four sessions was conducted. In fact these sessions were bargaining sessions five through eight for this group in Experiment 1. After the second period, another counterclockwise rotation of subjects took place. A third period, another rotation, and a fourth period followed. Notice that participating in four periods allowed each subject a chance to occupy the F position for a single period.

There were 16 distinct bargaining sessions for a four-person group participating in Experiment 1. This experiment was considered to be complete when all four of the four-person groups were through with the procedure described above. Since each group participated in 16 sessions, it follows that Experiment 1 consisted of a total of 64 bargaining sessions.

Results

The criterion variable is exchange rate $E_{f/g}$; this was calculated for each session in Experiment 1 in which blue and white counters were exchanged. Exchange rate is number of blues exchanged divided by number of whites. Notice that the theoretic maximum is $E_{f/g} = .9$, a rate very favorable to the gs. The theoretic minimum is $E_{f/g} = .1$, a rate very favorable to the f. In one of the 64 bargaining sessions, the subjects failed to negotiate any agreed upon exchange; no exchange rate could be calculated for this session.

For the remaining 63 bargain sessions, the mean exchange rate was .694; median exchange rate and mode for exchange rate were both .700. The standard deviation of exchange rate was .069; the minimum and maximum values were .433 and .833, respectively. The observant reader will have noticed that the prediction of an exchange rate of .500 for Experiment 1 was not accurate; the observed mean was .694; the g actors in this experiment were able to obtain exchanges more favorable than the theory predicted. More will be said about this in the discussion section below.

Was the exchange rate constant over sessions? The mean exchange rates (averaged across groups and sessions) for periods one through four were .688, .713, .670 and .702, respectively. A new variable was created by averaging data across groups for each of the 16 sessions in Experiment 1. There was no relationship observed between session number (which ranged from one through 16) and "average exchange rate" per session [Pearson correlation $r(15) = .07$, $p < .79$]. In short, the data from Experiment 1 belong to a "constant phase," as predicted.

C. Experiment 2

Method

Subjects

The subjects for this experiment were drawn from the same subject pool as those for Experiment 1. A total of 20 subjects participated in Experiment 2; they were divided into four different five-person groups. Subjects were told they would earn a minimum of $2 and an average of about $5.

Apparatus

The experimental situation for Experiment 2 was identical to that for Experiment 1, with the following exceptions: There was one additional peripheral chair and an additional wooden barrier between the added chair and the three peripheral chairs from Experiment 1.

Materials

Each subject in Experiment 2 was given a set of instructions identical to the set in Experiment 1, except for the addition of "structural rule 7." The new rule stated: "The F can exchange with all but one of the Gs during each bargaining session; the F may decide, as a consequence of the bargaining, which G to exclude; this G may be different each session."

Procedure

There were four different five-person groups for Experiment 2. Each group was subjected to procedures identical to those used in Experiment 1 with the following exceptions: (a) There was an additional subject. (b) This meant the experiment required each subject to participate in five (instead of four) periods of bargaining sessions. (c) Hence there were 20 (not 16) sessions in Experiment 2. (d) The new structural rule meant that a bargaining session ended when the F subject had made three negotiated exchanges (with three of the G subjects) and had excluded one of the G subjects for the session.

Results

Four five-person groups participated in 20 bargaining sessions each, yielding exchange rate data on a total of 80 bargaining sessions. The mean, median and modal values of exchange rates were .326, .300 and .200, respectively. The standard deviation, minimum and maximum of exchange rate were .155, .100 and .800. The maximum value of .800 was observed in only one of the 80 sessions; the mode (.2) and the minimum (.1) were observed ten times and five times, respectively. The exchange rate data were averaged across the four groups to produce 20 values of "average exchange rate," one for each of the 20 sessions in Experiment 2.

There is an obvious pattern of declining average exchange rate over sessions; this pattern can be seen in Figure II. The Pearson correlation coefficient between session number and average exchange rate is r (19) $= -.92, p<.001$. There is no question that Experiment 2 produced a "declining phase" for average exchange rate. Where is the "constant phase"?

Examination of Figure II indicates that sessions 13 through 20 could be treated as a constant phase. The minimum value of average exchange rate is .212 and this occurred in session 15. The values of average exchange rate in the last period of four sessions are *higher* than the values in the period just before the last period. Sessions 17 through 20, over four groups, average to an exchange rate of .255; sessions 13 through 16 average to an exchange rate of .224. In short, the exchange rates in the last period, on the average, are 14% higher than in the period before. This effect was also observed in Experiment 3 and will be discussed further below. The remaining analysis of results will treat the declining phase of Experiment 2 as ending with session 18.

A least-square regression line was used to summarize the relation between average exchange rate and session number, for the 18 data points in the declining phase. The regression equation is

$$E_s = .473 - (.015)s, \tag{4}$$

where E_s is the predicted average exchange rate, .473 is the intercept, $-.015$ is the regression coefficient, and s is session number. Comparison of the regression sum of squares to the residual sum of squares indicates a significant relationship

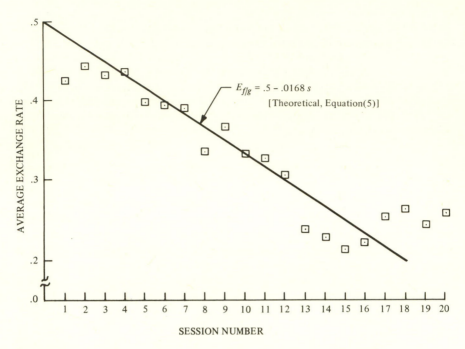

FIGURE II. Observed and theoretical exchange rate versus session number.

between average exchange rate and session [$F(1, 16) = 113.79, p < <.001$]. There is no theoretically interesting interpretation for the intercept value of .473; because of this, a second least-squares regression was calculated, this one forcing the intercept value to be .500. This intercept, of course, is the *theoretical beginning exchange rate* for the experiment. The new regression equation, for the declining phase, is

$$E_{f/g} = .500 - (.0168)s, \tag{5}$$

where $E_{f/g}$ is the predicted average exchange rate, .5 is the theoretically meaningful intercept, s is session number, and $-.0168$ is the regression coefficient estimated from the average exchange rate data for the sessions (one through 18) in the declining phase of Experiment 2. This puts us in a position to calculate the value of the constant of proportionality in Equation (1) (Section A, above). Comparison of Equation (5) and Equation (1) indicates that $-.0168 = -(1/3) k$. Solving for k yields $k = .0504$; we can round this to .050 and produce an equation to be used to predict results for Experiment 3. The equation is Equation (1) with our value of k based on the data from Experiment 2.

$$E_{f/g} = .5 + .050(C_g - C_f)s, \tag{6}$$

where $E_{f/g}$ is the system exchange rate, C_g and C_f are centrality indices for the g

and f actors respectively, and s is session number. Equation (6) will be used to analyze the data from Experiment 3 below.

D. Experiment 3

Method

Subjects

The subjects for this experiment were drawn from the same subject pool as were subjects for Experiments 1 and 2. A total of 24 subjects participated in this experiment; they formed four six-person groups. Subjects were told they would earn a minimum of $2 and an average of $5.

Apparatus

The experimental situation for this experiment was like that for Experiments 1 and 2, except that there were five "peripheral chairs."

Materials

Each subject was given a set of instructions like the instructions of Experiment 2; the only difference was a rule that the F exclude *two* of the G subjects from exchange in each bargaining session.

Procedure

The procedure for Experiment 3 was similar to that of Experiment 2, with the modification of adding a sixth period of four bargaining sessions. The subjects in each six-person group participated in 24 individual sessions and this allowed each subject to occupy the F position for four sessions.

Results

There were 96 bargaining sessions in Experiment 3. Mean, median and modal values of exchange rate were .216, .2 and .1, respectively. The standard deviation, minimum and maximum of exchange rates were .116, .1 and .633, respectively. For each session (one through 24) an average (across four groups) exchange rate was calculated. These values are plotted against session number in Figure III. Examination of Figure III shows a declining phase (sessions one through nine, inclusive) and a phase of much slower decline in average exchange rate (sessions ten through 20, inclusive). As in Experiment 2, the final period has higher average exchange rates than the period before it (sessions 17 through 20 average .129, whereas sessions 21 through 24 average .175).

There are differences between exchange rates in the declining phase and rates in the constant phase. The constant phase has less variation and is less favorable to the peripheral subjects. (a) For the declining phase, mean exchange rate is .288, standard deviation is .077, and there is a correlation between session

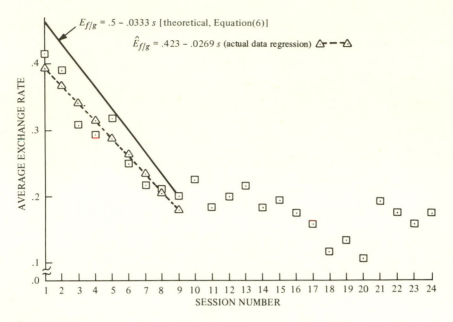

FIGURE III. Exchange rate versus session number, Experiment 3.

number and average exchange rate, $r(8) = -.96, p < .001$. (b) For the constant phase, mean of average exchange rate is .173, mode is .1, standard deviation is .034, and there is no significant relation between session number and average exchange rate, $r(14) = -.54, p > .01$.

Equation (6), presented in Section C above, can be used to calculate elementary theoretical values for average exchange rate in sessions one through nine of Experiment 3. Given $C_g = 1$ and $C_f = 5/3$, we have

$$E_{f/g} = .5 - .0333s, \tag{7}$$

which allows us to calculate average exchange rate $E_{f/g}$ from session number s. Table 1 presents values of observed average exchange rate and theoretical values, from Equation (7), for sessions one through nine of Experiment 3, the declining phase. There is a systematic error: the observed value is less than the theoretical for sessions one through eight. The end of the declining phase, session nine with rate .2, however, is correctly predicted with Equation (7).

A least-square regression line was used to summarize the relation between average exchange rate and session number for sessions one through nine (i.e., the declining phase). The calculated equation appears in Figure III. Comparison of the regression sum of squares to the residual sum of squares indicates a significant relationship between average exchange rate and session number, $F(1, 7) = 77.09, p < .0001$.

TABLE 1. Observed, Theoretical and Residual Average Exchange Rate, Declining Phase, Experiment 3.

Session Number	Average Exchange Rate Values		
	Observed	Theoretical[a]	Residual[b]
1	.4167	.4667	.0500
2	.3833	.4333	.0500
3	.3084	.4000	.0916
4	.2916	.3667	.0750
5	.3167	.3333	.0166
6	.2500	.3000	.0500
7	.2167	.2667	.0500
8	.2084	.2333	.0250
9	.2000	.2000	.0000

[a] Theoretical values are calculated from Equation (7).

[b] Residual = theoretical - observed.

E. Discussion

There are two major points which deserve emphasis in this discussion. (a) First, the mean exchange rates during constant phase for Experiment 1 and for Experiment 3 are .694 and .173, respectively. The comparison between modal exchange rates is more dramatic: .700 vs .100 for Experiment 1 and Experiment 3, respectively. In short the exchanges during the constant phase of Experiment 1 are at least *four times* as favorable for the *G* subjects than are the exchanges during the constant phase of Experiment 3. (b) Second, Equation (6) (see Section C above) was created with the elementary theory and with data from Experiment 2. This equation accurately predicted the slope and end point (i.e., final session) of the declining phase of Experiment 3.

All theoretic predictions (see Section A above) concerning declining phases were borne out by experimental results. (a) There is *no* declining phase in Experiment 1. (b) Experiment 2 has a declining phase. (c) Experiment 3 has a declining phase with slope twice that of the declining phase in Experiment 2.

The predictions concerning average exchange rate values for the constant phases were not as accurate as those concerning declining phases. The inaccuracies are in directions which can be interpreted using the additional elementary theory models below. There are at least three possible models that could account for the observed constant phase exchanges occurring at rates more favorable to the *g* actors than predicted: (a) negative symbolics from the *g*s, (b) collusion among the *g*s, and (c) altered costs of confrontation. We shall discuss these in order.

1. Negative symbolics such as "This game is not fair; I deserve a better exchange rate" were perceived by the experimenter to be emanating from *g* points in all three experimental situations. The experimenter's impressions were that, in Experiment 1, subjects in *g* positions frequently employed negative symbolics; these were observed in each bargaining session. The experimenter believes negative symbolics were far less frequent in Experiments 2 and 3. Notice that negotiated exchanges in these latter experiments were less "fair," where fair means favorable to subjects in *g* positions. Figure IV presents a model of a system with one *f* and three *g* actors; imagine that each actor has one "negative symbolic resource." The potential network shown in Figure IV indicates that the value of reception of any negative symbolic is negative. Notice that, if all actors transmit negative symbolics, the *f* actor receives three negatives but only transmits one negative. If negative symbolics were present as modeled, they could have raised the costs of confrontation for the *f* point three times as much as for the *g* points as a group. The consequent shift of the actors' resistance curves (see Chapter 7) would have altered the exchange rate upward (i.e., in a direction consistent with observed exchange rates in Experiment 1).

   The experimenter had the impression that groups in Experiment 1 took longer to bargain than did the groups in the two other experiments. The additional time seemed to be in part due to transmission of negative symbolics being more frequent in Experiment 1.

   The negative symbolics possible in Experiment 1 are of theoretic interest; there may be some "justice" process operating. Points 2 and 3 below are not as interesting theoretically and are more related to experimental design issues.

2. Although collusion among the *g* actors was a violation of the rules for the experiments, the experimenter perceived subjects in *g* positions, in Experi-

FIGURE IV. *Negative symbolics converge on f.* A typical possible network of negative symbolic sanction flow. Notice that each actor has only one negative symbolic sanction as an initial resource. Three negatives can converge on *f* who can send in return only one negative (in this figure to the point g_2) to the set of *g* points.

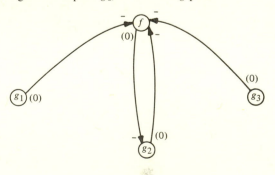

ments 2 and 3, communicating among themselves. These communications seemed to indicate a desire to collude while pretending to be communicating solely with the subject in the f position. The g actors have an interest in colluding to attain higher preference states through better exchange rates. Consider the following mental experiment for the model of Experiment 2. There are four g actors and only three will be allowed to exchange; if they compete for the chance to exchange, they will drive the rate down to one for ten as was shown above (see Section A). If, on the other hand, each of the gs agrees to voluntarily sit out one session of four, and if they all agree to rotate which actor sits out, they create a zero-exclusion situation similar to the one in Experiment 1.

If collusion is maximally successful, each g actor could receive as many as seven points a session; this would produce a total of 21 points for the series of four sessions (three sessions at seven points and one session at no points). If collusion is minimally successful, each g actor would receive two points each session for a total of six points. Either net preference alteration is better than the preference alteration, three, resulting from competition with other gs. Collusion on the part of the gs is a reasonable interpretation of the failure of average exchange rate to reach the theoretic minimum during the constant phases in Experiments 2 and 3.

3. Let us shift focus to costs of confrontation for the experiment taken as a whole. The procedure of rotating subjects through G and F positions was intended to minimize effects on exchange rate due to personality differences in bargaining. An artifact of this procedure was the possibility that a subject in a g position late in the experiment would lose interest in further bargaining and exchange. Imagine a g actor who already earned almost all points possible during earlier sessions. This subject already occupied the f position (and therefore benefitted from favorable exchanges). The reader will notice that this g subject will fail to gain points amounting to about ½% of current point total by reaching a confrontation now, rejecting a rate of only one for ten. This reduction in cost of confrontation, for gs late in the experiment, is an interpretation of the observed rises in average exchange rate for the final period of Experiment 2 and for the final period of Experiment 3.

The above interpretations of observed deviations from predicted exchange rates are not explanations. These features could be modeled, experiments could be run, and then results could be compared with theoretical predictions based on the models. For example, it would be possible to study collusion experimentally by running two experiments: (a) one allowing communications among gs and (b) one blocking completely any communication among them. Resulting exchange rates in the two experiments could then be compared to study collusion.

The purpose of laboratory experiments based on elementary theory models is to investigate the *scope* of the theory. The experimenter constructs instructions for the subjects, which are intended to generate preferences and beliefs in the subjects like those of the theoretic actors in the model to be investigated. The experimenter also constructs rules governing interaction, which make experimental structures like the structures of the model. Strong and weak structures were discussed above (see Chapter 7). The three experiments reported in this chapter are based on models of strong structures (Experiments 2 and 3) and of a weak structure (Experiment 1). We have investigated other types of systems in preliminary laboratory investigations. Elementary theory models have predicted outcomes of the following kinds of experimental structures: (a) centralized coercive, (b) collusion, (c) exchange systems (similar to those of this chapter) with counters (valued by f and g) initially given to g actors, instead of to f, and with counters (valued only by g) initially given to the f, and (d) hierarchical systems. In all cases theoretical predictions have been at least as accurate as those reported in this chapter. To date we have done no experiments with the direct intention of investigating normative systems (see Chapters 3 through 6). We have run no experiments combining models for two or more systems (e.g., a state, two "capitalists" and a set of "unemployed workers").

Others have argued that extremely high levels of variance accounted for are necessary to have a scientific sociology (Hamblin, Jacobsen and Miller, 1973: 6, 7). The elementary theory accounts for at least 90% of the variance in exchange rate data reported here. The theory offers suggestions for improvements in experimental technique that will allow even more accurate predictions in further experimental work.

The elementary theory is capable of generating models for a variety of social systems. This offers the experimenter a wide range of contrasting phenomena for investigation.

Reference

Hamblin, Robert L., R. Brooke Jacobsen and Jerry L.L. Miller
    1973   *A Mathematical Theory of Social Change.* New York: John Wiley and Sons.

12

Bo Anderson
Nanette J. Davis

This paper was first presented at the Pacific Sociological Society Meetings in Spokane, Washington, April 1978. A revised version was presented at the second annual networks conference, University of Kansas, June 1978. We want to thank Professors Fritz Heider, David Willer and Michael Loukinen for helpful comments.

ON BOUNDARY CROSSING
IN SOCIAL NETWORKS
On Some Unfinished Business for Exchange Theorists

A. Introduction

In his book *Philosophical Investigations* Ludwig Wittgenstein comments on the problematic nature of semiotic interpretation:

> And if there were, not a single sign-post, but a chain of adjacent ones or of chalk marks on the ground—is there only *one* way of interpreting them?

> [Und wenn statt eines Wegweisers eine geschlossene Kette von wegweisern stünden, oder Kreidestreiche auf dem Boden liefen,—gibt es für sie nur *eine* Deutung?]

What Wittgenstein implies in his reference to a chain of signs and chalk marks is that when dealing with language and language-carried transactions, the assumption that there is *one* stable meaning that is immediately and obviously given to participants is often erroneous. Our particular concern is with the phenomenon of *boundary crossing,* that is, movements from one context to another, when beliefs, values, rules, that is, the very grounds on which persons implicitly operate, begin to slide.

There are two kinds of boundary crossings: The first is the nonproblematic rule-guided crossings. Such crossings are guided by common assumptions, rules, and taken-for-granteds. Rules for bargaining, hierarchy and domination relations prevail. The customer–salesperson and professor–student exchanges are examples of this class of boundary crossings.

The second type of crossing is problematic, because it lacks clear-cut rules and a shared meaning system, and hence requires persons to construct rules and meanings in the course of their interactions. Rule work involves the development of some new language, as when social movement organizers must traverse class, caste, gender and other boundaries to seek social, ideological and material support.

The construction of reality in such situations is rarely very smooth. The interaction may rather be riddled with paradoxes, contradictions, misunderstandings and violations of taken-for-granteds. Although the actors may think that misunderstandings are matters of the differing uses of words, the distortion of communication, in fact, often occurs below the conscious levels in the minds of the speakers. Miscomprehensions reside in the failures of actors to understand those contexts within which words, gestures, facial expressions, social props and other signs make sense. An instance of this, observed by one of the authors, was an exchange between a police captain and a feminist in the late 1960s. After interminable wrangling, the captain stressing why women could not be admitted to the police ranks on an equal footing, and the feminist countering his logic with an alternative logic of equality, equal opportunity and other rationalistic stratagems, the police officer uttered his bottom-line statement: "But there are height and weight restrictions, and women just can't make those." The feminist countered, "So—now we know where to change the law—simply eliminate the physical restrictions." (This was, in fact, accomplished in subsequent legislation.) The captain regarded his statement as unchallengeable, taken-for-granted, the starting point of *any* rational argument about women's place in the police. When it was challenged, he found himself at loose ends, perceiving his opponent's argument as unrealistic and irrational. Often, indeed, boundaries consist largely of such unexamined but strongly held beliefs and conceptions of reality.

In this chapter, we shall examine boundary-crossing processes in situations that, although they are ubiquitously encountered in fieldwork and daily living, are rarely understood by sociological theorists. The *network* is a useful conceptual model when we deal with processes between systems. There are often actual or potential network links between persons in different organizations, communities, segments of communities, ethnic groups, social movements and other collectivities. These collectivities are bounded and boundary-maintaining, and transactions *across* boundaries present actors with the problems that provide the topic for this paper. Boundaries have not often been dealt with in contemporary social network theory. One major reason for this neglect is the prevalence of the graph-theoretic and matrix formalisms. Graph theory, although a topology, ignores the boundary concept: There either is or is not a path by which point i can be reached from point j; no provision is made for paths with barriers. And using matrix algebra, we are able to study whether two persons in a network are linked, by successively computing the powers of the matrix. But matrix multiplication recognizes no barriers or boundaries. Useful as the formal methods are, they clearly blind us to important sociological issues. Sociologists who do fieldwork, often unencumbered by formal theory blinders, are acutely aware of the existence of network boundaries and the barriers to communication across boundaries. A few examples suggest how common boundary obstacles are: the entrance of police from the ethnically dominant majority into minority communities, interethnic political rivalries, working-class utilization of the law and negotiating the services of the medical market by the poor, the young and minority women. Persons who run for political office often find that some segment of the community is closed to them unless they find a sponsor. The role of the sponsor is to help the candidate publicly across a boundary by interpreting him or her to the group.

We shall use the term "code" to indicate that we want to enrich the study of social exchange and exchange networks with ideas from structuralism, an orienting perspective that draws on semiotics, the general study of signs and their meanings. [See Eco (1979) for useful overviews.] Codes are the context-specific rules that are used for forming and interpreting speech and other meaning-carrying discourses. Very generally, we shall argue that the problems of crossing boundaries in networks give rise to and presuppose codes of a kind that are not necessary for transactions within local regions of networks. We shall draw upon and briefly comment on writings of Basil Bernstein (1974) and Mary Douglas (1976) since they, in particular, have attempted to think clearly about different kinds of codes. Jürgen Habermas's (1976) ideas about universal pragmatics and communicative competence are also of interest for the present discussion.

Crossing a boundary often involves actors in the creation of new boundaries as well as in the destruction of old ones. Each process of creating, crossing and destroying boundaries is accelerated during periods of social change. Rapidly changing epochs give birth to a variety of sects and movements that, at least in the early enthusiastic phase, work to eliminate old boundaries by exposing the taken-for-granted and by exhorting followers to turn to new values from old meaningless routines. In time, boundary work replaces value inventiveness as a sect becomes routinized, legitimized or coopted.

B. Boundaries and Codes

We shall assume that people cross boundaries or barriers not to chitchat but in order to try to accomplish somewhat concerted actions. The participants have stakes in one anothers' discourses, and must, hence, pay close attention to the verbal and cognitive codes used by the others. "Exchange," "arrangement," "agreements," "deal," "treaty" are some of the names used for the more or less stable outcomes of cross-boundary actions. The terms refer to *normative* or rule-directed arrangements; exchanges are *equitable* or *inequitable* deals, agreements more or less *acceptable,* and treaties more or less *binding.* Hence, one crucial aspect of cross-boundary social action must be *rule-work.* By this term we refer to the attempts by people in groups to clarify to themselves and others which norms or rules apply to the situation at hand and how, concretely, these norms are to be interpreted. For instance, before an agreement can be reached about what constitutes fair or just exchange in a particular situation, the relevant social properties of the situation have to be agreed upon or at least formulated in ways acceptable to the parties. The norms acquire concrete "operational" meanings; they are applied to a satisfactorily formulated reality. Agreeing and formulating are verbal activities and, hence, reflect and presuppose codes.

For norms to become activated or brought to bear in a situation, a good deal of norm-work may be necessary. Norms and rules appear to be brought into situations in highly schematic forms—the schemes require a good deal of filling in before they can be applied to the given concrete problems. Some must be agreed upon or at least formulated in ways acceptable to the parties.

Communications in *local* neighborhoods or regions in networks have some notable, interdependent properties that provide convenient starting points for our argument. *First,* they take place against backgrounds of taken-for-granted, assumed-to-be-shared meanings, relevancies, experiences and emotions, such as hopes, fears and identifications. Shared perspectives, orientations and actions can be accomplished with little speech, often in the nature of stock phrases, grunts, standard gestures,—for example, "How're ya doing, buddy?", "Screw it, a bummer of a day, uh?", "Same here." A variety of gestures, pointings, frownings, noddings or even staying silent supplements speech acts. *Second,* local system communications need not attempt to be context-free. Normally, when we say, "I'm going downtown," it is assumed that we mean, for instance, downtown East Lansing or downtown Portland, as the case may be, depending on where we are when we say it. *Third,* participants in local systems usually need not discourse *about* their communications, or formulate in words what they are doing. It is, for instance, very hard to get members of local communities to be specific about, to formulate "in so many words," the rules they practice in the exchange of gifts, help, visits and so forth. Speaking about these matters may even be seen as strange and inappropriate. In a Danish-American community known for strong localism that was studied by Knud Hansen reported in part in Chapter 4, the plan to ask informants to keep track of daily activity schedules (time-budgets) had to be abandoned—the people found it utterly impossible to translate their overt behavioral activities to a written code.

It is the first two properties that Bernstein primarily had in mind when he formulated the notion of *restricted/elaborated* code (Bernstein, 1974). The three properties are closely related: Participants are able to take a great deal for granted because they share a context and they do not need to discourse about their speech—for example, explain it to one another—because they share a taken-for-granted reality, or at least assume they do. In local systems, people are usually able "just to do," and to speak, often elliptically, counting on being understood and responded to (receiving nods, tokens of agreements, expected actions and reactions) in set ways.

When boundaries in networks are crossed, situations arise in which *none* of the above conditions may hold. In treaties and contracts, an effort is made to put everything in black and white—that is, to leave as little taken for granted as possible and to spell out the terms as explicitly as possible. In negotiations across boundaries, there is a good deal of formulating of accomplishments, intentions, expectations and anticipated reactions. Negotiators need to discourse upon their discourses—explain, reformulate, cancel, amend, qualify, past statements. By contrast, it is interesting to note that English does not seem to have any convenient label for regularly occurring, parallel arrangements in *local* systems. A man and a woman who have recently started to date are not likely to be said to negotiate their roles; *if* they do, we consider the situation semiotically *marked*—we say for instance, that "he is setting her up" or that "she is making trouble for him." And, members of traditional local systems, for instance those studied by Loukinen and Hansen, resist having their dealings called "exchange" and often deny that any accounts are kept of who owes whom what.

Full-fledged negotiations, deals, bargains and treaties, presuppose elaborate codes in Bernstein's sense. To say *this*, however, is *not* to answer our problem, for we want to know what happens when boundary crossings in networks first occur; the above terms presumably get used in their full senses when boundary crossings have become routine, institutionalized and hence, to some extent, unproblematical.

How then are boundaries *first* crossed? One common situation is that socially *marked* status or power-differences exist between the persons or groups on one side of the boundary and those on the other. One group may, for instance, be seen by itself or by both parties as experts. Or one group may have higher traditional status than the other—be male and not female, professionals and not laypersons, or Mestizo and not Indian in Mexico. In such cases, the more powerful group or the group with higher status will assume that *its* discourse should naturally dominate in the dealings between the groups. It is up to the second group to learn and to accept the first group's taken-for-granteds, to learn to understand *its* shorthand phrases and to formulate the situations that come up in the categories in *its* terminology. In the long run, the powerless or lower-status group may resent the hegemony and force a change if its consciousness has been raised, but we are speaking here about the arrangements that are likely to prevail initially. If the transactions can be made to occur on the physical premises of the powerful or higher-status group, the dominance of its code is most easily assured.

An example to help clarify the point: Control over agenda-setting is one familiar way in which the dominance of a code is promoted. One of the authors observed a group of parents, representing local elementary and other school district associations in a Midwestern community, participate in a "study" designed to find "answers" to various "problems" pertaining to school district boundaries, the use of school facilities and overcrowding in local schools. The school administration controlled the "study" by predetermining in detail both the agenda and the time-schedule. Parents who desired to include questions that were not on the agenda and who asked for information not conveniently available were literally and eloquently hectored by the top school administrator. A majority of the parent representatives loyally made sure that the school administration's points of view dominated the "study" by defining dissenters as "uncooperative." The categories and points of view of the educational "experts" were seen simply as the objective description of the situation at hand and as natural tools for formulating the social reality. The most interesting feature of this process was how *natural* it seemed to most of the participants. *Agenda control was not grasped but freely given.*

When a group cannot easily use dominance tactics to ensure that its own codes prevail, then it is faced with the difficult tasks of interpreting and translating the messages that come from the other side of the boundary and formulating its own messages in ways that are interpretable to the other group. This may force the group to reflect on and make explicit its taken-for-granted concepts, rules and speech. Some members of the group may become *code-brokers,* developing a new more elaborated code that enables them to speak about and relate the taken-for-granteds of *both* groups. Persons with complex role-sets could be expected to develop elaborated codes.

However, it is possible to imagine and to find empirically social systems where actors must cope with a good deal of role-set complexity and at the same time take much for granted, being able to communicate in shorthand phrases. A submarine at sea for months at a time or a small but highly differentiated and isolated community—for instance, an Antarctic research station—may be thought of as examples. And, is it not common that a person with a complex role-set communicates *separately* in *different* restricted codes with each member of the role-set? Translations may not be necessary and the elaborated code does not develop. It is when actors with different taken-for-granteds and codes are brought together simultaneously into the same situation in order to accomplish an unfamiliar but socially relevant task jointly that we should expect a good deal of code-elaboration to occur.

C. Boundaries and Depth-Structures

In two important papers, Jürgen Habermas (1976, 1979) has developed two notions that further this discussion: *communicative competence* and *systematically distorted communication.*

Habermas has drawn the "model" concept of undistorted communication from psychoanalysis. If we understand him right, he is focusing on the one case he regards as a somewhat unmuddled model of the phenomenon he wants to deal with. He wants to get a "beachhead" explication that can later be expanded and generalized. The communicative material dealt with in psychoanalysis—dream material, for example—does not signify its surface meanings. But the depth-structure meaning is not found through asking for clarifications, by encouraging the person being analyzed to try to restate, formulate, eludicate, amend, explicate or the like. These are, of course, practices that often work to clarify *nondistorted* communication. But, in psychoanalysis, the detailed scrutiny of the transference process *and* the theory of socialization enable the analyst to *re*construct the message behind the *dis*torted communication. Psychoanalysis is a *radical* root-seeking rather than a *routine* hermeneutic. We want to suggest that very often transactions across community or organizational boundaries involve instances of systematically distorted, misunderstood or mystifying communications. To analyze such communication we need models that demonstrate the *connections* between the *surface* meanings of messages sent and a *depth-structure* of intentions, beliefs, fears, avoidances, deflections and treacheries.

Habermas uses Chomskyan linguistics as a metaphor for his hermeneutic. But the code-elaborations, code-stiflings and code-destructurings that can be observed when people cross boundaries cannot, unfortunately, be cast simply as Chomskyan transformations.

A few illustrations are in order. The first illustration is drawn from the fieldwork of Michael Loukinen. Loukinen and his wife were visited by an elderly couple in a Finnish–American community. Visiting is an important social activity in the community and has to be done according to a well-specified although largely implicit set of rules. One of the rules says that coffee and cake are served toward the end of the visit and that visitors are expected to leave shortly after having taken coffee. The field-worker couple led their visitors to a nicely set table when they arrived for the visit without going through the preliminaries of couple and separate-sex interactions. The husband of the visiting couple became visibly disturbed, interpreting the serving of coffee as a sign that an early termination of the visit was requested. The wife explained to him, in Finnish, that no such message was intended by the young couple, and that the latter had merely misunderstood the subtleties of local customs. The older man stayed but remained somewhat perturbed for the remainder of the visit.

The urban couple, in attempting to cross the boundary between their own world and that of the rural Finnish–Americans, had unintentionally violated a rule of conduct. The visiting man was unable to perceive the friendly intentions of the urban couple; his was a literal interpretation of the early invitation to have coffee in terms of his own culture. His wife had a less restricted code and was able to perceive and translate the meaning of the displayed table setting. Her husband accepted the explanation, but he remained disturbed by the perceived incongruities of the situation. Semiotic proprieties and errors in boundary crossings are not merely cognitive matters that one can be flexible about, but often involve deeply held feelings about right and wrong.

The study of the abortion controversy provides many examples of distorted communication. Right-to-life and other antiabortion groups present a distorted message: On the one hand, the doctrine articulates religion, family, pro-life and a politically conservative order. On the other, it offers a tough-minded public relations movement: a well-organized, well-funded organization willing to engage in radical tactics to achieve goals—fire-bombing abortion clinics, chaining members to surgical beds in abortion wards and so on. The ostensible purpose is to revoke the law, thus ridding civilization of the "terror of abortion." Semiotics provides a more fundamental tool for exploration. It reveals a depth structure of resistance and resentment, opposed to emancipatory trends of dehierarchization of sex roles and women's expression of personal choice. The absolutist position, in its manifest statement a preoccupation with the status of the unborn, masks the underlying antisex message and the distrust of human autonomy and modernism. The pervasive fears and resentments that emerge revolve around the current loosening of the age-old social controls over women's sexuality and reproduction. At a basic level, the right-to-lifers reject women's right to determine the number of children they will bear. There is a double irony here. To reverse the permissive law, "pro-life" groups must use the law, a secular instrument, to enact a religious doctrine of life. The related traditional relationships of submission/ domination between women and men, in an explosively sexualized culture, leaves women psychically vulnerable and sexually unprepared, a situation very likely to result in unwanted pregnancies.

The distortions of communication in the abortion controversy are more fundamental that those that occurred in the example involving the rural and urban couples. In the latter case the wife of the older man acted as a code-broker and was able to explain the matter, although some emotion remained. But would a code-broker be able to bring proabortion feminists and right-to-lifers into the same discourse? The answer is, very likely, no. Generally speaking, when codes for speaking and interpretation are tied to absolutist polarities like good and evil, right and wrong, holiness and sin, we should expect the *cognitive* activities of code-brokers to be of limited usefulness. Habermas's utopia of social problem solving through the construction of situations in which the social and semantic barriers to communication—status differences, differences in linguistic competence—have been removed may be realizable only in those cases where these polarities are not activated.

D. Boundaries and Social Movements

Social movements provide some of the most important means by which the boundaries in social systems are rearranged. *First,* movements often profoundly affect the linguistic and behavioral codes so that boundaries become easier to cross than before. Feminism, for instance, has helped make it unacceptable in many contexts to publicly condescend to professional women by defining them as "girls" who by and large belong in the typing pool, even when they have professional credentials. Much unease accompanies such code changes, and new and subtler boundary defenses may be tried, but each woman who crosses into the previously all-male regions helps make the code-changes permanent by challenging the residues of the old code.

Second, by challenging exclusionary codes in one area a social movement may help weaken similar codes in other areas. There are multiplier effects associated with social movements. The civil rights movement concentrated on breaking down those codes that exclude blacks, but also indirectly helped weaken sexist codes. And once the volatile domain of exclusionary sex codes was challenged it has become more difficult to exclude homosexuals.

Third, social movements also erect new boundaries or strengthen old ones. Separatist groups may insist on exclusion of others because they fear cooptation or because code-reconstruction takes so much energy that the movement's vision cannot be allowed to be diluted. It is easy to see, for instance, how a group of blacks or women, concerned with radically reconstructing their collective self-identities, may become exclusionary in order to avoid dissipating the group's energies in pluralistic group politics.

There are several good examples in the literature of how social movements shape networks. One of the best comes from the work of Clifford Geertz on community schisms in Indonesia (Geertz, 1957).

Javanese villages often contain several religious factions. In a village studied by Geertz there were Moslems as well as persons who practiced cults based on indigenous Malayan beliefs and practices. Traditionally, religious differences have been played down in the interest of cooperation, and many Moslems have participated in indigenous cults like the *slamentan,* a ceremony that gives ritual expression to neighborhood solidarity (Geertz, 1960, Chapter 1). The village headman has traditionally officiated at funerals, regardless of the religious beliefs of the deceased. There has developed in Java, however, a movement advocating purification of the Islamic faith in the country, a return to orthodoxy, and a purge of nonislamic elements from the beliefs and practices of the Moslems. At the same time there developed a national political force, the Permai, which is a synthesis of Marxism and indigenous Javanese beliefs. In the village Geertz studied a young boy died. The funeral ceremony should have called for manifestations of neighborhood cohesion, but instead a bitter argument grew up regarding how the Moslem headman was to prepare the boy, from a Permai family, for burial. Was he to use some Moslem prayers? If he did, would these be interpreted as specifically Moslem or as just an element of Javanese village syncretism, which happened to be of Moslem origin?

Villagers became extremely disturbed. For one thing, it is believed that an unburied body attracts evil spirits and the danger increases the longer it is left lying before burial. The conflictive contrast (Moslem versus Permai) activated in a situation where more appropriately another solidary set (members of the kin group of the deceased, the neighborhood, fellow villages, the outside world) should have been activated. Solidarity of fellow villagers with the bereaved family was called for, but the latent conflict between two political factions was activated as a result of this "error" in the social construction of the situation.

Geertz suggested that the ideological polarization in Java between Islamic and other political forces was ultimately responsible for the events he described. Village life had traditionally been based on tacit agreements to play down religious cleavages; when the codes from *nationwide* politics were transferred to the *local* scene, confusion and culturally extreme and inappropriate behavior resulted.

From Geertz's case we may extrapolate three lines of thinking that are relevant to the development of exchange theory: (1) The semiotics of the face-to-face social system may be determined by a macrostructure, outside of the control of the local actors. The macropolitical divisions made it impossible for the headman to play his traditional mediating role. We learn from Geertz's analysis that the theoretical modeling of meaning systems must take account of societal *macroprocesses*. The interacting Self and Other in the scheme of G. H. Mead are sometimes unable to build stable meanings, in spite of honest desires and intentions. The production and maintenance of meanings have too long been treated as a topic for social psychology. If the present discussion is correct, the processes involve the larger social structure. (2) It is through the enthusiasm or *commitment* that the production of meaning systems presupposes and generates that social movements both break down and erect social boundaries. Abandoning familiar codes is difficult and learning new ones requires social support. The channeling of *personal* motivations—*resentment*, sexual boredom, job-related frustrations, curbed ambitions and so on, into the interpersonal commitments to a social movement provides much of the energy required to challenge codes. To illustrate briefly from our own work, women can be seen to break out of traditional sex-role boundaries to join feminist health collectives. The resulting *commitment organization* ends up being exclusionary and boundary maintaining. Liberation movements end up being construction movements. This *may* not be the full story, however. When one ponders Geertz's Javanese case and the experiences of social movements and commitment organizations in the United States, one suspects that the movement experiences give rise to groups of members and exmembers who have "seen it all," and who as a result now possess a language of boundary transcendence. (3) The most interesting implication of Geertz's Javanese case-study is that the symbolic values of the transmission and reception of some sanctions may be related to system boundaries. The different segments in the community did not share a common evaluation of the headman's burial ritual. In fact, it may be that fuss and disagreeements about the values of the transmission and reception values of symbolic sanctions are the best indication we have that a system boundary is in view.

References

Bernstein, Basil
  1974   *Class, Codes and Control*. New York: Schocken Books.

Douglas, Mary
  1976   *Implicit Meanings*. London: Routledge and Kegan Paul.

Eco, Umberto
  1979   *A Theory of Semiotics*. Bloomington and London: Indiana University Press.

Geertz, Clifford
  1957   Ritual and social change: A Javanese example, *American Anthropologist* 59.
  1960   *The Religion of Java.*, Glencoe, IL: The Free Press.

Habermas, Jürgen
  1976   Systematically distorted communication, in Paul Connerton (ed.), *Critical
          Sociology*. Harmondsworth, Middlesex, England: Penguin Books.
  1979   What is universal pragamtics? in Jürgen Habermas (ed.), *Communication
          and the Evolution of Society*. Boston: Beacon Press.

Lévi-Strauss, Claude
  1949   *Les Structures Elémentaires de la Parenté*. Paris: Presses Universitaires de
          France.

Mauss, Marcel
  1967   *The Gift*. New York: W.W. Norton.

13

David Willer
Bo Anderson

OUTLOOKS AND PROSPECTS

The works included in this volume have been based on a conception of science that is new to the social sciences. Central to that conception is the idea of a modeling procedure and its place in the development and use of theory. As has been seen, a modeling procedure is an interpreted geometry that is used to represent the abstract objects and events of the theory. Certain principles and laws were formulated that, when applied to those representations, generated dynamic interaction models. Beginning with simple models, procedures were introduced to generate increasingly complex ones. Because the elementary theory has this methodological form, it has been possible to construct a wide variety of models and to interpret particular empirical cases in light of those constructions.

There is nothing fundamentally new about this conception of theory, for it has been proven (and is today being proven) in use in exact sciences as well as diverse engineering fields. Until now, there has been no other attempt to develop a theory for the social sciences that fully exploits the procedures of modeling. But in the absence of modeling procedures, social theories must remain limited in scope.

If either interpretations or explanations are to be offered by a social theory, it must (in principle) have broad scope of application in at least the following sense. It must be possible to model from the point of view of the theory not just one kind of social structure and just one kind of social actor, but, instead, a variety of structures and actors the characteristics of which can vary independently from one another. Such a theory must contain a procedure for analysis so that complex structures can be broken into their component parts and must avoid distortions of the parts when separated from the whole. These procedures must be reversible such that the parts can be synthetically reassembled into a complex whole—a process in which the properties of any part can be transformed by that synthesis. This volume has provided an opportunity to examine some of these theoretic procedures as they are carried out with the elementary theory.

If interpretations and explanations are to be offered by a social theory, that theory must act as a guide for an integrated research program. Its integration rests upon the systematic investigation of the *scope* of the theory and cannot be limited to one or another research procedure. In this volume ethnographic, institutional and experimental research have been reported. The integration of the results of that research has rested not upon similarity of procedures or research outcomes, but upon the integrative capacity of the elementary theory through the models drawn from it. The studies reported here are few in number. There is a need to investigate further the variants of the systems discussed in this volume and to draw from the theory new models for systems yet to be considered. As research proceeds, it is hoped that an integration of historical, ethnographic, institutional and experimental research will emerge.

The isolation of these research methods from one another has been a consequence of pervasive empiricist biases in the social sciences, and (more recently) of the methodological limits of social theories. Consider the problem of integration of experimental and historical research. Experimental systems are constructed to be as simple as possible. The need for this simplicity rests not only upon our limited powers of control and observation, but also upon the extreme difficulties that are faced by the theorist as the complexity of any formally drawn model increases beyond a certain point. But theories are by no means limited in their use to formal applications. More complex models can be imagined whose derivation would entail massive calculative complexities. Yet these models can be thought through to reasoned conclusions. Thus the elementary theory can be applied for interpretation of historical cases. Moreover, the less formal application of the theory to historical cases can gain rigor from more formal work, for the component parts of these complex models can be simpler systems whose initial conditions, dynamics and final conditions have been investigated under controlled laboratory conditions; thus the prospect of integration of these hitherto isolated research methods.

But the formulation of complex theoretic models need not be limited to paper-and-pencil techniques. It is possible to conceive of a computer modeler that would be a tool for the theorist/researcher. Such a modeler could be used to construct a variety of structure and actor types and to combine them into complex systems of interaction wherein that construction proceeded from no more than the specification of the appropriate initial conditions by the theorist/researcher. With the modeler successive runs of a variety of systems could be compared to one another and compared to empirical cases, thereby extending the formal application of the theory to systems which up to that point had been dealt with less formally.

But the purpose of any scientific theory is not to introduce complexities but to simplify our understandings of the world. Perhaps the elementary theory can make a contribution to a simplification of understanding at least in the following sense. Consider normatively controlled social exchange systems, state controlled market systems, centralized coercive systems and dyadic exchange systems. Each of these systems has its typical structure and (under certain actor conditions) its typical dynamics. Thus models for these and other systems can be used to *identify* ongoing empirical cases. That identification is the beginning point of an understanding of the cases in question. Considerable variation of form and content is possible for each system type. Yet, each system has its typical "inputs" and "outputs" and certain minimal conditions for its reproduction. Thus, systems can be linked together in thought and the reproduction of each investigated in light of its place in the system as a whole. In this volume, we have begun the consideration of the relations between normatively controlled social exchange systems and larger (exploitative) systems. Under what conditions can mutual benefit systems continue in modern societies? How do the pressures upon these systems differ in capitalistic and noncapitalistic countries? Thus the identification of typical systems furthers our understanding of social structures and also leads to research which would add considerable precision to those understandings.

As Toulmin (1953) has rightly emphasized, theory must first explain facts that are already known. Properly understood, scientific discovery consists not of finding new facts but of theoretically explaining the facts we already know. Up until now, exchange theory in its economic, sociological and anthropological forms has seen exchange as effectively independent from coercion. Marxists and Weberians and most economic historians properly object to that view and have pointed out that property and property relations must be understood in light of the role of state structures. Using its modeling procedure, application of the elementary theory to this issue has allowed a more formal understanding of the relations of exchange and (potential) state coercion than had been offered up until now.

But it would be surprising indeed to find that a new theory was introduced that did not uncover (and interrelate) facts of a new order. We feel that the model for normative control presented, applied and discussed in Section I of this volume does uncover and interrelate new facts. The further investigation of strong structures offers similar prospects.

Space will not be taken at this point to review the studies of this volume. Seen in a larger perspective, these studies are but a beginning. That they have been concerned with widely differing structures does not imply that the elementary theory is now "proven valid" for that scope of application. But the scope of application does support the position that widely different systems can be investigated from the point of view of a single social theory.

This volume is not a complete report of research that has been completed under the elementary theory. Completed experimental research includes exchange systems similar to the ones reported here but in which peripherally placed subjects were allowed to communicate and in some instances to sanction one another. With the development of this "collusion" the exchange rates of the strong (but not the weak) structures were significantly changed in a direction favorable to the peripherals. Coercive analogues of the reported systems were studied of both strong and weak types with results consistant with the models for the systems. Historical research in progress includes study of the Hittite empire, the "hierocratic" structure of pre-Columbian Maya and the transformation of ancient civilization into feudalism.

Theoretic issues are being pursued. We are beginning to understand the meaning of the idea of boundaries of a group or structure, and to realize that those boundaries are not simply reflections of the conceptions of group limits held by the persons involved. It is now clear that groups are bounded by beliefs as they are expressed in the restricted codes of the actors. To investigate this issue further, concepts for belief *systems* must be introduced. Groups are also bounded structurally, as for example by the system of normative control in social exchange systems or by the state in economic exchange systems. Of course, all these boundaries are permeable, but relations across the boundaries (if the idea of boundaries is to be meaningful at all) are always in some regards distinct from relations within the system.

In commenting on the capabilities of modern physics, Einstein pointed out that

> the physicist has to limit himself very severely: he must content himself with describing the most simple events which can be brought within the domain of our experience; all events of a more complex order are beyond the power of the human intellect to reconstruct with the subtle accuracy and logical perfection which the theoretical physicist demands. (Einstein, 1954:225–226)

The recognition of the import of this point is of the greatest possible significance for the development of scientific theory in the social sciences. Even allowing for the subjectivity of the idea of "simple events"—for that which would be simple to Einstein or to another who was well schooled in a theory may seem hopelessly complex to one who was unschooled—it has remained true that the precise formal application of any theory has been limited to systems seen as simple from its point of view. If this limit holds for developed sciences, are not the theories of less-developed ones subject to greater limits? But the recognition of the limits of scientific theory stands in the strongest possible contrast with the kinds of demand for explanation typical of the social sciences. In the case of the elementary theory, the simplest possible model for any system contains only reflective actors, that is, actors with effectively full and accurate information and only material interests that are a consequence of their position in the system. Sociologists may feel that such systems are hopelessly oversimplified, yet ongoing work on the theory has established that such systems can be formally treated. We do not now know that systems of considerably greater actor complexity can be formally treated by paper-and-pencil techniques—although there is good intersubjective agreement among theorists who have worked less formally with more complex actor models. Yet, were we to follow the experiences in other sciences (as characterized by Einstein for physics), these limits need not be discouraging at this point in time.

But the approach to social phenomena that emphasizes complex structures and simple actors runs counter to what must be the main current of thought in sociology and related fields. With some important exceptions social scientists see behavior in systems as different because the people of the systems differ, but that position is excessively reductionist. In contrast, *the first step in the use of the elementary theory is to attempt to account for differences of behavior in light of differences in the structures in which the actors are found.* Only after structural conditions are exhausted would one turn to nonstructurally related conditions of value and belief to account for any case in question. This approach follows from the internal logic of the theory and particularly from the fact that the simplest model is always one with reflective actors.

From the point of view of the elementary theory, modern social sciences are almost totally lacking in a concept for *social structure*, a fact that is masked to some extent by the imprecise use of that term. To some extent, we have the founders of our field to blame for the absence of structural concepts and the consequent excessive idealism of modern social interpretation and explanation. To some extent we also have the dominance of systematic empiricism to blame for the lack of progress toward concepts of social structure. It seems high time to throw off these ghosts of the past and take a fresh look at social phenemona and the structural conditions under which they occur.

References

Einstein, Albert
    1954   *Ideas and Opinions*. New York: Crown Publishers.

Toulmin, Stephen
    1953   *The Philosophy of Science*. New York: Harper and Row.

Ann Morris

A GLOSSARY OF TERMS
OF THE ELEMENTARY THEORY

I. Concepts for Actors

   A. *Social actor:* defined by the properties attributed to it: (1) the property of meaning and (2) the property of resources.

      1. *Meaning:* a property of a social actor consisting of three properties: (1) preferences, (2) beliefs and (3) decisions.

         a. *Preferences:* one of three properties of the meaning system attributed to a social actor consisting of a weak ordering from most to least valued of the system states believed by that actor to be potential to a given action system in relation to the actor's position in that system.

         b. *Beliefs:* one of three properties of the meaning system of a social actor which are statements concerned with the information that an actor has which are relevant to its action system at a given point in time. An actor's beliefs are a totality of attributed beliefs relevant to a given system of action which may consist of beliefs concerning the preferences, beliefs and resources of other actors, communications from other actors, calculations concerning possible actions by others, and information concerning the structure in which it is acting.

         c. *Decision procedures:* one of three properties of the meaning system attributed to a social actor which are the means through which an actor selects its contingency rules and its action in light of its preferences, beliefs and the structure of the system. These decision procedures are interpreted by means of the first and second principles of the theory.

2. *Resources:* a property of an actor as conditioned by its relational system.

   a. *Material resources:* the physical things held by an actor that may be used and/or consumed on the one hand or transmitted to other actors on the other. A complete theoretic formulation for material resources would include at its core the biophysical modeling of the actors and their relevant environment on the one hand and a formulation for property rights on the other.

   b. *Symbolic resources:* the symbolic resources that may be transmitted by an actor are the elements of that actor's beliefs.

II. Concepts for Acts

A. *Social action:* an action conditioned by an actor's preferences and by its beliefs concerning at least one element of at least one other actor's meaning system.

B. *Social acts:* sanction flows, communication and information flows that can or do occur within social relationships.

   1. *Sanction:* a social action transmitted by one actor and received by another that alters the preference state of the actor receiving the sanction.

      a. *Positive sanction:* a social act that increases the preference state of the actor receiving the sanction flow.

      b. *Negative sanction:* a social act that reduces the preference state of the actor receiving the sanction flow.

      c. *Material sanction:* a social act that affects the preference state of the actor receiving the sanction flow through changes in that actor's physical system or resources.

      d. *Symbolic sanction:* a social act that affects the preference state of the actor receiving the sanction flow through that actor's beliefs and thus can be modeled cognitively.

   2. *Information flow:* any transmission from an actor the content of which can be any believed or disbelieved condition of a system and any derivation from the conditions.

      a. *Communication:* an information flow that affects the beliefs of an actor receiving the flow.

      b. *Veracity:* an attribution made by an actor to another actor in its network that any designated statements or communications by the second actor would be believed to be true by that actor.

      c. *Expertise:* an attribution of accurate knowledge made by an actor to another actor in its network.

      d. *Influence:* the phenomenon resulting when a communication changes the beliefs of the receiving actor who has, prior to the communication, attributed veracity and expertise to the actor transmitting the communication.

C. *Typology of social acts*
  1. *Sanctions:* see II.B.1.

    a. *Positive sanctions:* see II.B.1.a.

    b. *Negative sanctions:* see II.B.1.b.

  2. *Subtypes of sanctions affecting the preference state of both the transmitter and the receiver of a sanction:*

    a. *Negative–positive:* reduces the preference state of the transmitter and increases the preference state of the receiver.

    b. *Positive–positive:* increases the preference state of both the transmitter and the receiver.

    c. *Negative–negative:* reduces the preference state of both the transmitter and the receiver.

    d. *Positive–negative:* increases the preference state of the transmitter and decreases the preference state of the receiver.

  3. *Subtypes of sanctions affecting the preference state of the receiver only:*

    a. *Zero–Positive:* does not alter the preference state of the transmitter and increases the preference state of the receiver.

    b. *Zero–negative:* does not alter the preference state of the transmitter and decreases the preference state of the receiver.

  4. *Acts affecting the preference state of the transmitter only:*

    a. *Negative–zero:* decreases the preference state of the transmitter and does not alter the preference state of the receiver.

    b. *Positive–zero:* increases the preference state of the transmitter and does not alter the preference state of the receiver.

  5. *Communications* (see II.B.2.a).

    a. *Truthful-believed:* an information flow consistent with the transmitter's beliefs, preferences and resources (i.e., a truthful statement) which is believed by the receiver and added to its beliefs.

    b. *Truthful-disbelieved:* an information flow consistent with the transmitter's beliefs, preferences and resources (i.e., a truthful statement) which is disbelieved by the receiver. The disbelieved information flow does not become incorporated into the receiver's beliefs.

       c. *False-believed:* an information flow inconsistent with the transmitter's beliefs, preferences and resources (i.e., a lie, false communication, etc.) which is believed by the receiver and added to its beliefs.

       d. *False–disbelieved:* an information flow inconsistent with the transmitter's beliefs, preferences and resources (i.e., a lie, false communication, etc.) which is disbelieved by the receiver. The disbelieved information flow does not become incorporated into the receiver's beliefs.

III. Concepts for Social Relationships

  A. *Social relationship:* two or more social actors acting socially toward one another, (those actions being conditioned by meanings each has attributed to the other, the structure of the system of action and other relevant initial conditions).

  B. *Three ideal types of social relationship:* three types of dyadic sanctioning social relationship in which only two sanctions are potential.

    1. *Exchange:* a dyadic social relationship where both sanctions are positive.

    2. *Conflict:* a dyadic social relationship where both sanctions are negative.

    3. *Coercion:* a dyadic social relationship where one sanction is positive and the other negative.

  C. *Types of exchange systems*

    1. *Economic exchange:* a system of social relationships consisting of negative–positive sanctions.

    2. *Social exchange:* a system of social relationships consisting of positive–positive sanctions.

  D. *Exchange rate:* a ratio of quantities of sanction flows. (Rate of coercion—see Chapter 9.)

  E. *Contingency rule:* a statement that can conditionally relate the actions of two or more social actors.

    1. *Rule:* a possible contingency rule.

    2. *System rules:* contingency rules that actually govern the actions of at least one actor in a social relationship.

    3. *Fully general system rules:* contingency rules that govern the action of all actors in the system (such as prices and laws).

    4. *Agreement:* the adoption of common and consistent contingency rules by two or more actors in a system of social relationships.

    5. *Confrontation:* the adoption of distinct and inconsistent contin-

gency rules by two or more actors in a system of social relationships.

IV. Network Concepts

A. *Networks:* geometric constructions that can represent elements of
social actions, social relationships and social structures.

B. *Actor points:* points of a geometric model that are interpreted as
social actors. These points may represent a single actor or a set of
actors.

C. *Square points:* the term applied to the squares in a geometric model
that are interpreted as biophysical properties for a network.

D. *Dashed points:* the term applied to the dashed circles in a geometric
model that are interpreted as cognitive properties for a network.

E. *Flow:* the term applied to the events that occur along the path of an
arc in a geometric model.

F. *Arcs:* arrows in a geometric model connecting points and representing paths along which events occur. These are interpreted as social
acts.

Sanctions	Positive	+ (arc)
	Negative	− (arc)
Subtypes of Sanctions	Negative–Positive	(−) +
	Positive–Positive	(+) +
	Negative–Negative	(−) −
	Positive–Negative	(+) −
	Zero–Positive	(0) +
	Zero–Negative	(0) −
Communications	Truthful–Believed	$I^{(+)}$ I^{+}
	Truthful–Disbelieved	$I^{(+)}$ I^{-}
	False–Believed	$I^{(-)}$ I^{+}
	False–Disbelieved	$I^{(-)}$ I^{-}

1. *Social action arcs*

2. *Reflexive arcs:* arcs that originate and terminate at a given point representing a social actor's relation to either biophysical events or cognitive events.

    a. *Packed reflexive:* a reflexive that is modeled as originating and terminating at a given point.

    b. *Unpacked reflexive:* a square or dashed point and associated arcs in a model representing a reflexive.

G. *System:* a set of points and arcs considered together in a geometric model and representing a system of social relationships.

H. *Potential network* (N_p): a system of social relationships that contains all of the social acts that are theoretically considered for a given instance, some, none or all of which may occur in the relationship.

I. *Maximum possible network* (N_m): the network that contains an actor and the maximum number of actors with which the actor has an interest in relating.

J. *Possible network:* a general term for any subset of a potential network.

K. *System state:* a conditioned possible network.

L. *Actual network:* any system state or set of system states that occur in a system of social relationships.

V. Principles and Laws

A. *First principle:* All social actors act to maximize their expected preference state alteration.

B. *Law 1:*

In a number of theoretically important systems each actor can transmit one type of sanction flow and can receive one type of sanction flow. When the preference state alteration of transmission and reception is independent, and when the subscripts t and r represent transmission and reception then the first law can be stated as

$$L_1: \quad P_a = v_{t_a} x_{t_a} + v_{r_a} x_{r_a},$$

and by removing the restriction on numbers of flows, when all preference alterations are independent, t is the index set of sanctions transmitted and r is the index set of sanctions received,

$$L_1: \quad P_a = \sum_{i \in t} v_i x_i + \sum_{j \in r} v_j x_j.$$

C. *Second principle:* compromise occurs at the point of equiresistence for undifferentiated actors in a full information system.

D. *Law 2:*

$$L_2: \quad R_a = \frac{P_{a_{max}} - P_a}{P_a - P_{a_{con}}},$$

where R_a is the resistance for actor a, where $P_{a_{max}}$ is the most preferred preference state alteration for an actor, where P_a is any preference state alteration potential to the system for an actor, and $P_{a_{con}}$ is the preference state alteration of the system state of confrontation.

The numerator represents the interest a social actor has in gaining the most favorable system state of an interaction and the denominator represents the interest an actor has in avoiding a confrontation.

VI. Structural Concepts

A. *Bilateral monopoly:* a dyadic system in which each actor has only the other actor as a member of its potential network.

B. *Unilateral monopoly:* a system of social relationships in which a centrally placed actor has more than one other actor as a member of its potential network and any peripherally placed actor has only the centrally placed actor as a member of its potential network.

C. *Central actor:* an actor whose centrality index is greater than one.

D. *Peripheral actor:* an actor whose centrality index is one.

E. *Centrality index of an actor:*

$$C = n_a/m_a$$

where n_a is the size of the potential network of actors with which an actor could potentially establish relations and m_a is the maximum number of actors with which an actor has an interest in relating.

F. *Differential centrality system:* a system containing both central and peripheral actors.

G. *Structurally determined system:* a system in which confrontation conditions are differentially allocated structurally and the information conditions are such that the differential allocation of the costs of confrontation are a determinate of the process of interaction. Typical conditions for structural determination are strong structure and reflective actors.

VII. Process Concepts. (Note: each type of social relationship involves its own process and individual reference should be made to each one.)

A. *Bargaining:* an interaction process governed by the interests of each actor in gaining the best agreement possible and avoiding the costs of disagreement (confrontation). The end point of a bargaining process may or may not be a contingency rule mutually agreed upon which relates the behavior of the actors.

B. *Overwhelming malefactions:* a condition of the dyad in which the unfavorable consequences of disagreement for the first actor so exceed those of the second actor that no bargaining process occurs such that an agreement is reached which is favorable to the second actor.

C. *Iteration:* a process of interaction in which the resistance of one or more actors is dissolved and the resistance of one or more other related actors is increased. The end point of a process of iteration for a system of reflective actors is a fully general system rule.

D. *Influence:* See definition II.B.2.d.

VIII. Derived Concepts

A. *Interest:* a *comparative* term which has as its referent the preference system of the actor. For any system an actor has an interest in attaining its first-ranked system state as compared to any other system state, an interest in attaining its second-ranked system as compared to any system state ranked lower and so forth.

   1. *Complement of interests:* a social relationship in which at least some of the ordered elements of the actors' preference systems correspond.

   2. *Opposition of interests:* a social relationship in which there is reversal of the order of at least some of the elements of the preference systems of the actors.

   3. *Opposed but complementary interests:* a social relationship in which at least some of the ordered elements of the actors' preference systems correspond and in which there is reversal of the order of at least some of the elements of the preference system of the actors.

B. *Costs of confrontation:* the comparison of the preference state alteration for an actor in a state of confrontation with other preference state alterations. (Typically the base line from which the alteration is calculated is the state of agreement potential for the relationship.) The comparative level of alteratives (when relevant) must be an element of the foregoing calculation.

C. *Costs of agreement:* the comparison of the preference state alteration for an actor in a state of agreement with other preference state alterations.

D. *Differential costs of confrontation:* a system of social relationships in which the costs of confrontation are less for one actor or set of actors than are the costs of confrontation for another actor or set of actors.

E. *Distribution of costs of confrontation:* an analysis of a system that compares the preference state alterations of agreement and confrontation for the actors engaged in the relationship.

F. *Equiresistance:* the point at which resistance curves cross.

G. *Unambiguous interest:* a condition of the actor-system such that an actor selects a particular contingency rule regardless of the interest and potential action of any other actor in the system.

IX. Formulations

A. *Full information systems:* systems in which all actors' information is complete and accurate.

B. *Reflective actor:* an actor with full information and only material interests. Material interests are generated from a preference system that takes into account only the standardized units of material flows and the sanction signs.

C. *First-order model:* the simplest model that can be constructed which preserves the structures and interaction dynamics of interest in the formulation. Typically, first-order models have few actors. When the interest is sociological, not psychological, first-order models typically have simple actors as, for example, actors with full information or reflective actors.

D. *Second-order model:* any model more complex than a first-order model. In empirical applications, although first-order models give approximate explanations to a broader range of phenomena, second-order models, although narrower in scope, give more precise explanations (and predictions).

INDEX